NEW ESSAYS ON JOHN CLARE

John Clare (1793–1864) has long been recognized as one of England's foremost poets of nature, landscape and rural life. Scholars and general readers alike regard his tremendous creative output as a testament to a probing and powerful intellect. Clare was that rare amalgam – a poet who wrote from a working-class, impoverished background, who was steeped in folk and ballad culture, and who yet, against all social expectations and prejudices, read and wrote himself into a grand literary tradition. All the while he maintained a determined sense of his own commitments to the poor, to natural history and to the local. Through the diverse approaches of ten scholars, this collection shows how Clare's many angles of critical vision illuminate current understandings of environmental ethics, aesthetics, Romantic and Victorian literary history, and the nature of work.

SIMON KÖVESI is Professor of English Literature at Oxford Brookes University.

SCOTT MCEATHRON is Associate Professor of English at Southern Illinois University.

NEW ESSAYS ON JOHN CLARE

Poetry, Culture and Community

Edited By
SIMON KÖVESI
Oxford Brookes University

and

SCOTT McEATHRON
Southern Illinois University

CAMBRIDGE
UNIVERSITY PRESS

University Printing House, Cambridge CB2 8BS, United Kingdom

One Liberty Plaza, 20th Floor, New York, NY 10006, USA

477 Williamstown Road, Port Melbourne, VIC 3207, Australia

4843/24, 2nd Floor, Ansari Road, Daryaganj, Delhi - 110002, India

79 Anson Road, #06-04/06, Singapore 079906

Cambridge University Press is part of the University of Cambridge.

It furthers the University's mission by disseminating knowledge in the pursuit of education, learning and research at the highest international levels of excellence.

www.cambridge.org
Information on this title: www.cambridge.org/9781108439091

© Cambridge University Press 2015

This publication is in copyright. Subject to statutory exception and to the provisions of relevant collective licensing agreements, no reproduction of any part may take place without the written permission of Cambridge University Press.

First published 2015
First paperback edition 2017

A catalogue record for this publication is available from the British Library

Library of Congress Cataloging in Publication data
New essays on John Clare : poetry, culture and community / edited by Simon Kövesi and Scott McEathron.
    pages cm
Includes bibliographical references and index.
ISBN 978-1-107-03111-1 (hardback)
1. Clare, John, 1793–1864 – Criticism and interpretation. I. Kövesi, Simon, editor. II. McEathron, Scott, 1962– editor.
PR4453.C6Z84 2015
821'.7–dc23
2015008281

ISBN 978-1-107-03111-1 Hardback
ISBN 978-1-108-43909-1 Paperback

Cambridge University Press has no responsibility for the persistence or accuracy of URLs for external or third-party internet websites referred to in this publication, and does not guarantee that any content on such websites is, or will remain, accurate or appropriate.

Contents

Notes on contributors	*page* vii
Acknowledgements	x
List of abbreviations	xi
Introduction Simon Kövesi and Scott McEathron	1
PART I: POETRY	15
1 John Clare's colours Fiona Stafford	17
2 John Clare, William Cowper and the eighteenth century Adam Rounce	38
3 John Clare's conspiracy Sarah M. Zimmerman	57
PART II: CULTURE	77
4 John Clare and the new varieties of enclosure: a polemic John Burnside	79
5 Ecology with religion: kinship in John Clare Emma Mason	97
6 The lives of Frederick Martin and the first *Life of John Clare* Scott McEathron	118
7 John Clare's deaths: poverty, education and poetry Simon Kövesi	146

PART III: COMMUNITY   167

8 John Clare's natural history   169
   Robert Heyes

9 'This is radical slang': John Clare, Admiral Lord
   Radstock and the Queen Caroline affair   189
   Sam Ward

10 John Clare and the *London Magazine*   209
   Richard Cronin

Select bibliography   228
Index   239

Notes on contributors

JOHN BURNSIDE teaches at the University of St Andrews. His poetry collections include *Feast Days* (1992), winner of the Geoffrey Faber Memorial Prize; *The Asylum Dance* (2000), winner of the Whitbread Poetry Award; and *Black Cat Bone*, (2011) which won both the Forward and the T. S. Eliot Prize. In 2011, he received the Petrarca Preis for poetry. His novels include *The Devil's Footprints* (2007), *Glister* (2008) and *A Summer of Drowning* (2011). He is also the author of two collections of short stories – *Burning Elvis* (2000) and *Something Like Happy* (2013), which was the Saltire Society's Scottish Book of the Year, as well as the winner of the Edge Hill Short Story Prize. His memoirs to date include *A Lie About My Father* (2006), also a Saltire Book of the Year, and *Waking Up in Toytown* (2010). John Burnside's latest poetry collection is *All One Breath* (2014). A new prose book, *I Put A Spell On You: Several Digressions On Love and Glamour*, was recently published. He was writer in residence at the DAAD (Deutscher Akademischer Austauschdienst), Berlin, for 2014–15.

RICHARD CRONIN is Professor of English Literature at Oxford Brookes University. He began his career as a Shelley scholar but has subsequently written widely on nineteenth-century literature. His most recent books are *Romantic Victorians: English Literature 1824–1840*; *Paper Pellets: British Literary Culture after Waterloo*; and *Reading Victorian Poetry*. With Dorothy McMillan he has edited *Robert Browning* for Twenty-First Century Authors, and *Emma* for Cambridge University Press's new edition of Austen's work; he also co-edited a *Companion to Victorian Poetry*. He is currently working on a biography provisionally entitled *George Meredith: A Life in Writing*.

ROBERT HEYES was born and grew up in Lincolnshire, initially in Grantham and later in the villages of Metheringham and Scopwick. His first degrees were in Chemistry. His professional life was spent as a schoolteacher, mainly at a village primary school in Kent. Forty years ago he began to collect books and manuscripts by, and about, John Clare; eventually this resulted in what was probably the finest Clare collection in private hands. After taking early retirement, he began to disperse his collection, and the emphasis shifted from collecting to research. This resulted in the award of a PhD from the English department at Birkbeck College, for a thesis entitled *'Looking to Futurity': John Clare and Provincial Culture*. He contributed an essay to *John Clare: New Approaches* (2000) and has published essays and book reviews in the *John Clare Society Journal*, *English* and *Romanticism*. For many years he was the book review editor of the *John Clare Society Journal*.

SIMON KÖVESI is Professor of English Literature at Oxford Brookes University. He edited two prefatory collections of Clare's poetry – *Love Poems* (1999) and *Flower Poems* (2001) – and, with John Goodridge, co-edited *John Clare: New Approaches* (2000). His study of the contemporary Glaswegian writer, *James Kelman* (2007), was shortlisted for the Saltire Scottish First Book of the Year Award in 2008. He is editor of the *John Clare Society Journal* and has published essays on Clare, ecology, copyright, editing and Romantic literary culture.

EMMA MASON is Professor of English and Comparative Literary Studies at the University of Warwick. Her publications include *Elizabeth Jennings: The Collected Poems* (2012); *The Cambridge Introduction to Wordsworth* (Cambridge University Press, 2010); and *Women Poets of the Nineteenth Century* (2006). She is the editor of *Reading the Abrahamic Faiths: Rethinking Religion and Literature* (2014), and a 'new perspectives' issue of *La Questione Romantica* on William Wordsworth (with Elena Spandri; 2014). Her book *Christina Rossetti: Poet of Grace* is forthcoming.

SCOTT MCEATHRON is Associate Professor of English at Southern Illinois University. He has written extensively on the relationship between labouring-class poetry and canonical Romanticism, and, more recently, has published a series of essays on Romantic-era painters and paintings with links to Lamb, Hazlitt and Keats. He is the editor of *English Labouring-Class Poetry, 1800–1830* (2006) and *Thomas Hardy's Tess of the d'Urbervilles: A Sourcebook* (2005). His current projects include work on the nineteenth-century labouring-class elegy and on the treatment of labouring-class poets by the Royal Literary Fund.

ADAM ROUNCE lectures at the University of Nottingham. He has written extensively on various seventeenth- and eighteenth-century writers, including Dryden, Pope, Churchill, Joseph Warton and Johnson. He is co-editing two volumes of the ongoing Cambridge edition of the writings of Jonathan Swift, as well as writing a separate Chronology. He has recently published a monograph on literary culture and lack of success in the long eighteenth century: *Fame and Failure, 1720–1800: the Unfulfilled Literary Life* (Cambridge University Press, 2013).

FIONA STAFFORD is Professor of English at the University of Oxford and a Fellow of Somerville College. Her recent books include *Reading Romantic Poetry* (2012) and *Local Attachments* (2010). She edited *Lyrical Ballads* and *Pride and Prejudice* and a collection of essays on *Burns and Other Poets* (2012). She has also written and delivered two series of 'The Essay' for BBC Radio 3 on 'The Meaning of Trees'. She is currently working on *The Oxford History of English Literature: Volume Seven, The Romantic Period* and on a book about trees.

SAM WARD is an Honorary Visiting Fellow in the Centre for Regional Literature and Culture at the University of Nottingham and teaches at Nottingham Trent University. He worked as an associate editor on *The Letters of Robert Bloomfield and His Circle* (2009) and parts 1–4 of *The Collected Letters of Robert Southey* (2009–13), and has recently edited Bloomfield's final volume of poetry, *May-Day with the Muses*. He is Archivist of the John Clare Society and is currently working on a book-length study entitled *John Clare, Ownership and Appropriation*.

SARAH M. ZIMMERMAN is Professor of English at Fordham University. Her work on the Romantic lyric includes *Romanticism, Lyricism, and History* (1999), which focused on Charlotte Smith, William Wordsworth, Dorothy Wordsworth and John Clare. She has also published essays on the lyric poetry of Smith, Clare and Keats. Her work on performance includes essays on Percy Bysshe Shelley's *The Cenci*, Samuel Taylor Coleridge's public lectures, and women writers in the Romantic lecture room. She has completed a study of the Romantic literary lecture that features Coleridge, John Thelwall, Thomas Campbell, William Hazlitt and their women auditors, including Mary Russell Mitford, Catherine Maria Fanshawe and Lady Charlotte Bury.

Acknowledgements

For access and help with archival materials, the authors are grateful to the British Library; the New York Public Library; the National Archives, Kew; the Bryn Mawr College Library; the Central Library, Peterborough; and the John Clare Collection of the Northamptonshire Central Library, Northamptonshire Libraries and Information Service.

We thank the Trustees of the British Museum for the reproduction of 'August', after Peter DeWint, 1827, which appears on p. 26, and is copyright © The Trustees of the British Museum. The front cover image is Samuel Palmer's 'The White Cloud', *c.* 1833–4 (detail), reproduced by kind permission of the Ashmolean Museum, © Ashmolean Museum, University of Oxford.

Abbreviations

Bate	Jonathan Bate, *John Clare: A Biography* (London: Picador, 2003)
By Himself	*John Clare By Himself*, ed. Eric Robinson and David Powell (Ashington and Manchester: MidNAG/Carcanet, 1996)
Critical Heritage	*Clare: The Critical Heritage*, ed. Mark Storey (London: Routledge & Kegan Paul, 1973)
Early Poems (I–II)	*The Early Poems of John Clare 1804–1822*, ed. Eric Robinson and David Powell, assoc. ed. Margaret Grainger, 2 vols. (Oxford: Clarendon Press, 1989)
Eg.	British Library, Egerton Manuscript
Haughton	*John Clare in Context*, ed. Hugh Haughton, Adam Phillips and Geoffrey Summerfield (Cambridge: Cambridge University Press, 1994)
JCSJ	*The John Clare Society Journal*, vols. 1–33 (2014), continuing series
Later Poems (I–II)	*The Later Poems of John Clare 1837–1864*, ed. Eric Robinson and David Powell, assoc. ed. Margaret Grainger, 2 vols. (Oxford: Clarendon Press, 1984)
Letters	*The Letters of John Clare*, ed. Mark Storey (Oxford: Clarendon Press, 1985)
LM	*London Magazine*, various editors and publishers (London: 1820–9)
Major Works	*John Clare: Major Works*, ed. Eric Robinson and David Powell, with an Introduction by Tom Paulin (Oxford: Oxford World's Classics, 2004)
Middle Period (I–V)	*John Clare, Poems of the Middle Period 1822–1837*, ed. Eric Robinson, David Powell and

	P. M. S. Dawson (Oxford: Clarendon Press. vols. I–II: 1996; vols. III–IV: 1998; vol. V: 2003)
Natural History	*The Natural History Prose Writings of John Clare*, ed. Margaret Grainger (Oxford: Clarendon Press, 1983)
New Approaches	*John Clare: New Approaches*, ed. John Goodridge and Simon Kövesi (Helpston: John Clare Society, 2000)
Nor.	Northampton Manuscript, John Clare Collection, Northamptonshire Libraries and Information Service, as listed in [David Powell], *Catalogue of the John Clare Collection in the Northampton Public Library* (Northampton: County Borough of Northampton Public Libraries, Museums and Art Gallery Committee, 1964)
Pet.	Peterborough Manuscript, Central Library, Peterborough, as listed in Margaret Grainger, *A Descriptive Catalogue of the John Clare Collection in Peterborough Museum and Art Gallery* ([Peterborough]: [Peterborough Museum Society], 1973)
Sales	Roger Sales, *John Clare: A Literary Life* (Basingstoke: Palgrave, 2002)
Tibbles (1972)	J. W. and Anne Tibble, *John Clare: A Life* (London: Michael Joseph, 1972)

Introduction

Simon Kövesi and Scott McEathron

In his biography of Charles Dickens, John Forster quotes from a now lost letter which contains Dickens' only known reference to John Clare. It is not the kind of response we might have expected from a novelist so well regarded for sympathetic, nuanced portrayals of the effects and dimensions of poverty. Forster defends his subject:

> A dislike of display was rooted in [Dickens] ... His aversion to every form of what is called patronage of literature was part of the same feeling ... These views about patronage did not make him more indulgent to the clamour which with which it is so often invoked for the ridiculously small. 'You read that life of Clare?' he wrote (15th of August 1865). 'Did you ever see such preposterous exaggeration of small claims? And isn't it expressive, the perpetual prating of him in the book as *the Poet*? So another Incompetent used to write to the Literary Fund when I was on the committee: "This leaves the poet at his divine mission in a corner of a single room. The Poet's father is wiping his spectacles. The Poet's mother is weaving." – Yah!' He was equally intolerant of every magnificent proposal that should render the literary man independent of the bookseller, and he sharply criticized even a compromise to replace the half-profit system by one of royalties on copies sold.[1]

Dickens' scorn is really aimed at Frederick Martin's 1865 biography of the poet, the single most significant Victorian-period Clare publication.[2] Nevertheless, that Dickens should have been so sweepingly dismissive of Clare's 'small claims' while taking umbrage at the perceived excesses of a biographer he regards as a mere hagiographer comes as a disappointment. As with John Keats, Robert Bloomfield, William Wordsworth and Alfred Tennyson – all of whom Clare might readily have met in person but did not – Dickens' failure to appreciate Clare feels like yet another missed opportunity for a fruitful meeting of minds, albeit at a distance.[3] Yet his remarks can help us unpack a dominant problem in the history of Clare's critical reception. At the heart of the matter – as always in English life, it seems – lies class; and for Clare in particular, class seems to render problematic almost every relationship he and his work might forge to the polite world of letters. By the time Dickens issued his sarcastic attack on Martin's extravagances, while swatting away, as one might an irritating midge, the very notion that Clare could be a writer of enduring interest, the eighteenth-century model of patronage had all but disappeared – with the hardest-working exemplar of the newly professionalized writer being Dickens himself. A *Times* editorial of 1964 memorably cut to the quick in explaining why excessive acclaim of Clare tended to come off as demeaning: 'Praise of his verses had about it a ring of the Johnsonian reaction to a dog walking on his hinder legs – it is not done well, but you are surprised to find it done at all.'[4]

Whereas the mid-Victorian Dickens could bid a blithe good riddance both to literary patronage and to those he felt had never deserved it, the Romantic era in which Clare was born, and into which his poetry first emerged in public, was a transitional period wherein a deferential, partisan mode of sponsored authorship was gradually replaced by one in which writers could independently exploit the newly capitalized economy of the book trade. Clare was both beneficiary and victim of this change. His income from a rather old-fashioned trust fund set up for him by a collaboration of publishers and patrons (of varying political hues) could theoretically have been substantial enough to cover his living expenses, yet in practice never quite did so. The publishing of collections of his own verse, and of individual poems in magazines, periodicals, annuals and anthologies, would seem to have augured financial health, but in fact did not appreciably boost his income. Any great expectations Clare had to be free of reliance on benefactors were persistently and repeatedly dashed; any monies he might have expected from his early successes never proved sufficient to stop feverish worries over the subsistence of his home and family. To his long-term correspondent and London helpmeet, the lonely middle-class Eliza Louisa Emmerson, Clare wrote in 1832: 'all I wish now is to stand upon my own bottom as a poet without any apology as to want of education or any thing else & I say it not in the feeling of either ambition or vanity but in the spirit of common sense'.[5] Commonsensical and reasonable such a wish may have been; realistic or realizable it was not.

In 1837 it was clear to Matthew Allen, the doctor who ran the asylum in Essex, that a root cause of Clare's psychological problems was that he simply did not eat enough.[6] As with many of his peers, it is likely that Clare was persistently malnourished. It is both no surprise and a sharp irony that

Clare never ate as well or as regularly as he did in the asylums in the final third of his life, so that by the time the only known photograph of Clare was taken in 1862 in Northampton, he looks healthily bulky.[7] But this stature was an accident of his being a private patient in both institutions – the fees for which were covered by his trust fund. No amount of effort of the 'historical imagination' can help us grasp what protracted hunger must have meant to Clare – to his body, his mind and so to his writing. For us this also stands as a critical problem, not least because he does not write about it much at all. There is always a fraught relationship between a critical subject-position of relative privilege (verging, some might say, on academic decadence) and a working-class object of study. This gulf of material experience can itself bring about the sort of over-praise that Dickens found so distasteful; indeed, the hagiography still informing some responses to Clare is no less a classist phenomenon than now-obsolete dismissals of his value. As Alan Porter observed as early as 1928,[8] neither Dickens nor the 1920s editor of the new edition of Forster's biography dealt fairly with Clare; but it remains true that Dickens's scorn could be redirected at many puff pieces in favour of Clare written in the century and a half since his death.

Hugh Haughton and Adam Phillips lamented in 1994 that Clare 'is mainly famous for being neglected',[9] neatly summarizing a predominant critical noise about Clare: that somehow the sort of misfortunes he suffered in life continue to beset his literary legacy due to a lingering snobbery and elitism towards his class and education; his rural, humble subject matter; and his language. Of course, those who locate their criticism solely in relationship to this neglect risk putting themselves in the dubiously heroic position of chastising others' class prejudices. Indeed, in twentieth-century reshapings of Clare's reputation it has sometimes been this protectionist posture, more than excessive praise, that has slowed the development of critical, creative and editorial work. But while rage over the unjust neglect of Clare still flares up occasionally, the first decades of the twenty-first century have stabilized most critics' sense to the extent that we can now put those past injuries to rest.

Still, it is worth reviewing here the steps that have brought us to this point, not least because the history of the reception of Clare offers insights into the effects class has on the diverse agendas of criticism. No special pleading is necessary: the critical reception of working-class writers is always beset with such problems, from Stephen Duck's and Mary Collier's era through to our own. In Clare's case, being presented to the world as an uneducated peasant meant that his work suffered the type of sweeping dismissal that Charles Mackay included in his anonymous 1869 *All the Year Round* essay 'An English Peasant', five years after Clare's death and a year before the death of Dickens:

> If there be any class of the English people that is pre-eminently unknown to itself and to all other classes, it is that of the farm labourer. The squire or other great landed proprietor of the neighbourhood knows them after a certain fashion, as he knows his cattle; but of the labourer's mind he has as little idea as he has of that of the animal which he bestrides in the hunting-field. He knows the peasant to be a useful drudge, like the horse that draws the plough, but unlike the horse, to be a burden upon the poor-rates, either present or prospective ... In the southern shires, the condition of the peasant is virtually that of the slave. He is tied to his parish by circumstances too formidable to be overcome by any such small and weak agencies as he can employ ... Why the English peasantry, the border men excepted, should be inferior in energy, or in the art of bettering themselves, to their compeers in Scotland, Ireland, and Wales, has never yet been satisfactorily explained ... Whatever may be the cause, there is a lack of imagination among them that leads to lack of enterprise, and that seems somehow or other to run in the blood of those portions of the British people that are not of Celtic origin or intermixture. The peasantry of Saxon England have among them but two poets, Robert Bloomfield, the author of the Farmer's Boy, and John Clare, author of the Village Minstrel; neither of them a poet with any claims to the first or even to the second rank, while Scotland's poets, sprung from the agricultural and labouring classes, are to be numbered by scores, including Robert Burns, a greater than fifty Bloomfields and Clares rolled into one, and a long bead roll of genuine bards and minstrels, of whom it is sufficient to name Allan Ramsay, the barber, William Ferguson, the sailor, James Hogg, the shepherd, Robert Tannahill, the weaver, Hugh Miller, the stonemason, and Jean Glover, the strolling tinker.[10]

Here the Scottish poet, journalist and editor Mackay does condemn the hopeless trap of peasant life – lumping together the reputations of two quite different English labouring-class poets as he does so – but he is as condemnatory of the 'innate sluggishness of blood' of the southern English peasant as he is of rural poverty. He castigates peasants for 'making serfs of themselves by their ignorance and limpet-like tenacity in sticking to the parish in which they were born' more than he does an economic system which allows a farmer to regard the peasant 'on a par with the concern he has for his inanimate tools'.[11] For Mackay, as it seems was the case for his editor Dickens, 'small' Clare, like all English peasants, is eminently forgettable.

Mackay's essay can stand as a low point in Clare's critical reception – though in truth it is actually one among many examples we might have chosen to focus upon, as Victorian writers such as Mackay wrestled with the political and cultural presence, and growing influence, of an increasingly unified, and unionized, working class. It is instructive that in his vituperative 1867 essay 'The Working Classes', Mackay trumpets his opposition to the Trades Union movement, the campaign for universal manhood suffrage, and 'the organisation of labour – Communism, Socialism, Fourierism, Proudhonism or whatever else it may be or has been called'.[12] Thus, Clare is just a baby thrown out with the dirty working-class bathwater. Nevertheless, for every Mackay there was a counteracting Edwin Paxton Hood or Samuel Smiles, Victorian gentlemen prominently praising Clare as a prime example of just what an educated labourer might become even in the toughest of circumstances: both a model of industry and an example of the power of literacy. For Hood in 1851, Clare was 'the Wordsworth of Labour', while Smiles in 1861 thought the poet was 'entitled to a high place, if not to the highest, among the uneducated poets of England.'[13] Writers and commentators of all stripes returned again and again to Clare throughout the late nineteenth century – though Roger Sales rightly notes that Clare appears most often as just one name among many in 'litanies of humble geniuses'.[14] Clare was a low-key yet persistent presence in late nineteenth-century assessments of the literary landscape, and this fact accounts for a small but significant crop of editions after the turn of the twentieth century. The first of these, a 1901 collection edited by the poet Norman Gale,[15] met with a brutal dismissal in the Tory *Spectator*:

> Clare had just the amount of ability which is most dangerous to a man's character. It was enough to lift him out of his place; it did not lift him high enough. His verse was remarkable as written by a farm-labourer; it was never really good. Mr. Gale thinks that the public which refused to praise, or even to read, him were 'blind bats.' It may be so; we must own to the same blindness. The verse has the common fatal fault of not being interesting. It is not thoughtful; it is not even sonorous; one never feels disposed to read it aloud. It is not even minutely true to Nature.[16]

After this violent knock-back – which was probably as much a coded rejection of the then deeply unfashionable 'Bodley Head' 1890s poet Gale[17] as it was of Clare – the twentieth century would prove far friendlier to Clare's work. The story of the emergence of biographies and editions has been told many times, starting with the groundwork laid by Frederick Martin and J. L. Cherry[18] in the nineteenth century, and proceeding through collections of increasing breadth and editorial quality by a succession of poets – Arthur Symons, Alan Porter with Edmund Blunden and then Blunden on his own.[19] The editorial baton was next picked up by the educationalist academic J. W. Tibble and his remarkably prolific partner Anne Tibble, who also co-edited Clare with Leonard Clark and Kelsey Thornton.[20] The Tibbles' substantial efforts were complemented by two editions from the influential all-round man of letters – and notoriously scathing reviewer – Geoffrey Grigson.[21] Such charismatic figures, with their increasingly solid scholarship, built a platform for a series of committed academic editors from the 1960s onwards. Initiated by Geoffrey Summerfield, an editing project which was joined by Eric Robinson in the early 1960s produced new editions and marked a sea-change in the way Clare was presented.[22] Textual primitivism – that is, transcription of original handwritten manuscripts into published type, yet with an ostensibly minimalist level of editorial intervention (no grammatical correction, no indentation, no additional punctuation, no orthographic regularization) – had starkly arrived. Summerfield and Robinson's early partnership led in turn to Robinson's forty-year-long editing project with David Powell, Margaret Grainger and Paul Dawson that by 2003 had produced the monumental nine-volume Oxford Clarendon edition of the complete poems, to which we will return below.[23]

The corrective we offer to this well-rehearsed history is that while Clare's work certainly suffered its share of academic marginalization and neglect, there was no dramatic opening of Tutankhamun's tomb, as it were, in which Clare was gloriously rediscovered after having been buried and locked away. To imagine any single watershed moment of this kind is to deny Clare's commonality with many writers whose fortunes have risen and fallen with fluctuations in literary-critical taste and curatorial practice. As we have said above, since his death in 1864 Clare has received quiet yet constant attention, both despite and because of his uneasy periodicity. Never quite accepted as one of the great male Romantic poets, he has also been perceived (mistakenly) as having been out of contact with the swift changes of Victorian literary culture, by virtue of having been institutionalized in the same year that the young Queen was crowned. There are of course other literary categories and typologies we might use to frame our understanding of Clare but, as David Simpson pointed out in 1999, they never seem to fit him very well:

> Economic hardship, sexual and emotional deprivation, physical discomfort, geographical displacement, a sense of place made no-place by enclosure and by just growing up – these are the coordinates of Clare's poetry. Many of the compensatory gestures – the patriotism, the conformity to convention, the nods to other poets and poems so evident in the 1820 *Poems Descriptive of*

Rural Life and Scenery – either register as hollow or unfelt or require for their elucidation a deep literary historical knowledge that is seldom to be found and is therefore seldom taught. The sheer complexity of the mix makes it very hard to reduce Clare to the 'historical generalisations' identified in a fine essay by Nicholas Birns as the stuff of most historical criticism. Too literate for a primitive, not just a dialect poet, too patriotic for a 'radical', too psychologically complex for a passive victim of repression, and too nostalgic for a realist, Clare makes a difficulty for any of the obviously contending categories by which we might make him familiar ... The love of books and writing that takes Clare 'out' of the laboring class does not comfortably insert him into any other group, least of all that of guild of professional writers.[24]

Yet, owing in part to the critical reflexivity his situation has always demanded, Clare's ongoing status as an uncategorizable literary and social misfit might in the end have served him well. Clare's work is now more highly regarded, more widely considered and his name more broadly recognized and referred to, than at any time since the mostly warm reception his first book received in 1820. Perhaps we no longer need be concerned about Clare's place in the canon. The inclusion in Romantic and Victorian period study of writers of similar social class to Clare – along with the serious study of the work of women, servants and slaves, and of texts couched in regional or dialect languages and eschewing 'polite' forms – has done much to expose the baldly ideological nature of academic literary canon formation in general. The cultural processes of valuation that once excluded Clare do not now form a valid or settled model of literary or academic taste. By the same token, Clare scholars have tended of late to extend their scepticism of a fixed Romantic canon towards any fixed listing of Clare's 'best' poems – fittingly, perhaps, given Clare's many lurching stops and starts in the making of his own career. It might not be so much that Clare is no longer on the margins, but rather that any centrally agreed ground has been dissolved.

Clare has become a central part of – and a leading inspiration for – the ongoing 'recovery' of many other working-class, labouring-class, regional, dialect or otherwise socially marginalized writers of the eighteenth and nineteenth centuries. We now appreciate that contemporary tastes, social mores, fashions and historically determined prejudices influence which texts are read and which forgotten, rather than any council-of-elders' agreement over eternal verities of literary value. Access to Clare is now guided by a plurality of scholarly and popular editions and by Jonathan Bate's critical biography, as well as by a range of interpretive approaches taking in psychology, music, creative writing, dialect and language, literary genre and form, folklore, cultural materialism, botany, ornithology, eco-criticism and environmentalism, geography and local history. It is no surprise, then, that his work has enjoyed a surge of rich, diversifying and popularizing attention.

Given the shift in the quality and range of interest in Clare across the past twenty years or so, we felt it was high time for a newly commissioned set of critical essays on the poet. It is now more than two decades since the first major critical essay collection focused on the poet – the Cambridge University Press collection of 1994.[25] Since that collection, critical work has expanded exponentially,[26] while access to the poetry has been dramatically improved by the completion of the Oxford Clarendon edition of the poetry, which amounts finally to nine weighty volumes published between 1984 and 2003. Other collections from the same team – and latterly from editors sometimes with contrasting editorial and interpretative regimes – have given the study of Clare a firm if, at times, contested textual foundation for further critical advances. The monumental impact of the Oxford edition is beyond doubt: it is an extraordinary achievement of determined, committed scholarly labour. Editing Clare is hard work indeed. His manuscripts are notoriously and riotously ungovernable, and often unreadable. Some are even disintegrating due to the corrosiveness of Clare's homemade ink – his written words have become looping, sometimes indecipherable, holes in paper. Yet the unsettled nature of Clare's textual life remains a dominant and idiosyncratic feature of the study of this poet. Presentations of his work include the textually primitivist extreme of the Oxford edition of the poetry; Margaret Grainger's edition of the *Natural History Prose Writings* and Mark Storey's edition of the letters,[27] both textually primitivist in their own ways; and the Mid-Northumberland Arts Group (MidNAG) and Carcanet editions of poetry and prose[28] (similarly primitivist though with some variance). More editorially liberal agendas are seen in the parallel texts of Tim Chilcott's Carcanet edition of *The Shepherd's Calendar* (showing transcriptions in tandem of both manuscript and 1827 published versions), and in the lightly polished selections such as those edited by Kelsey Thornton (the selection used to teach Clare in English secondary schools) and Jonathan Bate[29] (who argues there and elsewhere for a polished text[30]). An altogether different realm of textual reproduction is found online, where one may find complete facsimiles and transcriptions of the original lifetime publications; though of varying quality and reliability, these online versions of the poems comprise as important an entry point to Clare as any other today. This textual and editorial complexity – which is politicized, sometimes heatedly, and even fought over via lawyers' letters – means that still more critical and theoretical attention will have to be paid by future Clare scholars to the ways in which his texts might best be presented to an ever-widening readership. There remains a lot of work to do. The more plural the audience becomes for Clare – and the more varied its demands at different points and levels of access to his world and work – the more multifarious the editions and presentations of his work will necessarily become. This is beginning to happen, and the prospect of this next stage in the developing history of Clare's life and texts is an exciting one indeed. This is a good time to be interested in Clare.

This collection of new work charts some of the breadth of Clare's diversity, featuring essays which range from Clare's engagement with poetic tradition to his contemporary presence as a beacon for environmental thinking. In Adam Rounce's hands, Clare's encounter with his eighteenth-century poetic forebears Thomson and Cowper has 'benefits and limitations', yet remains foundationally significant. Sam Ward grapples with the complex, subtle politics of Clare's relationships with patrons and promoters – especially with the sometimes toxic, yet hugely supportive, presence of Lord Radstock in Clare's early writing life. Richard Cronin newly assesses Clare's place in the vibrant London and *London Magazine* scene, which Clare was both a part of and apart from. Fiona Stafford on colour, and Sarah Zimmerman on birds' nests, distinctively pursue the poetic complexity of Clare's delicate, artful presentations of nature, while John Burnside looks to Clare as an insightful commentator on his own times, and on our contemporary ecological and social issues. Emma Mason is the first critic to consider how Clare's celebrated green politics might be informed by his understanding of divinity and faith, while Robert Heyes seeks to dispel some green myths with a detailed account of Clare's natural history prose, and the rich social contexts out of which such knowledge emerged. Scott McEathron and Simon Kövesi consider the reception and presentation of Clare, through the career of his first biographer Frederick Martin, and the framing imprint of death, respectively. One hundred and fifty years after Clare's death, the literary riches he left to us all are proving far from small.

This inventory confirms the current consensus that critical responses to Clare need no longer be framed by justifications of his work's value, or even by preliminary discussions of the phenomenon of labouring-class poetry. Instead, we find at this moment a sense of interpretive capaciousness that Clare himself, who told the Northampton physician Dr P. R. Nesbitt that his poetry 'came to him whilst walking in the fields – that he kicked it out of the clods', might have found appealing. Indeed, if there is one principle uniting the essays collected here, it is that all proceed from the conviction that, as Nesbitt noted, Clare possessed traits 'we are in the habit of associating with ... the highest order of intellect'.[31] This is a position that frees us from the false dichotomy of Clare as either importunate peasant or martyred genius, and that helps us recognize the striking variety of topics and issues to which Clare responded as a thinking artist. The spirit of this collection is to look directly at these interests, and to confront their inevitable remaking and appropriation in still-emerging contexts of reception.

Notes

1. John Forster, *The Life of Charles Dickens*, ed. J. W. T. Ley (London: Cecil Palmer, 1928), pp. 820–2. Forster's biography was first published 1872–4.
2. For an overview of the reception of Frederick Martin's 1865 biography, and then J. L. Cherry's *Life and Remains* of 1873, see *Critical Heritage*, pp. 15–16. For an account of Martin's career, see the essay by Scott McEathron in this volume, pp. 118–45.
3. John Lucas draws some interesting parallels between Dickens' fiction and Clare's life in his *John Clare* (Plymouth: Northcote House, 1994), pp. 2 and 7.
4. *The Times*, 20 May 1964, p. 13. This leader would most likely have been written by the paper's editor at the time, William Haley. The Samuel Johnson witticism was originally aimed at women, so Haley's redirection suggests there are parallels between the status of women and working-class people with intellectual aspirations. James Boswell recollects: 'I told him I had been that morning at a meeting of the people called Quakers, where I had heard a woman preach. JOHNSON. "Sir, a woman's preaching is like a dog's walking on *his* hind legs. It is not done well; but you are surprised to find it done at all."' *The Life of Samuel Johnson*, 9th edn, 4 vols. (London: T. Cadell et al., 1822), vol. 1, p. 408. For a feminist assessment, see Alan Richardson, 'Romanticism and the Colonization of the Feminine', in Anne K. Mellor (ed.), *Romanticism and Feminism* (Bloomington and Indianapolis: Indiana University Press, 1988), pp. 13–25 (p. 14).
5. *Letters*, p. 604.
6. The authoritative account of Allen's asylum, and his care for Clare, is by Pamela Faithfull, *An Evaluation of an Eccentric: Matthew Allen MD, Chemical Philosopher, Phrenologist, Pedagogue and Mad-Doctor, 1783–1845* (University of Sheffield: PhD Thesis, 2001), especially pp. 173–88. For further discussion see Chapter 7 by Simon Kövesi in this volume, pp. 146–66.
7. 1862 is the date ascribed by the National Portrait Gallery, London, to W. W. Law's photograph. National Portrait Gallery number: P1101.
8. In his review of Ley's new edition of the Forster biography of Dickens, poet and editor Alan Porter writes that 'a concentration upon one literary figure

seems often to forbid knowledge of others; editors become too obvious partisans. It is to be hoped that, if a new edition of the book is called for, Mr. Ley will see his way to alter his note on John Clare; it is both unsympathetic and inaccurate.' *Spectator*, 30 June 1928, p. 27. Ley's only note reads 'John Clare, "the peasant poet." Born, a labourer's son, 1793; died in Northampton lunatic asylum, 1864. His book, *Poems, Descriptive of Rural Life*, was published in 1821, and had a good reception. Despite the aid of many friends (including the Marquess of Exeter), he never prospered.' *Life of Charles Dickens*, p. 843, n. 492a. Other than its inaccuracy (it should be 1820 not 1821), it is hard to see quite what upset Porter so much. Porter had co-edited a groundbreaking edition of Clare's poetry with Edmund Blunden, *Poems, Chiefly from Manuscript* (London: Cobden-Sanderson, 1920), which was reissued in 1934.

9. Hugh Haughton and Adam Phillips, 'Introduction: Relocating John Clare', in Haughton, pp. 1–27 (p. 13).
10. 'An English Peasant', *All the Year Round*, I.6 (9 January 1869), 132–6 (132–4). Published anonymously, as were all items in this publication, and attributed to Charles Mackay by Ella Ann Oppelander, *Dickens' All the Year Round: Descriptive Index and Contributor List* (Troy, New York: Whitston Publishing, 1984), p. 213.
11. Mackay, 'An English Peasant', pp. 133, 132.
12. Charles Mackay, 'The Working Classes', *Blackwood's Edinburgh Magazine*, February 1867, pp. 220–9 (p. 229).
13. Edwin Paxton Hood, 'John Clare, The Peasant Poet', in *The Literature of Labour: Illustrious Instances of the Education of Poetry in Poverty* (London: Partridge and Oakey, 1851), pp. 128–64 (p. 155). Extracted in *Critical Heritage*, pp. 257–66. Samuel Smiles, 'John Clare', in *Brief Biographies* (Boston: Ticknor and Fields, 1861), pp. 432–9 (p. 438).
14. Sales, p. 99.
15. *Poems by John Clare*, ed. Norman Gale (Rugby: George E. Over, 1901).
16. Anonymous reviewer, *Spectator*, 25 January 1902, p. 40.
17. The pastoral poems of Norman Gale (1862–1942) were always on the remotest fringes of the more decadent and fashionable Bodley Head publishing coterie of London – a *fin-de-siècle* group which included the influential poet and critic Arthur Symons, who went on to edit Clare himself a few years later (see note 19 below). By the time Gale turned to edit Clare, he was a thoroughly ignored poet, a situation that continues to this day, with the exception of Michael Seeney, *A Six Foot Three Nightingale: Norman Gale, 1862–1942: A Biographical Essay and Check-List*, Occasional Series 7 (Oxford: Eighteen Nineties Society, 1998). Seeney lists, but does not discuss, the Clare edition.
18. J. L. Cherry, *Life and Remains of John Clare* (London: F. Warne, 1873).
19. *Poems by John Clare*, ed. Arthur Symons (London: H. Frowde, 1908); *Poems, Chiefly from Manuscript*, ed. Edmund Blunden and Alan Porter (London: Cobden-Sanderson, 1920); *Madrigals and Chronicles: Being Newly Found*

Poems Written by John Clare, ed. Edmund Blunden (London: Beaumont Press, 1924); *Sketches in the life of John Clare*, ed. Edmund Blunden (London: Cobden-Sanderson, 1931).
20. J. W. Tibble and Anne Tibble, *John Clare: A Life* (London: Cobden-Sanderson, 1932); *The Poems of John Clare*, ed. J.W. Tibble (London: J. M. Dent, 1935); *The Prose of John Clare*, ed. J. W. Tibble and Anne Tibble (London: Routledge & Kegan Paul, 1951); *The Letters of John Clare*, ed. J. W. Tibble and Anne Tibble (London: Routledge & Kegan Paul, 1951); J. W. Tibble and Anne Tibble, *John Clare: His Life and Poetry* (London: Heinemann, 1956); *Selected Poems of John Clare*, ed. Leonard Clark and Anne Tibble (Leeds: E. J. Arnold & Son, 1964); John Clare, *The Midsummer Cushion*, ed. Anne Tibble and R. K. R. Thornton (Ashington and Manchester: MidNAG/Carcanet, 1979); John Clare, *The Journal; Essays; The Journey From Essex*, ed. Anne Tibble (Ashington and Manchester: MidNAG/Carcanet, 1980). Even this list does not capture all of the Tibbles' Clare publications.
21. *Poems of John Clare's Madness*, ed. Geoffrey Grigson (London: Routledge & Kegan Paul, 1949); *Selected Poems of John Clare*, ed. Geoffrey Grigson (London: Routledge & Kegan Paul, 1950).
22. *The Later Poems of John Clare*, ed. Eric Robinson and Geoffrey Summerfield (Manchester: Manchester University Press, 1964); John Clare, *Selected Poems and Prose*, ed. Eric Robinson and Geoffrey Summerfield (Oxford: Oxford University Press, 1966); John Clare, *The Shepherd's Calendar*, ed. Eric Robinson and Geoffrey Summerfield (Oxford: Oxford University Press, 1973).
23. For full bibliographic details of these volumes see 'Abbreviations', pp. xi–xii.
24. David Simpson, 'Is the Academy Ready for John Clare?', *JCSJ*, 18 (1999), 70–8 (74). The essay by Nicholas Birns that Simpson refers to is in Haughton, pp. 189–220.
25. *John Clare in Context*, ed. Hugh Haughton, Adam Phillips and Geoffrey Summerfield (Cambridge: Cambridge University Press, 1994). The same year saw the publication of another excellent collection of papers, edited by John Goodridge, entitled *The Independent Spirit: John Clare and the Self-Taught Tradition* (Helpston: John Clare Society and Margaret Grainger Memorial Trust, 1994).
26. Since 1994, book-length highlights in the critical study of Clare include Ronald Blythe, *Talking About John Clare* (Nottingham: Trent Books, 1999); John Goodridge and Simon Kövesi (eds.), *John Clare: New Approaches* (Helpston: John Clare Society, 2000); Roger Sales, *John Clare: A Literary Life* (Basingstoke: Palgrave, 2002); Alan Vardy, *John Clare, Politics and Poetry* (Basingstoke: Palgrave Macmillan, 2003); Paul Chirico, *John Clare and the Imagination of the Reader* (Basingstoke: Palgrave Macmillan, 2007); Mina Gorji, *John Clare and the Place of Poetry* (Liverpool: Liverpool University Press, 2008); Sarah Houghton-Walker, *John Clare's Religion* (Farnham: Ashgate, 2009); John Goodridge, *John Clare and Community* (Cambridge: Cambridge University Press, 2013). Many more academic studies feature chapters on, or considerations of, Clare, and his work is a much

more frequent presence in academic journals, reviews and the press – and indeed in English education at primary, secondary and tertiary levels, and in creative work – than it has ever been. For an overview of how Clare studies has developed across thirty years in the *John Clare Society Journal*, since its first issue in 1982, see Greg Crossan, 'Thirty Years of the *John Clare Society Journal*: A Retrospective Survey', *JCSJ*, 31 (2012), 5–22.

27. *The Natural History Prose Writings of John Clare*, ed. Margaret Grainger (Oxford: Clarendon Press, 1983); *The Letters of John Clare*, ed. Mark Storey (Oxford: Clarendon Press, 1985).
28. John Clare, *The Rural Muse*, ed. R. K. R. Thornton (Ashington and Manchester: MidNAG/Carcanet, 1982); John Clare, *The Midsummer Cushion*, ed. R. K. R. Thornton and Anne Tibble (Ashington and Manchester: MidNAG/Carcanet, 1990); John Clare, *Cottage Tales*, ed. Eric Robinson, David Powell and P. M. S. Dawson (Ashington and Manchester: MidNAG/Carcanet, 1993); John Clare, *Northborough Sonnets*, ed. Eric Robinson, David Powell and P. M. S. Dawson (Ashington and Manchester: MidNAG/Carcanet, 1995); John Clare, *By Himself*, ed. Eric Robinson and David Powell (Ashington and Manchester: MidNAG/Carcanet, 1996); John Clare, *A Champion for the Poor: Political Verse and Prose*, ed. P. M. S. Dawson, Eric Robinson and David Powell (Ashington and Manchester: MidNAG/Carcanet, 2000).
29. *John Clare*, ed. R. K. R. Thornton (London: J. M. Dent, 1997); John Clare, *The Shepherd's Calendar: Manuscript and Published Version*, ed. Tim Chilcott (Manchester: Carcanet, 2006); *'I Am': the Selected Poetry of John Clare*, ed. Jonathan Bate (New York: Farrar, Straus and Giroux, 2003). See also Chilcott's experimental 'calendrical' edition *John Clare: The Living Year 1841* (Nottingham: Trent Editions, 1999).
30. See, for example, Jonathan Bate, Review of *John Clare: Poems of the Middle Period 1822–1837*, vols. 3 and 4, *JCSJ*, 18 (1999), 79–83, and Bate, 'Appendix: Clare's Text', *Biography*, pp. 563–75. For further consideration of editorial policies, see the introductions to any of the Oxford Clarendon editions listed above, and Zachary Leader, *Revision and Romantic Authorship* (Oxford: Oxford University Press, 1996), pp. 206–61; R. K. R. Thornton, 'What John Clare Do We Read?', *PN Review*, 31.4 (March–April, 2005), 54–56, and 'The Raw and the Cooked', *JCSJ*, 24 (2005), 78–86; and Simon Kövesi, 'Beyond the Language Wars: Towards a Green Edition of John Clare', *JCSJ*, 26 (2007), 61–75.
31. P. R. Nesbitt to Frederick Martin, 15 April 1865, Nor. 58.

PART I

Poetry

CHAPTER I

John Clare's colours

Fiona Stafford

In his third 'Natural History Letter', John Clare remarked that 'I love to look on nature with a poetic feeling which magnifys the pleasure'.[1] Clare not only looked frequently and directly at the natural world, but loved what he saw and was not afraid to say so. If the precise details of the external world were of prime importance to his poetry, his perception was nevertheless highly individual and emotional. The same letter expresses both intellectual frustration over the 'ignorance of nature in large Citys' (prompted by the failure of a London 'gentleman and lady' to recognize a song thrush) and also pained dismay at the practices of 'naturalists and botanists', who 'dry the plant or torture the Butterflye by sticking it on a cork board with a pin'.[2] Clare was well aware that not everyone sees things in the same way and his poetry, accordingly, combines convincing observation of a known world with deeply personal responses. For him, seeing meant feeling – and both were part of an experiential wholeness that was, at the same time, open to fresh possibility.

Unlike the scientists whose pursuit of truth seemed at odds with life itself or those who failed to notice the natural world at all, Clare's was an essentially creative response and the feeling that magnified his pleasure was more akin to that of a certain kind of visual artist. Clare admired the modern landscape painters who not only looked with clear eyes at the real world, but also seemed to share his delight in what they saw, transforming quite ordinary stretches of countryside into glowing fields of light. In his own endeavour to recreate the world in words, Clare's powerful, subjective response to his immediate environment found expression in the language of colour, which he used just as adventurously as did his artistic contemporaries. Here was a means to express the dynamic reciprocation between the imaginative impulse and objective reality, without the deadening tones of philosophical analysis. In Clare's hands, the use of colour seems natural and intuitive: a deceptively simple means to express a living world. Once seen in the context of Romantic painting, however, Clare's highly distinctive use of colour emphasizes the experimental qualities of his art and its affinities with the modern, progressive aesthetic movements of his day.

For Clare, the fullness of the natural world demanded an equivalent response and so, in many of his poems, visual detail is inseparable from verbal delight. The second stanza of the relatively late lyric beginning 'The wind blows happily on everything' conveys a passion for natural phenomena through the simple recurrence of the word 'green', which gradually seems to flood the monochrome, two-dimensional printed page with fresh colour. The power of the poet's impulse to 'magnify' what he sees compels the repetitions with increasing force:

> I love the luscious green before the bloom
> The leaves & grass & even beds of moss
> When leaves gin bud & spring prepares to come
> The Ivys evergreen the brown green gorse
> Plots of green weeds that barest roads engross
> In fact I love the youth of each green thing
> The grass the trees the bushes & the moss
> That pleases little birds & makes them sing
> I love the green before the blooms of spring
> (lines 10–18; *Later Poems*, I, 205)[3]

Not every poet would risk the same, simple word six times in a nine-line stanza, but here 'green' seems to grow in intensity with every new instance, linking the lines acoustically, visually and imaginatively. The final line returns to the tenth, but now transforming what had seemed a spontaneous response to natural surroundings into a fully justified statement. This is the culmination of a poem full of disparate details, which yet are made all of a piece. The dominant colour of the stanza, the 'luscious green before the bloom', seems to spread unstoppably through the alliterative lines – 'leaves & grass', 'leaves gin bud', 'brown green gorse', 'barest roads engross' – as the sounds of the repeating consonants herald the inexorable arrival of spring.

The absence of punctuation adds to the sense of interconnection, for the leaves in line 12 seem to be springing up as well as budding, until the rest of the line suggests that a new subject – spring – has appeared. Similarly, the 'Ivys evergreen' (line 13) may be the object of the speaker's love, but if 'evergreen' is also working as a verb, it can convey the effects of ivy plants on brown trunks and dead leaves. So much depends on where the reader places the pauses in the long, unbroken passage, and whether any pauses are really needed in a stanza in which everything is green. Despite this pervasive colouration, each detail is still distinguished: the 'evergreen' of the Ivy is not the same as the 'brown green' of the gorse (if 'brown' is qualifying 'green') or the 'luscious green' of the leaf buds, blades of grass and beds of moss. The very consciousness of difference only adds to the overall sense of the season, stemming as it does from carefully observed, but also *habitual* experience. These are not the words of someone who is seeing the spring for the first time – the reassurance of the lines, the foundation of the love that is being expressed so emphatically, lies in their repetition. The passionate delight in immediate physical experience is magnified by the familiarity arising from seeing the same fields, bushes and trees day after day and week after week. This is the annual renewal of tender feeling – all the more marvellous for being instantly recognizable. Green is not a symbol for spring, but a pledge that spring is about to arrive, affirmed and reaffirmed with every bud. In another poem from the same period, beginning 'How beautiful is Spring!', fresh shoots appear 'in promise to the sun' ('Spring', line 11; *Later Poems*, I, 378). Recurrent greenery suggests the rising sap of the new growing season: gradually, the natural world is waking up, visible, tangible, and still preliminary, about to burst into a multitude of soft, fresh colours.

In Clare's poetry, 'green' has many meanings, ranging from the numerous subtle shades of leaves on different trees, flowers or mosses to the varied moods that the word seems to carry. The 'deader green' of 'The Flitting' (line 54; *Middle Period*, III, 481) offers a very different emotional charge from that of the 'sunny air right green & young' in 'Old Poesy' (line 19; *Middle Period*, IV, 197) or the 'green/In some warm nook' in 'The Gipsies Evening Blaze' (lines 3–4; *Early Poems*, I, 33). In 'Out of Door Pleasures', Clare focuses on the special quality of the summer 'green', the colour seemingly intensified by its association with new-mown grass:

> The meadows are mown, what a beautiful hue
> There is in green closes as I wander through
> A green of all colors, yellow, brown and dark grey
> While the footpaths all darkly goes winding away
> (lines 5–8; *Later Poems*, I, 342)

We can almost smell the 'beautiful hue'. And yet, the knowledge that the long grass has been cut also reminds us of the perpetual changes in the rural world: green may be recurrent in Clare's poetry, but it is not constant. Meadow grass turns rapidly to hay. Again, the syntax in this passage adds to the ambiguity of its greenness, because it is difficult to determine whether the 'green of all colours' includes tints of 'yellow, brown and dark grey' or whether green is, of all colours, the most beautiful. Since the adjective turns almost imperceptibly into a noun, it is equally unclear whether 'A green' (line 7) still refers to the hue, or whether it has now become a grassy space or greensward. In a later summer sonnet, Clare describes how 'The silver mist more lowly swims/And each green bosomed valley dims' making 'Green trees look grey, bright waters black' ('Sonnet', lines 1–2, 5; *Later Poems*, I, 350). In *The Shepherd's Calendar*, too, 'August' begins with direct reference to the changing year, as registered in the colour of the fields: 'Harvest approaches with its busy day/The wheat tans brown & barley bleaches grey' (lines 1–2; *Middle Period*, I, 118). Given Clare's acute sensitivity to the transitory qualities of natural colour, the run of 'yellow, brown and dark grey' in 'Out of Door Pleasures' may well anticipate a similar fading of bright spring greens as the year grows older. On the other hand, in that poem – and many others – thoughts of future decay also accentuate the beauty of the present. Whether the other colours are immediate tints or hints of what's to come, Clare's lines invite multiple simultaneous possibilities.

Since the evocation of colour is especially challenging for the artist whose medium is language, such ambiguities are only too appropriate. As soon as we begin to visualize a particular green, as these lines encourage us to do, we realize that whatever we are imagining must be highly subjective. Again and again, Clare's poetry teases us with its vivid sense of objective physical reality and simultaneous emphasis on the personal nature of perception, memory and interpretation. From an early age, Clare had been conscious that his responses to the world were somewhat unusual, as he recalled in the autobiographical 'Sketches', composed in 1821: 'I thought somtimes that I surely had a taste peculialy by myself and that nobody else thought or saw things as I did'.[4] Of all the aspects of daily experience, few are more subjective than colour; although everyone possesses an idea of 'green', who can be sure that his particular shade corresponds exactly to what others might think of as 'green'? What appears to be commonsensical may in fact be highly individual – but this is what makes Clare's use of colour so effective. 'Red', 'yellow', 'blue' and 'green' are among the earliest adjectives learned by children to make sense of the world, and yet colour remains mysteriously elusive, exercising the powers of physicists, philosophers and psychologists in the struggle to determine its nature and meaning.[5]

Clare's own interest in children's natural attraction to brightly coloured phenomena emerges in his letter on 'Pooty shells' – the brilliant yellow, red and black shells of landsnails, which he had loved to collect since his schooldays. For Clare the adult observer, the pleasure in pooty shells was deepened by memories of 'happy hours' spent hunting for them in youth.[6] They were in a way Clare's equivalent of Wordsworth's rainbow – reminding him that the child was father of the man: fresh discovery of shells as colourful as those gathered years before meant recovery of an earlier self that often seemed in danger of slipping away. The long description of bright pooty shells thus helps to illuminate the colours in Clare's poetry, not least the recurrent green, which frequently trails clouds of childhood glory. Adult awareness of the ever-turning seasons, however, meant that the joy of childhood memories was rarely undiluted. A 'green' summer's day was not only tinged with recollections of paler, sharper, spring greens, but also with the deeper fullness of deciduous trees in harvest months. The natural details are at once vividly present and reassuringly habitual, but they are also capable of delivering pangs of wistfulness for remembered greens, irretrievable as childhood. Clare's colours have the capacity to convey the passage of time, even as they capture a fully realized moment. In 'Out of Door Pleasures', the spontaneous response to a fine day in June is magnified by the simple names of colours, carrying thoughts of cooler months and earlier years.

Clare and painting

Colour is a vital but fluid element in Clare's art – acting in some respects as a visual counterpart to the unpunctuated poetry of his manuscripts. Just as the successive phrases in his poems run on, unhindered by full stops and semi-colons, so the recurrent images of colour mingle imperceptibly. Greens can blend into yellows, browns, greys and blues, lighting up under a pervasive sun or fading through silver mists. Everything is vividly realized and yet slipping away from hard lines and limits. In 'Pleasant Places' Clare celebrates the absence of clear definitions in the 'Old stone pits with veined ivy overhung' (line 1), or the 'Old narrow lanes where trees meet overhead' (line 4), concluding with his praise of the wind:

> While painting winds to make compleat the scene
> In rich confusion mingles every green
> Waving the sketchy pencil in their hands
> Shading the living scenes to fairey lands
> (lines 11–14; *Middle Period*, IV, 225)

The wind is a natural artist, setting everything in motion and defying fixed distinctions. Clare's lines, too, complete the scene conjured in the sonnet, with a syntactical confusion over whether it is the mingled 'green' or the 'sketchy pencil' that is 'shading' the rest. The scene is 'moving' not only because of the physical force of the wind, but also because of the poet's delight in what he sees and recreates for others. Clare's poem draws parallels between the arts of the poet, the visual artist and Nature – an imaginative celebration of creative forces, fused together in the word 'scene'. This suggests a visual depiction of landscape *and* a dramatic piece, as well as the natural creation. Though rather less emphatic than Coleridge's references to the 'mighty Poet' in 'Dejection: An Ode', Clare is employing the wind, a common Romantic metaphor for divine inspiration, to suggest connections between the creative impulses of human beings and God. The play on 'scene' also reiterates the importance of what is being 'seen', overwhelming the visual distinctions with acoustic unity – just as the wild wind so often does.

The resistance to boundaries, evident in 'Pleasant Places', is couched in the language of the Picturesque, with its well-established opposition to classical lines and regularity. Uvedale Price, for example, had rejected the old aesthetic rules separating 'the sublime' from 'the beautiful', in favour of the principles of 'harmony, and connection', arguing for the superiority of more natural 'unimproved' landscapes because 'symmetry and regularity are particularly adverse to the picturesque'.[7] Clare's own attraction to visual analogies and the language of painting derived partly from their power to unsettle clear divisions and challenge the limitations of convention. In a fragmentary 'Essay on Landscape', for example, he wrote admiringly of the paintings of his contemporary, Peter DeWint:

> there is the simplest touches possible giving the most natural possible effects the eye is led over the Landscape as far as a sunbeam can reach & the sky & earth blends into a humanity of greetings & beautiful harmony & symetry of pleasant imaginings – There is no harsh stoppage no bounds to space or any outline further then there is in nature – if we could possibly walk into the picture we fancy we might pursue the landscape beyond those mysterys (not bounds) assigned it so as we can in the fields – so natural & harmonious are his perceptions & tints & lights & shadows[8]

Clare's response to DeWint sheds helpful light on his own aesthetic ideals and the deployment of highly visual images – especially colour – in his poetry. The way in which DeWint's landscape is seen to blend 'into a humanity of greetings' is strongly reminiscent of Clare's sense of the 'poet's feeling', which 'magnifys the pleasure' of looking at the natural world. Crucial to DeWint's effects are both his 'natural & harmonious' perceptions – and his 'tints & lights & shadows'. The painter's reliance on 'the simplest touches' also recalls Clare's unabashed use of the plain vocabulary of colour. In that apparent simplicity, however, a whole world opens up. DeWint's scene is without any 'harsh stoppage', or 'bounds', or 'any outline further than there is in nature' – and because he achieves such a sense of boundlessness in a small, two-dimensional space, the viewer is welcomed into his art, as if into a series of endless fields. In her pioneering essay on 'John Clare and DeWint', Lynn Banfield Pearce suggests that Clare's admiration for the boundlessness of DeWint's art was related to his anxieties about enclosure, and his attraction to wilder spaces, such as those evoked in 'The Mores'[9]. However, we might also fruitfully explore his remarks on DeWint's landscapes in relation to his own artistic endeavour – his own desire to create 'natural & harmonious' poems, in which there were no stoppages or bounds, and into which the viewer might be encouraged to enter imaginatively, discovering a new, hidden world.

Early reviewers of Clare's poetry were struck by the resemblance between his approach to the rural world and its portrayal by the contemporary artist George Morland. Josiah Conder, writing in the *Eclectic Review* in 1822, thought that Clare's poems 'breathe of Nature in every line', going on to suggest that they were 'like Morland's inimitable drawings, not studies from nature, but transcripts of her works'.[10] The poet himself, however, was much more taken with DeWint: 'The only artist that produces real English scenery in which British landscapes are seen and felt upon paper with all their poetry and exillerating expression of beauty about them is Dewint'.[11] This praise of DeWint's art can be read in tandem with Clare's substantial poem 'Shadows of Taste', which dwells on the process whereby the natural world is transcribed onto the page to become a fully embodied imaginative landscape:

> In poesys vision more refined & fair
> Taste reads oerjoyed & greets her image there
> Dashes of sunshine & a page of may
> Live there a whole life long one summers day
> A blossom in its witchery of bloom
> There gathered dwells in beauty & perfume
> The singing bird the brook that laughs along
> There ceasless sing & never thirsts for song
> A pleasing image to its page conferred
> In living character & breathing word
> Becomes a landscape heard & felt & seen

> Sunshine & shade one harmonizing green
> Where meads & brooks & forrests basking lie
> Lasting as truth & the eternal sky
> (lines 63–76; *Middle Period*, III, 305–6)[12]

The ideal of the true artist, whether working with words or watercolour, was the creation of a 'landscape heard and felt and seen' (line 73). And if the image on paper seemed to live and breathe, it offered a truth as eternal as nature's own. If spring was the 'Poesy of seasons! Scripture of the year!' ('Spring', line 10), DeWint could be lauded as a fellow scribe, transferring the creations of nature to virtual life on paper. Unlike the classically trained artists of the Royal Academy, who were taught to follow nature through studying the perfect statuary of ancient Greece, DeWint seemed to be responding directly to the English countryside, creating paintings with a new kind of truth: 'admirers of nature will admire his paintings – for they are her autographs & not a painters studys from the antique'.[13] DeWint seemed to make painting an 'out of door pleasure' and his clear-sighted observation of natural phenomena, under the constantly shifting light of the sun, offered very different possibilities from the lamp-lit figures and drapery of the formal studio. In fact, DeWint had taken classes at the Royal Academy and originally trained as an engraver and portrait painter, but what Clare recognized in his mature landscapes was a kindred delight in the natural world for its own sake.[14] The feeling in the painting depended not just on an accurate reproduction of a pleasing view, but also on the passionate response of the artist. Creation of a painted landscape that could be 'heard and felt and seen' required the combined effort of eye, ear, hand, heart and mind.

What Clare loved about DeWint is articulated most clearly in a letter he wrote in 1829, requesting from the artist

> one of those rough sketches taken in the fields that breathes with the living freshness of open air & sunshine where the blending & harmony of earth air & sky are in such a happy unison of greens & greys that a flat bit of scenery on a few inches of paper appear so many miles[15]

Although the letter does not seem to have had the desired effect on DeWint, it demonstrates again Clare's admiration for a kind of art that flourishes in the open air, responsive to natural harmonies and capable of enlarging what is being perceived through the brilliantly blended colours of living freshness. As his sonnet 'To Dewint' would subsequently emphasize, these were paintings marked by 'the sunny truth/Of nature' (lines 7–8, *Middle Period*, IV, 198). Far from imprisoning the landscape in a fixed frame, or turning it into a series of separate parts, DeWint's paintings encouraged the discovery of imaginative immensity in the most ordinary places. Even the flattest fenland seemed brimming with life and possibility, when the 'greens & greys' were in 'happy unison'. Clare knew only too well that the ordinary observer of Lincolnshire's 'level pastures' saw 'nothing deemed divine', but in DeWint the unlikely county found 'a worshipper' who

> worked such rich surprise
> That rushy flats befringed with willow tree
> Rivald the beauties of italian skies (lines 12–14)

When it came to creating a frontispiece for *The Shepherd's Calendar*, with its direct descriptions of rural life and celebrations of the inexhaustible pleasures of the turning months, DeWint was the obvious choice (see Figure 1). In 1827, the technology for mass colour printing had yet to be developed, however, so the image gracing Clare's collection was a black and white engraving. Though grateful for the illustration, which he described as 'a very beautiful thing', Clare's letter still betrays a lurking disappointment as he judges the cask-like drinking vessel in the reaper's hands 'too big for the company in fact' and 'too big for a bottle at all'.[16] The oversized 'stout hooped bottle' (line 102) is certainly very visible in the small group of figures, completely obscuring the face of the reaper who is drinking from it. Clare's comments express unease over its clear predominance – a predominance DeWint ensures by directing slanting beams of light from distant clouds to the drinking labourer. Unlike many of DeWint's beautiful landscapes, this is not a scene free from outlines and stoppages, in which everything is boundless and harmonious. Indeed, it is a scene depicting 'stoppage' itself, as the farm workers are shown seated and refreshing themselves, reclining against hay in an idyllic harvest field. Yet in *The Shepherd's Calendar*, the harvest month of 'August' is portrayed as the most action-packed and strenuous of the entire year, so for the frontispiece to foreground a rare pause in the back-breaking work was hardly representative.

The lines that relate most closely to the image are also far less peaceful than DeWint's drawing suggests, coming immediately after a disturbing cameo in which a 'rude boy or churlish hearted swain' chases terrified mice from the fresh straw, spreading 'an instant murder all around' (line 82). After a scene 'so cruel' that the young female labourer 'forgets her song' (line 86), the cessation of work seems more like the aftermath of a massacre than a pastoral idyll:

Figure 1 'August', 1827, a group of figures resting beside a pile of corn in a field, including a young woman facing to front, dog and a man drinking from a barrel, workers in the fields beyond at right; after Peter DeWint, frontispiece to John Clare's *The Shepherd's Calendar*. ©The Trustees of the British Museum

> They seek an awthorn bush or willow tree
> For resting places that the coolest be
> Where baskets heapd & unbroached bottles lye
> Which dogs in absence watchd with wary eye
> To catch their breath awhile & share the boon
> Which beavering time alows their toil at noon
> All gathering sit on stubbs or sheaves the hour
> Where scarlet poppys linger still in flower
>   Next to her favoured swain the maiden steals
> Blushing at kindness which his love reveals
> Who makes a seat for her of things around
> & drops beside her on the naked ground
> Then from its cool retreat the beer they bring
> & hand the stout hooped bottle round the ring
> Each swain soaks hard – the maiden ere she sips
> Shreaks at the bold whasp settling on her lips
> That seems determined only hers to greet
> As if it fancied they were cherrys sweet
>   (lines 89–106; *Middle Period*, I, 122–4)

Far from being carefree and content, the workers are parched, exhausted and beset by wasps. Whether the 'swain' is the same man who had been murdering the mice a few lines earlier is unclear, but the rapid turn from unnecessary slaughter to soaking beer unsettles any sense of peace. The movement of the lines, running from moment to moment and shifting from dogs to flowers to humans, suggests a wholeness of experience and multiple perspectives. The harvest scene is also splashed with red – scarlet poppies, blushing cheeks and cherry lips all recall the destruction of the mice and highlight energies that still seem to be surging throughout. Clare's scene is moving, three-dimensional and internally connected – readers can feel the blood coursing through, even at a moment of apparent rest. Indeed, his disappointment with the illustrated title page may also have had something to do with the hardening of DeWint's art into clear lines – and the draining of colour necessitated by the impersonality of print.

Colour in art

The primacy of colour in the visual arts may now seem obvious enough, after a century of experimentation with non-representational chromatic painting and photography. In the early nineteenth century, however, the old aesthetic question of whether line or colour was the foundation of great art was still being hotly contested. In sixteenth-century Italy, Titian's revolutionary creation of form through colour had reignited a classical debate over '*disegno versus colore*', with Michelangelo's skill in drawing increasingly coming to be seen as the defining quality of his genius.[17] During the eighteenth century, admiration for the luminous colours of Titian and Rubens had to compete with the influence of Winckelmann and Flaxman, whose elevation of classical lines and ideal forms gained materially from the fashion for collecting the white marble statuary of ancient Greece and Rome.[18] French Romantic art, too, divided between the neoclassical emphasis on line advocated by Ingres and Delacroix's radical experimentation with colour. During the Romantic period, colour in painting started to be associated primarily with personal emotion and with the direct representation of real life. Although artists inherited a set of religious and cultural meanings for particular colours, they were increasingly finding ways of representing individual moods and feelings through combinations of shade and hue. The twentieth-century artist Bridget Riley, whose own abstract paintings show a deep, practical understanding of colour, has explained that it is the absence of guiding principles and firm theories relating to colour that allows 'each individual artistic sensibility ... a chance to discover a unique means of expression'.[19] In the early nineteenth century, debates were still raging over the very nature of colour, as Newton's spectrum was tested and questioned by German philosophers and artists, including Goethe and Runge, who developed their own alternative theories and increasingly emphasized the relationship between the perception of colour and the individual mind. For Goethe, art was 'an effusion of genius' and colour was as much part of inner experience as a quality of the external world.[20] Uncertainty about the very nature of colour militated against fixed aesthetic rules, freeing artists to use colour for expressing personal feeling, just as contemporary poets were developing their own new expressive aesthetic. As John Gage has commented, 'it is precisely the uncertainties and instabilities in the interpretation of colours that fit them especially for the expression of unstable emotions'.[21]

When he lectured to students at the Royal Academy in 1769, Sir Joshua Reynolds had avoided the old debates over colour and line by announcing that 'The power of drawing, modelling and using colours, is very properly called the Language of Art' – in other words, all were equally necessary to equip the budding artist for whatever he might wish to accomplish.[22] His later praise of Titian reveals a deep pleasure in colour, but is still qualified by a sense of the artist's one deficiency, in failing to correct 'the form of the model by any general idea of beauty in his own mind'.[23] Those who made colour their fundamental principle were those whose art did not aspire fully to the world of ideal forms, remaining too close to the real world of flesh and blood. Six years later, however, in 1788, Reynolds paid tribute to the genius of his recently deceased colleague, Thomas Gainsborough, whose chief strength lay in colour: 'Gainsborough having truly a painter's eye for colouring, cultivated those effects of the art which proceed from colours'.[24] Though in Reynolds's eyes Gainsborough's failure to strive for the grand style of Michelangelo meant relegation to the lower ranks of genius, his ability to find subjects 'every where about him ... in the streets and in the fields' and his skilful use of colour to recreate his 'new and higher perception of what is great and beautiful in Nature' still gave him sufficient stature to merit an entire discourse – unlike any other modern artist.[25] Reynolds's ideas about art were rooted in European traditions, but the sympathetic turn to Gainsborough in his late 'Discourse' is indicative of the new aesthetic trends that would gradually turn landscape painting into a genre worthy of the most talented artists of the nineteenth century.

The new movement of landscape painting, with its aspiration towards accurate representation of the natural world, meant that colour began to gain ascendancy as the crucial medium for the artist. As Gage observes, 'it was in landscape, from Rubens to Constable, the Pre-Raphaelites and Monet, that fidelity to the colours of the outdoor scene became a central aesthetic objective'.[26] The great enthusiasm for landscape painting sent artists out among the Cumbrian Lakes, the Scottish glens, the Welsh mountains, the East Anglian rivers and the fields of the Midlands, often equipped with watercolours to capture the shifting effects of the light most rapidly. Traditionally, watercolour paintings had tended to rely on line as much as colour, the sepia washes being largely subordinate to pen-and-ink drawings of buildings, churches or tree-lined riverbanks. With the new emphasis on accurate representation of nature in all her moods – and the concurrent movement to allow paintings to express the personal feelings of the artist in the scene – colour began to dominate and watercolour painting took on a much more varied spectrum. Where for eighteenth-century artists such as Paul Sandby, drawing had remained fundamental to topographical art, a new generation of watercolourists, including John Cozens, Thomas Girtin, J. M. W. Turner, Cornelius and John Varley, John Constable and John Sell Cotman, began to paint in such a way that their landscapes depended primarily on colour.[27] By the time the Society of Painters in Water-Colours was founded in 1804, their exhibitions displayed luminous skies, navy seashores, yellow waterways and hillsides formed from subtle greens and greys. Colour, not line, seemed best suited to recreating the British landscape in all her variety.

In some of Peter DeWint's watercolours the shapes of the landscape are created entirely by the application of darker washes over a lighter base. 'The Staith, Lincoln', for example, presents an entirely convincing image of the River Witham, winding away towards the horizon through banks that consist only of layers of amber and burnt-umber washes.[28] The river itself shines luminously in the foreground, reflecting the great expanse of pale sky above, which is all of the same creamy base colour. In paintings such as this there are no stoppages or hard outlines, and the entire scene is conveyed through subtle banks of colour, contours raised or levelled by the skilful stroke of another brush. Indeed, Pearce has suggested that the sense of boundlessness in DeWint's painting, so admired by Clare, owed much to his skills as a watercolourist.[29]

At first, the idea of a connection between landscape painting and the poetry of John Clare might lead to thoughts of pastoral escapism, especially since landscape art is often regarded as a largely elegiac genre, symptomatic of modern humanity's 'sense of alienation from its original habitat'.[30] To equate early nineteenth-century landscape art, whether verbal or visual, with nostalgia is, however, to neglect both the forward-looking and self-renewing qualities of the pastoral mode *and* the radical novelty of landscape art in the early nineteenth century. When Clare began to publish, landscape painting was regarded as a quintessentially modern art – popular with the public, but at odds with the artistic establishment. Constable's well-known difficulty over having paintings accepted for Royal Academy exhibitions is indicative of the uncertain status of landscape art and its unsettling novelty. The foundation of the Society of Watercolourists, too, was prompted by frustration over the Academy's resistance to recognizing the importance of contemporary watercolour landscapes. Far from pointing backwards, the parallel between contemporary landscape painting and Clare's poetry therefore underlines the innovative character of each.

Clare's 'Essay on Landscape' reveals a serious interest in modern art and the new kind of painting that eschewed traditional lines and rules to achieve a truthful, personal expression of the feelings inspired by natural beauty. The essential role of colour in landscape art, with its attendant power to express personal feelings, meant that while such paintings were direct responses to the living world of nature, their vitality derived as much from the artist as from the fields or streams. As John Lord has observed, the directness of a watercolour sketch 'had a sense of spontaneity which evoked the artist's emotional engagement with his subject'.[31] Clare's own distinctive use of colour in his poetry can fruitfully be seen not merely as a sign of his unquenchable yearning for childhood, but rather of an adventurous, experimental artistic ambition. Landscape art was modern and forward-looking – it conjured ideas of distant, imperceptible horizons, of fields beyond what was immediately visible. And while this may seem unlikely to appeal to a poet whose own sense of space was so firmly centred on a relatively small local area, once Clare is credited with the sophistication of a viewer who sees in paintings not just a real world, but rather a *representation* of a real world, perceived and reimagined by the creative artist, then the attraction of such views becomes much easier to understand.

It is evident from remarks on DeWint's paintings in the 'Essay on Landscape' that what Clare admired was the sense of enormous possibility embodied in a small, unassuming space: the invitation to walk in and pursue the landscape beyond what was immediately visible. Here was an art that spoke to the imagination as much as to the eye – offering a chance to enter a world beyond the surface and encouraging the celebration of mental freedom. When considering the visual dimensions of Clare's poetic art, then, it is fruitful to focus not just on poems that recreate landscapes or employ the language of the picturesque, but also those most laden with hidden possibility, with worlds within worlds. The poems that come closest to the aesthetic ideals set out in the 'Essay on Landscape' are probably the bird poems, because they so often include a world within, suggested and yet hidden, promising something evermore about to be. And crucial to their success as a series is Clare's innovative use of colour.

Bird poems

As quickly becomes apparent to any reader of the bird poems, among their many striking features is a fascination with eggs and nests. Not content with describing the bird's appearance, habits or distinctive call, Clare frequently includes the discovery of a nestful of eggs in his poems. And it is often at this revelatory point that the poem magnifies and flushes with colour, as in 'Hedge Sparrow':

> It makes a nest of moss & hair & lays
> When een the snow is lurking on the ground
> Its eggs in number five of greenish blue
> Bright beautiful & glossy shining shells
> Much like the fire tails but of brighter hue
> (lines 7–11; *Middle Period*, IV, 237)

Hidden at the centre of the poem, as if in a nest of lines and words, lie those 'Bright beautiful and glossy shining shells'. In the cold dregs of winter, in the midst of dead moss and discarded hair, lies the astonishing surprise of the season, arresting the eye with unexpected colour. It is almost like a nativity scene, especially as there are five eggs – the strange, mystical number, regarded by Clare as the sign of 'natures wonder & her makers will' in 'The Eternity of Nature' (line 99; *Middle Period*, III, 531). In 'The Thrushes Nest', the nest is formed gradually by the mother bird's

> secret toils from day to day
> How true she warped the moss to form her nest
> & modelled it within with wood & clay
> & bye & bye like heath bells gilt with dew
> There lay her shining eggs as bright as flowers
> Ink spotted over shells of greeny blue
> (lines 6–11; *Middle Period*, IV, 187)

The thrush is made something like a natural alchemist, toiling with mundane materials until suddenly the eggs, 'like heath bells gilt with dew', appear to dazzle the observer. In sonnets such as this the bird takes on the role of the artist, while the poet apparently gazes in admiration, witness to 'natures minstrels' (line 13) and their 'ink-spotted' creations. We now know that the distinctive markings on birds' eggs are part of the process of laying – the lines and spots are not inscriptions, but traces of pigment secreted by the hen bird.[32] The markings on some birds' eggs readily suggest the appearance of writing or pen-and-ink drawing, so Clare's description of the 'ink-spotted' thrush's eggs is visually accurate as well as reflective of personal preoccupations. In 'The Yellow Hammers Nest', the connection between bird and poet is even more explicit, and it is the eggs that provide the site of connection:

> —Five eggs pen-scribbled over lilac shells
> Resembling writing scrawls which fancy reads
> As natures poesy & pastoral spells
> They are the yellow hammers & she dwells
> A poet-like (lines 13–7; *Middle Period*, III, 516)

The passage suggests both direct, spontaneous response to the natural world, and the expression of a poet whose deep feeling for what he sees is inseparable from his own inner life. The sense of connection with the pen-scribbling bird-poet overcomes conventional boundaries to create a moment of deep joy at the heart of the poem. Even the sharp observation of markings that appear as scribbles and scrawls suggests kinship with a fellow labourer, whose creations may be involuntary, but nevertheless require great effort. If parallels between poets and birds had become commonplace in the Romantic period, Clare's special attention to the visual rather than purely aural dimensions of avian life made his work highly individual and innovative.[33]

That the yellowhammer is characterized primarily by colour is obvious from its popular name, but, as Clare's description of the 'pen-scribbled lilac shells' makes plain, recognition of the eggs is even more colour-dependent. Though there is considerable variety in size and some variation in the shape of birds' eggs, the basic oval of hedge or tree-nesting species makes it difficult to tell one from another: mere outline is insufficient to distinguish the chaffinch egg from the thrush. So too for the poet, the word 'egg' offers only a general image for the reader, but as soon as colour is introduced it becomes a real, textured object, shining on the page and in the imagination. Clare's descriptions of eggs, accordingly, need colour in order to affirm the individuality of the particular kind of bird. Both the hedge sparrow and the thrush lay eggs of 'greenish blue', but the wryneck's are 'white as snow' ('The Wry Necks Nest', line 6; *Middle Period*, IV, 290). The pettichap – or chiffchaff – has a tiny clutch, covered in 'spots as small/As dust – & of a faint & pinky red' ('The Pettichaps Nest', lines 25–6; *Middle Period*, III, 518), while the yellow wagtail's are 'sprinkled oer with spots of grey' ('The Yellow Wagtails Nest', line 19; *Middle Period*, III, 474). Birds are the only creatures whose eggs are coloured, and so Clare's remarkable poems – like the notes in his extensive 'Bird List' – celebrate a natural wonder of the world, hidden within a tiny compass.[34]

Not all of Clare's eggs are as visually captivating as those of the thrush or yellowhammer. Rather less eye-catching, for example, are the robin's 'brun-coloured eggs' ('The Robins Nest', line 99; *Middle Period*, III, 536) or the 'deep blotched' clutch of 'The Land Rail' (line 56; *Middle Period*, III, 554). But of all the birds, it is the nightingale that seems to produce the least showy eggs, characterized by 'deadened green or rather olive brown' ('The Nightingale's Nest', line 90; *Middle Period*, III, 461). Yet it is these muted tones that make the nightingale's eggs so remarkable. The distinctive colour of eggshells is not merely a sign of nature's immense variety or the individuality of a particular kind: it also serves the practical function of providing camouflage. The nightingale's eggs are especially elusive, often located in obscure and unlikely places like the old thorn bush in Clare's poem, a spot he discovers only after several hours of searching. Instead of revealing a sudden treasure-like cluster of shining shells, the nest, when finally exposed, contains dull eggs that are barely distinguishable from the surrounding 'dead oaken leaves' (line 78) and 'velvet moss' (line 79). When the nightingale's hidden home is uncovered, both nest and eggs seem as much a part of the woodland clump as the prickly thorn bush that guards them. The colour of the shell is therefore its glory – and its protection.

Clare's portrayal of the poet in pursuit of the secretive nightingale includes uneasy references to the bird's 'choking fear' (line 60), as the impatient observer finally closes in ('there put that bramble bye/Nay trample on its branches & get near' [lines 55–6]). Here, the 'deadened green' reminds us not only of the bird's instinct for survival, but also of the probable consequences of being discovered. A search for birds' eggs in the nineteenth century did not generally end with a poem, but with a raid – whether the eggs were destined for the kitchen or the collector's case. Clare's bird poems frequently acknowledge the threat from human beings, whether intentional or indirect. In 'The Fern Owls Nest', the weary, homeward-bound woodman doesn't care whether 'he tramples near its nest' (line 8; *Middle Period*, IV, 300), while the woodlark is given to inadvertently betraying her home by fluttering out just when someone happens to be passing. In many of the poems, however, the threat is overt. Snakes, cats, foxes and birds of prey lurk in these poems, ready to snap or pounce or swoop; but the greatest and most consistent predator is man. The boys in 'The Land Rail' search 'in every tuft of grass' and 'every bush they pass' (lines 25–7), those in 'The Reed Bird' throw 'a jelted stone' at the nestlings (line 10; *Middle Period*, IV, 321), while others take away eggs 'every day' ('Birds in Alarm', line 5), unmoved by the agitation of the parent birds. Any idea that Clare idealizes childhood must be complicated by the frequent encouragement to imagine a bird's eye view of these terrifying 'boys'. In the later birds' nest poems, written at Northborough, the fate of the eggs is even more disturbing, with the Nuthatch being prey to both jays and boys ('The Nuthatch') and the rook succumbing to the 'reaching poles' ('The Rooks Nest', line 13), while the partridge is witness to children who 'throw the eggs abroad/And stay and play at blind egg on the road' ('The Partridges Nest', lines 9–10). The fragility of birds' eggs is brought home again and again.

Clare's ability to offer different perspectives on a particular scene was not readily available to the contemporary landscape painter, who had to select a single viewpoint and particular moment in time for his image. Nevertheless, DeWint's creation of a sense of boundlessness that invites viewers *into* his painted landscapes can still illuminate Clare's poetic technique, for in exposing the birds' fears so sympathetically, Clare was also emphasizing the desirability of their eggs, and thus suggesting uncomfortable parallels between the predators within the poem and its readers. As we share the poet's delight in the bright 'shining eggs', we become aware of their preciousness – and their vulnerability. The description of the wryneck's eggs as 'curious' ('The Wry Necks Nest', line 6) not only appeals to the reader's imagination, but also recalls contemporary cabinets of 'curiosities', those strange collections of manmade and natural phenomena often featuring items seized from creatures' homes and habitats to be sold or put on display. By aligning the boys on their bird-nesting expeditions with natural predators such as snakes or jays, Clare also reminds us of a natural world in which living things survive by preying on one another. The remaining partridge eggs that are carried home in hats will probably provide a much-needed meal for the boys who found them. Clare's poems are therefore encouraging awareness of the many different ways of looking at the same small objects, of the essentially subjective nature of human perception. As in DeWint's inviting landscapes, readers are being taken inside the scene, where things can be viewed from another side and then another. Colour is key to Clare's technique because it catches the reader's attention and then encourages awareness of both the beauty of the sharply visualized exterior and the less immediately obvious possibilities within.

In his natural history letter on pooty shells, snails are celebrated for their glorious colour – but in one of Clare's natural history notes, the sight of pooty shells 'thickly litterd round a stone' is taken as evidence of their irresistible appeal to hungry blackbirds and thrushes.[35] Eggshells can be signs of fragmentation and transience, just as much as fullness and hope. And yet, it is this sense of multi-dimensional experience that gives Clare's poetry such power. There is nothing sentimental about the descriptions of shining eggs, because their discovery is always attended by an awareness of its own unlikelihood and the fragility of the future. Birds' eggs are poised between two births – the moment of being laid and the moment when the chicks hatch. They lie, quiet and mysterious, promising new life from within their smooth forms. Their perfect colour is spotted and scrawled as the egg emerges into the world, and remains as a shield until destroyed by the young bird bursting into independent life. Clare was fascinated by the egg in the nest – the moment of promise. Like the luscious green before the bloom, the glistening shells were pledges of endless renewal, defying the ravages of late frosts, hungry jays and even schoolboys. Birds' eggs were not such obvious heralds of the spring as budding twigs and blossoms, but their colour was all the more precious for being hidden, their inaccessibility more stimulating to active, imaginative observation. Two years before Clare's death, Delacroix noted that 'Colour gives the appearance of life', but Clare had long since realized that it was evidence of life itself.[36]

Notes

1. *Natural History*, p. 38.
2. Ibid., p. 39. Hugh Haughton has discussed Clare's role as a 'poetic naturalist' in relation to this letter in 'Progress and Rhyme'; see Haughton, pp. 51–86 (p. 58). See also Douglas Chambers, '"A love for every simple weed": Clare, botany and the poetic language of lost Eden', Ibid., pp. 238–58.
3. All internal references to Clare's poetry are from the Oxford edition of *The Poems of John Clare*, gen. ed. Eric Robinson, with line numbers included in the body of the chapter.
4. *By Himself*, p. 17.
5. For a wide-ranging introduction to the issues and approaches of different disciplines, see Trevor Lamb and Janine Bourriau, *Colour: Art and Science* (Cambridge: Cambridge University Press, 1995) and John Gage's excellent *Colour in Art* (London: Thames and Hudson, 2006). For the philosophical meaning of colour, see Johann Wolfgang von Goethe, *Theory of Colours* (1810), translated by Charles Lock Eastlake (London, 1840); Ludwig Wittgenstein, *Remarks on Colour*, ed. G. E. M. Anscombe, translated by Linda McAlister and Magarete Schättle (Oxford: Blackwell, 1978); Joseph Westphal, *Colour: Some Philosophical Problems from Wittgenstein* (Oxford: Blackwell, 1987).
6. 'Natural History Letter X', *Natural History*, p. 64. See also 'The Crab Tree', *Middle Period*, IV, p. 189.
7. Uvedale Price, *Essays on the Picturesque* (London, 1810), pp. 62, 169.
8. 'Essay on Landscape', *The Prose of John Clare*, ed. J. W. Tibble and Anne Tibble (London: Routledge & Kegan Paul, 1951), p. 211–15 (p. 211).
9. Lynn Banfield Pearce, 'John Clare and Peter DeWint', *JCSJ*, 3 (1984), 40–9 (41).
10. Review of *The Village Minstrel; Eclectic Review*, ns. xvii (January 1822), 31–45; in *Critical Heritage*, p. 169.
11. 'Essay on Landscape', *Prose*, p. 212.
12. For a reading of this poem in relation to natural history, see Sarah Weiger, '"Shadows of Taste": John Clare's Tasteful Natural History', *JCSJ*, 27 (2008), 59–71.
13. 'Essay on Landscape', *Prose*, p. 212.
14. Harriet DeWint, *A Short Memoir of the Life of Peter DeWint and William Hilton RA*, in John Lord, *Peter DeWint 1784–1849: 'For the Common Observer of Life and Nature'* (Aldershot: Lund Humphries, 2007), pp. 78–89 (pp. 78–9).
15. *Letters*, p. 488: Clare to DeWint, 19 December 1829.
16. Ibid., p. 399: Clare to DeWint, 14 October 1827.

17. John Gage, 'Disegno versus Colore', in *Colour and Culture* (London: Thames and Hudson, 1993), pp. 117–38.
18. For the long running history of the drawing/colour debate, see Mosche Barasch, *Theories of Art*, 3 vols. (London and New York: Routledge, 2000), I, pp. 355–72; II, pp. 265–78, pp. 348–61.
19. Bridget Riley, 'Colour for the Painter', in Lamb and Bourriau, pp. 31–65 (p. 63).
20. Barasch, vol. II, p. 274; Gage, *Colour and Culture*, pp. 201–4.
21. Gage, *Colour in Art*, p. 83.
22. Joshua Reynolds, *Discourses on Art*, ed. R. Wark, 2nd edn (New Haven and London: Yale University Press, 1997), p. 26.
23. Ibid., p. 196.
24. Ibid., p. 259.
25. Ibid., pp. 253, 251.
26. Gage, *Colour in Art*, pp. 165–6.
27. *Paul Sandby: Picturing Britain*, ed. John Bonehill and Stephen Daniels (London: Royal Academy, 2009); Lord, *Peter DeWint*, pp. 11–15; David Blayney Brown, 'Nationalising Norwich', in Brown, Andrew Hemingway and Anne Lyles, *Romantic Landscape: The Norwich School of Painters* (London: Tate Gallery, 2000), pp. 24–35.
28. 'The Staith', pre 1829, is part of the DeWint collection at the Usher Art Gallery, Lincoln. It is reproduced in Lord, *Peter DeWint*, p. 113.
29. Pearce, p. 44.
30. Malcolm Andrews, *Landscape and Western Art* (Oxford: Oxford University Press, 1999), pp. 21–2.
31. Lord, *Peter DeWint*, p. 12. For the parallels with poetry, see Richard Sha, *The Verbal and the Visual Sketch in British Romanticism* (Philadelphia: University of Pennsylvania Press, 1998).
32. Rosamund Purcell, Linnea Hall and René Corado, *Egg and Nest* (Cambridge MA: Harvard University Press, 2008), p. 123.
33. See Haughton, p. 70; John Goodridge, *John Clare and Community* (Cambridge: Cambridge University Press, 2013), pp. 138–42.
34. 'Bird List' in *Natural History*, pp. 118–64 (see especially 'Quail', p. 153; 'Heron', p. 154; 'Peewit', p. 158; 'Water hen', p. 159; 'Coot', p. 160).
35. *Natural History*, p. 76.
36. Delacroix, notebook entry, 1852, Barasch, vol. II, p. 360.

CHAPTER 2

John Clare, William Cowper and the eighteenth century

Adam Rounce

When Francis Palgrave included William Cowper's 'The Poplar-Field' (1785), in his 1861 anthology the *Golden Treasury*, he had Tennyson's approval: according to Palgrave's manuscript notes the Laureate 'especially admired its sweet flow – said he did not know why, but it seemed as if no such verses could be written now.'[1] This suggestive sentiment – an expression of nostalgic regret for the lost possibilities of a poetry of nostalgia – serves to remind the reader of how English poetry had changed during the lifetime of John Clare. Clare, who would die three years later, was born less than ten years after Cowper had lamented the loss of the eponymous poplars, where 'the tree is my seat that once lent me a shade', in the sort of poem – wistful, full of generalized sentiments and euphony – which would help make Palgrave's enterprise so successful. It is the sort of lament that seems to connect intimately to Clare's own poetry and his aesthetic, with its melancholy detailing of rural despoliation and its consequences. Clare's reverence for Cowper is well documented, yet this connection is also marked by a disjunction: Tennyson sagely noted that the 'sweet flow' of Cowper's lines seems to make them belong immutably to the past, and would simply not be possible to write in the world of the mid-nineteenth century. Much of Clare's poetry follows the same pattern as that of Cowper and other eighteenth-century forebears (such as James Beattie and Oliver Goldsmith), but then veers off into its own very specific territory. It is the point of the present chapter to describe this movement by Clare from sympathetic identification with, and near emulation of, Cowper, to a clearly defined, sometimes apparently slight – but always precise – distinction from him. The general premise will be to indicate the degree of empathy between Clare and eighteenth-century poetry, to show how much he absorbs from this poetic tradition, and what he adds to it. It is useful to start with a brief consideration of the general influence of eighteenth-century poetry upon Clare, with specific reference to the example of James Thomson.

John Clare, William Cowper and the eighteenth century

I

The relationship between Clare and the poetry of the eighteenth century has become, in some ways, an established part of the narrative of his career, from the sentimental anecdote (the inspirational discovery of Thomson's *Seasons*) to more recent critical attention to the connection with and dissonance between Clare and his forebears in the poetry of pastoral landscape (in the work of John Barrell and others). It is inevitable, of course, that the large-scale recovery of Clare's poetry in the last half-century has created various conflicting readings of his place in any poetic narrative of the eighteenth century and Romanticism. This is, doubtless, partly the result of narratives of literary history and their often procrustean needs, but also a reflection of some cogent qualities in Clare's large poetic canon: specifically, his fecundity, and his mode of composition in a variety of forms and genres. In a related vein, Clare often composed poetry close to his forebears in a spirit of pastiche, or homage, or a mixture of the two (the use of Beattie in the Spenserian 'Village Minstrel' and the much later asylum parodies of *Don Juan* and 'Childe Harolde' are notable examples). The result is a poetry that manages to borrow from, imitate, acknowledge the weight of and also transcend its eighteenth-century influences. Or, to use Bridget Keegan's summary, the

> heteroglossic nature of Clare's poetry both invites and precludes his comparison with and assimilation into a variety of literary idioms, ranging from that of the late eighteenth century loco-descriptive poets, to that of his Romantic contemporaries (in particular, Wordsworth), to that of the natural historians.[2]

Clare is thus impossible to pin down, as he shows so many influences as to resist identification with any one poetic movement or moment, defying any easy placing of him within a tradition.

What can be shown, though, are the ways in which Clare borrows elements from the literary past, including Thomson's Miltonic recreations of landscape and Cowper's meditative poems and lyrics of the later eighteenth century, in order to encompass a mindset that is increasingly beleaguered in its relations with the world. Clare especially shares with Cowper an interest in the revaluation and reshaping of traditional lyric forms.

Clare's relation to the eighteenth century has been a matter of some critical dispute, partly because it has been assumed to be part of a literary historiographic model whereby Romanticism frees itself from poetic predecessors; alternately, Clare has been held up as an example of veneration of the past at the expense of the present. A leading figure in this dispute is

Clare's first poetic idol, James Thomson. As has often been discussed, Thomson's influence on Clare was always obvious, and John Taylor broadcast it in the 'Introduction' to his first published volume: 'He was thirteen years of age when another boy shewed him Thomson's Seasons. They were out in the fields together, and during the day Clare had a good opportunity of looking at the book. It called forth all the passion of his soul for poetry.'[3] This discovery is repeatedly seen as an epiphany – albeit one that was as much a marketing device as a statement of poetic inspiration – in its representation of Clare as follower of an established model.

John Barrell's reading of Clare and Thomson sees the latter as a model from which Clare had to extricate himself. Barrell emphasizes the difficulties of what landscape Clare as a subject could freely visualize and explore imaginatively. For Barrell, Thomson was therefore an influence that had to be shaken off: Clare's mature poems were

> written as a deliberate and a considered alternative to the style of landscape description he had encountered in Thomson and other eighteenth-century descriptive poems. In his earliest books of poetry, Clare had made a number of more or less successful attempts to write in the mode of Thomson, but had turned away from these attempts, because he decided that Thomson's descriptive procedures could not be used to represent his own sense of place, his own consciousness, and the mutually constitutive relations of the two.[4]

The problem with this line of argument is that, retrospectively, Clare's departure from Thomson's style can be more of a natural lessening of influence in proportion to Clare's own poetic development and needs: it is possible to argue that Thomson's 'descriptive procedures' did not suit Clare for a number of reasons (particularity versus the general, for one). The counter-argument to claims of Clare writing himself away from the eighteenth century – suggesting instead a poetics of veneration – is offered by James McKusick, in accounting for the lack of congruence between Clare and his most famous contemporary:

> Far more important than the Wordsworthian influence on Clare, especially in his early career, was his affectionate imitation of the poets of Sensibility: Thomson (whose *The Seasons* was the first book of poetry that Clare ever possessed), Cowper (whose fondness for small defenceless creatures especially appealed to Clare), Gray and Collins. Clare admired these poets not because they were (or once had been) fashionable, but because for him they constituted an alternative poetic tradition, one that exalted the rural landscape and the rural sense of community over the anomie of urban existence.[5]

This genial model of influence, in turn, does not question the extent of Clare's affection. It risks over-determining the poetry of urban anomie (which would hardly be recognized by Clare as a distinct body of work), and simplifying the diversity of Gray, Collins and the rest: after all, Collins's highly allegorical and obscure odes do not replicate Gray's *Elegy* in exalting the rural landscape and community (if, indeed, that is what Gray's famous poem does).

It is possible to see both sides, and accommodate Clare's poetic requirements within the benefits and limitations of past influences. In a practical sense, Clare did follow Thomson, like most other writers of topographical poetry, whilst moving away from his example in tangible and almost tactile ways. As a reminder of what Clare was responding to, it is worth looking back at a passage from *Winter* (1726), in which Thomson's description of the arrival of snow suggests earthly uncertainty:

> Earth's universal Face, deep-hid, and chill,
> Is one wild dazzling Waste, that buries wide
> The Works of Man. The Labourer-Ox
> Stands cover'd o'er with Snow, and then demands
> The Fruit of all his Toil. The Fowls of Heaven,
> Tam'd by the cruel Season, croud around
> The winnowing Store, and claim the little Boon,
> Which Providence allows.[6]

Thomson's verse is built around following the strikingly universal impulse with the particular; the obvious qualities that mark this passage as being of the first part of the eighteenth century are both the diction and constructions – the descriptive register that includes the 'Labourer-Ox' and the King James Version's 'Fowls of Heaven' – though the 'winnowing Store', ostensibly an example of the sort of ornate diction that would become notorious for its superfluity, is simply describing the process of sorting the wheat. Clare's poetic perspective is often described as inherently more localized, and therefore naturally less abstract and removed than such a landscape tradition; his writings in this vein do not seem ostensibly different, but in the level of their detail the change becomes apparent, as in an 1820s piece such as 'Snow Storm':

> What a night the wind howls hisses & but stops
> To howl more loud while the snow volly keeps
> Insessant batter at the window pane
> Making our comfort feel as sweet again
> & in the morning when the tempest drops
> At every cottage door mountanious heaps

> Of snow lies drifted that all entrance stops
> Untill the beesom & the shovel gains
> The path—& leave a wall on either side—
> The shepherd rambling valleys white & wide
> With new sensations his old memorys fills
> When hedges left at night no more descried
> Are turned to one white sweep of curving hills
> & trees turned bushes half their bodys hide
>
> (lines 1–14; *Middle Period*, V, 213)

The onrushing of sensory impression here and the concomitant accumulation of effects and sensations are, alongside the enjambed, unpunctuated lines, the most significant alteration from Thomson's method of description. Paul Chirico captures the feeling of these lines in referring to their 'visual intensity' and method of description which 'is defamiliarising, even uncanny', part of his larger argument that 'Although Clare is usually described as a poet of place, of precise, localized natural description, his landscapes are in fact repeatedly transformed, their familiarity undermined by disorientation or by an excess of detail.' The problem, in some ways, is 'the troubled and unresolved relationship between precise, yet diverse and constantly changing, natural observations and their fixed and limited representation in poetry and memory'.[7] There is also, in this example, alongside Clare's customary reluctance towards blank verse, the anthropomorphic feel in the trees at the end, which leads to a sense of intimacy and informality, and a perspective that is both generalized and local in its range.

To say as much is to point out that Clare's uniquely off-kilter description, combined with the diction and tone that reflects his closeness to his subject-matter, means that he follows eighteenth-century poetic landscapes in outline, but makes them seem more familiar, domestic, intimate and therefore empathetic in their details. He is not at odds with Thomson, but the latter was generally aiming for a poetic decorum that Clare found unsuitable, and not entirely reflective of the impression that he was trying to make. In this sense, there is a distance between them, in that the ingenuous informality and intimacy that Clare creates was not generically open to Thomson – and it was also not surprising that Thomson's mode of address in most of his poetry reflected the manners of a bygone age, and therefore was not available to Clare, even had he wished to avail himself of it. Thomson was not a shadow from which Clare had to extricate himself, but part of a tradition that was open to him to a certain extent.

What is needed, perhaps, is a *via media* between general perceptions of Clare's recent poetic past as ultimately either oppressive or sympathetic. John Goodridge has recently challenged the 'common critical view' which holds the eighteenth-century influence on Clare to be 'a slightly embarrassing literary adolescence through which he must pass to find his own authentic voice', offering instead 'more positive aspects' of such influence, and viewing Clare's relations with the past as not a 'restraining or intimidating presence' upon him, but rather 'a new door to open'.[8]

Goodridge disputes the bald idea that Clare moved from hackneyed and commonplace copying of the eighteenth century to find simplicity and the natural in his own environment and style. He instead offers influential texts and paratexts as examples of where the eighteenth century made a direct, detailed contribution towards Clare's poetic apprenticeship. John Pomfret's 'The Choice' (1700) – that hugely popular Horatian message of desired retirement and ease – lies behind Clare's early 'wish' poems. Along with the debts to Goldsmith and Beattie,[9] Goodridge also identifies the once-widely read pastorals of John Cunningham as a positive source for Clare's own writing, helping him to absorb the octosyllabic line (as did John Dyer's 'Grongar Hill', 1756). Goodridge also presents Gray's *Elegy* as a sort of ur-text for Clare's attempts throughout his career to understand the fate of the labouring-class writer.[10] For Goodridge, 'a key challenge in Clare's literary development was that of accommodating in his style both the "high" literary culture to which he aspired, and the rich narratives and songs of folk and popular culture with which he had grown up'.[11] Goodridge's laudable general aim is to represent, where possible, the specific details of comparison and contrast between Clare and his 'high' predecessors. The following readings of Clare's interactions with Cowper (and by implication, as least some of the eighteenth-century poetic past) will try to emulate this spirit of detailed enquiry.

II

For all Thomson's general influence, especially early in Clare's career, there are fewer shared factors between the two poets than are common in Clare and the later William Cowper, a poet whose range of styles and characteristic themes reflect Clare's own restless generic and formal invention. The closeness of Clare and Cowper has been touched upon many times: Clare himself addressed lines to 'Cowper the Poet of the field', and while the more genteel Cowper had a slightly different experience of a field, the biographical points of similarity between the two are hard to gainsay: apart from their mental difficulties, both fell back upon and wrote about solitude, retirement and isolation from a community. Cowper's was chosen, a result of mental difficulties and a near-paranoid sense of religious guilt; Clare's was enforced, given his repeated levels of conflict with and antipathy towards many in his community, at certain stages of his life.[12]

Clare's attitude towards Cowper was always plain. On his trip to Huntington in March 1820 en route to his first visit to London, he was shown Cromwell's house, as well as 'the parsonage with its mellancholy looking garden', Cowper's former residence, 'which was far the most interesting remembrance to me tho both were great men in the annals of fame'.[13] In terms of poetry, the appeal of Cowper to Clare as a model would encompass rather darker and more troubled areas, but it could well have originated in the (relative) informality of *The Task*, that long meditation on everything and anything that, like so much of Clare's work, is rooted in the associations, values and feelings of landscape, and the relaxed mood of the conversation poem. In this respect, one cogent area of comparison between the two poets is the shared sense of the pleasures of sometimes necessary retirement from the noise and follies of the world: in the asylum period, in the 'Lines on Cowper', Clare refers to the reading of books five and six of *The Task*: 'The "Winters walk" and "Summers Noon"/We meet together by the fire' (lines 17–18; *Later Poems*, II, 871). This joy in retirement is also shown in the poets' respective descriptions of winter, where the pleasure of reading is a compensation for necessary confinement. Cowper apostrophizes the season thus:

> I crown thee King of intimate delights,
> Fireside enjoyments, home-born happiness,
> And all the comforts that the lowly roof
> Of undisturb'd retirement, and the hours
> Of long uninterrupted evening know.[14]

It is this sense of intimacy that retirement gives which Clare also captures in another late piece, 'The Winters Come', when describing the relish and passion for reading, and the implicit release from the cares of the world that the season enables:

> 'Tis Winter! and I love to read in-doors,
> When the moon hangs her crescent upon high:
> While on the window shutters the wind roars,
> And storms like furies pass remorseless by,
> How pleasant on a feather bed to lie,
> Or sitting by the fire, in fancy soar,

> With Milton, or with Dante to regions high,
> Or read fresh volumes we've not seen before,
> Or o'er old Barton's 'melancholy pore.'
>
> (lines 19–27; *Later Poems*, II, 929)

The register is slightly more informal, and the bookish delight a childish pleasure at the familiarity of the well-worn and the new. It is also a reminder of Clare's relish of the world of the bookish retreat: as Richard Cronin has suggested, Clare, more often than his contemporaries, 'presents himself in his poems as a reader, as a man who when he returns home from a walk' picks a book from the shelves.[15] The idiomatic spelling of Robert Burton aside (like Samuel Johnson, Clare apparently appreciated *The Anatomy of Melancholy* as one of the great books to dip into), the sublimity of Milton is accompanied by Dante, whose reception in English was in its relative infancy.[16] The jarring metre of the line, however, is odd given Clare's perfect ear for scansion, and it is possible he did not intend 'Dante' to be pronounced with more than one syllable. Yet the passage shares with Cowper a paramount sense of the joy of the solitary experience – of the season as a fortunate excuse for the natural retreat towards books and the fire by certain temperaments.

Such temperaments are drawn to the meditative, and this is why Cowper, a poet of profound levels of introspection (albeit leading him to estrangement and alienation), is a helpful prism through which to view Clare, not least in considering how close Clare is to Cowper's style, and how clearly he moves away from it. To stay with the descriptive powers of both on the subject of winter, Cowper is appropriately more grounded in an eighteenth-century blank verse tradition:

> Forth goes the woodman leaving unconcerned
> The cheerfull haunts of man, to wield the axe
> And drive the wedge in yonder forest drear,
> From morn to eve his solitary task.
> Shaggy and lean and shrew'd, with pointed ears
> And tail cropp'd short, half lurcher and half cur
> His dog attends him. Close behind his heel
> Now creeps he slow, and now with many a frisk
> Wide-scampering snatches up the drifted snow
> With iv'ry teeth, or ploughs it with his snout;
> Then shakes his powder'd coat and barks for joy.[17]

What is so marked here is the level of detail that Cowper is striving towards, expressed, inevitably, through the Latinate syntax that he would pursue in most of his mature blank verse, as a conscious homage to Milton, and which would lead to his Homer translations. Here, this explains the allusion to the fall of Mulciber, the architect of Pandemonium in *Paradise Lost*, in 'from morn to eve'.[18] Although this is thirty-five years before Clare's first publications, despite the syntactic constructions and the somewhat ornate diction ('frisk', 'ivory' and 'powder'd coat') Cowper is after the sort of detail that Clare would later delineate. Clare's own descriptions are in a similar if somewhat less formal register. Take the asylum sonnet from the Epping forest period (mainly, and rarely for Clare in this period, in blank verse), 'The Gipsy Camp':

> THE snow falls deep; the Forest lies alone:
> The boy goes hasty for his load of brakes,
> Then thinks upon the fire and hurries back;
> The Gipsy knocks his hands and tucks them up,
> And seeks his squalid camp, half hid in snow,
> Beneath the oak, which breaks away the wind,
> And bushes close, with snow like hovel warm:
> There stinking mutton roasts upon the coals,
> And the half-roasted dog squats close and rubs,
> Then feels the heat too strong and goes aloof;
> He watches well, but none a bit can spare,
> And vainly waits the morsel thrown away:
> 'Tis thus they live – a picture to the place;
> A quiet, pilfering, unprotected race.   (*Later Poems*, I, 29)[19]

The final 'unprotected', with its support for the underdog and compassionate reaching for the margins of society, could come from few, if any other poets of the period, or the preceding century. It is the only point of judgment; hence, it stands apart from the near-documentary realism of the poem. Alan Vardy has described the poem as a 'realistic delineation of a series of moments' that nonetheless acts as a profound kind of 'imaginative sympathy' with its marginalized subjects. Vardy continues:

> Not only is Clare not interested in judging the gypsies, the only language of judgment is directed back at the reader as a challenge to his or her habitual notions about gypsies. The fact of their 'pilfering' is not denied, but rather is presented in the context of the description of the camp, and the other descriptive adjectives that surround it.[20]

The apparent neutrality of landscape description (more honoured in the breach anyway) is reframed as a test of the reader's prejudices; the three adjectives of the final line can act as a goad, a gently provocative defence of the downtrodden, and a sharply impressionistic and repeated focus on the gritty detail of the sort of lifestyles dismissed by sweeping judgment. It is in small, radical details such as this that Clare defined his own poetic space, akin to, but slightly at a remove from, Cowper: both poets are willing to represent and sympathize with the outcast and the marginal, but Clare's perspective on such figures tends to challenge the reader's preconceptions.

III

For all that the naturalism of Clare's gipsy-camp is more visceral than any realistic external landscape described by Cowper, the comparison between the two poets remains fruitful. Both identified with the destruction of the solidity of natural scenes, places and objects as a metonym of wider attacks upon the communal and the individual by specific parts of modernity. For each poet, this resulted in an upheaval both of the quotidian and – more profoundly for the individual – of the existential surety that such venerated places represented. Here, too, Clare diverges from Cowper in important ways.

Cowper's attitude towards rural despoliation is summarized by Tim Fulford, recounting Cowper's response to one such action, the removal of what he called the Spinney:

> In July 1785 a local landowner felled trees, removed scrub, and re-organized as an orderly plantation a wood near Olney through which had run one of Cowper's favourite walks. He mourned for its loss in terms that make of the picturesque glade a sanctuary of spiritual community shared between Cowper and his domestic circle:
>
> > I have promised myself that I will never enter it again. We have both pray'd in it. You for me, and I for you, but it is desecrated from this time forth, and the voice of pray'r will be heard in it no more.

Fulford concludes that, as the quoted letter implies, for Cowper, 'Rural beauty ... is sacramental, an earthly form in which spiritual presence can be encountered. Despoliation of nature is made to seem sacrilegious. And despoliation also threatens the self.'[21] These threats would never be negated, and would be expressed through the spiritually tortured poems that Cowper wrote, especially in the 1790s, from 'On the Receipt of my Mother's Picture out of Norfolk' to 'The Castaway'. Yet, for all the genuine torment of these works, the automatic link between the destruction of the trees as a blasphemy and act of sacrilege in Cowper's letter here seems on one level a melodramatic, almost self-parodic expression of a particular kind of dissenting excess. The destruction of the solace of the walk for Cowper and his spiritual community may have been disappointing, but such a violation does not, arguably, possess the wider symbolic consequences that he suggests; he elevates an act of vandalism to a desecration perpetuated by the heathen.

This strange perspective is muted and transformed, beautifully, in 'The Poplar-Field', written late in 1783 and published in 1785, in response to the felling of the trees in a familiar field next to the river Ouse in nearby Lavendon. The musicality of the anapaests may derive from its being designed as a setting for the favourite tunes of Cowper's friend Lady Austen.[22] The content is formed around the conventional themes of the vanity of human wishes, and *vitae summa brevis*:

> The black-bird has fled to another retreat
> Where the hazels afford him a screen from the heat,
> And the scene where his melody charm'd me before,
> Resounds with his sweet-flowing ditty no more.
>
> My fugitive years are all hasting away,
> And I must e'er long lie as lowly as they,
> With a turf on my breast and a stone at my head
> E'er another such grove shall arise in its stead.
>
> 'Tis a sight to engage me, if any thing can,
> To muse on the perishing pleasures of man;
> Short-lived as we are, yet our pleasures, we see,
> Have a still shorter date, and die sooner than we.[23]

The defiance and outrage of Cowper's letter is here replaced by a fatalistic sensibility, rendered in a very subdued poetic key, whereby meditation and melancholy use the loss of the stability of the locale to conclude in *sententiae*, which crucially seems divorced from the putative loss of the poplars. The result is a sentimental nostalgia that is always universal (which is indeed the source of its strength and appeal) but is wistfully separated from the object of its original protest. Moreover, it appears to accept its premise – that life and its pleasures are as transitory and fallible as any natural site threatened by 'improvement' – without hope of any alternative, in a manner which could be described as complacent, or solipsistic.

To say as much is not to expect a poet as constitutionally melancholy (and for such deep-seated reasons) as Cowper to add a happy ending, but it brings into light the most important contrast between him and Clare. For Clare, the destruction of an almost spiritual sanctuary leads not to resignation, but to a more complex blend of loss and recompense. Clare conveys a quietly defiant sense of a natural order that cannot be obliterated and that offers connections even amidst seemingly alien milieux, as in the closing lines of 'The Flitting':

> & why—this 'shepherds purse' that grows
> In this strange spot—In days gone bye
> Grew in the little garden rows
> Of my old home now left—And I
> Feel what I never felt before
> This weed an ancient neighbour here
> & though I own the spot no more
> Its every trifle makes it dear
>
> The Ivy at the parlour end
> The wood bine at the garden gate
> Are all & each affections friend
> That rendered parting desolate
> But times will change & friends must part
> & nature still can make amends
> Their memory lingers round the heart
> Like life whose essence is its friends
>
> Time looks on pomp with careless moods
> Or killing apathys disdain
> —So where old marble citys stood
> Poor persecuted weeds remain
> She feels a love for little things
> That very few can feel beside
> & still the grass eternal springs
> Where castles stood & grandeur died
>
> (lines 193–216; *Middle Period*, III, 488–9)

The workings of time and nature, and their genial contempt for the pretensions of civilization, act as a corrective to nascent despair, binding the poet to the solace of the imagination and its empathetic understanding of the underlying natural order. Much of Cowper's later work is a spiritual autobiography with nature repeatedly visualized as the symbol of his guilt and perceived damnation, and even in the gentle rhythms of 'The Poplar-Field' he is denied consolation. Clare is never so bereft. The sweep of time and nature, vast though they are, still nurture the 'little things/That very few can feel'.

It is, in one sense, Clare's refusal to accept the limiting terms of alienation and persecution that moves him away from Cowper and makes him a poet of localized, individual protest, not content to simply bemoan his fate, or to generalize around and thereby mystify the conditions under which he has been alienated from his environment. With Cowper, whether or not this reflects his more detached relationship to the process of labour and the land, it is possible to find in his poetry meditations upon change, the ravages of time and the shortcomings of human attempts to alter and control his environment; yet these usually lead to a symbolic debate, whereby it is Cowper's lasting lack of spiritual nourishment, and his perceived alienation from God's mercy, which is the latent source and the end of his writing. The result, often, is that the details of the landscape, object or vista of his subject are individualized, or latently act out parts of his lasting spiritual dilemma.

An example of this is 'Yardley Oak' (1791), the unfinished blank-verse meditation on history and the understanding of the past that is one of Cowper's most profound explorations of his place within the world of time and nature. The old tree of the title, a survivor, like the poet, of many past struggles, has lost much in the transition from youth to age. Yet the potentially uplifting pastoral salute to its endurance does not last. The very aspects of the tree that so fascinate the poet – its longevity in the face of adversity, its symbolic place in a transitory world – lead him to ruminate on questions that undermine such surety: mention of the oracle of the sacred oak tree at Dodona leads him to consider that, given such a chance to discover such truths,

> I would not curious ask
> The future, best unknown, but at thy mouth
> Inquisitive, the less ambiguous past.
> By thee I might correct, erroneous oft,
> The clock of history   (lines 42–6)

This indicates a desire to live outside of the temporal world, and its harmful effects, and to confront only the certainties of the past. The conventional reflection on time and its workings becomes in Cowper's hands a graver deliberation on the mutability that has brought the tree to its ruined state: 'The rottenness which Time is charged to inflict/On other mighty ones found also thee'. Change is portrayed as natural, but destructive, and hardly reassuring:

> Change is the diet on which all subsist
> Created changeable, and change at last
> Destroys them. Skies uncertain, now the heat
> Transmitting cloudless, and the solar beam
> Now quenching in a boundless sea of clouds,
> Calm and alternate storm, moisture and drought,
> Invigorate by turns the springs of life
> In all that live, plant, animal, and man,
> And in conclusion mar them.[24]

This depiction of the cycles of nature is not unusual in the movement of a meditative poem, yet the mood created – the stressing, through the syntax of the sentence's ending in destruction and marring – is one of sublime but disturbing grandeur: the fragment of the tree elegized so magnificently, but with such clear emphasis on the inevitability of its being ruined, almost gives the impression of a world without rationale, or controlling force. Some readers, such as Fulford, have found that the poem is a Burkean 'living monument to a shared sense of common ancestry',[25] but it is also a witness to Cowper's far less communal fears about the changes wrought by history and time, and his inability to exercise any control over them.

A comparison with Clare's 'The Fallen Elm' is suggestive, yet slightly awkward: Cowper's poem was a source, but an extensive parallel between the two founders a little.[26] Clare bases his poem upon an opposition between the neutral workings of time and the proportionate placing of blame for the tree's destruction upon flawed human motives. Time alters the tree, but does not destroy it:

> Old favourite tree thoust seen times changes lower
> Though change till now did never injure thee
> For time beheld thee as her sacred dower
> & nature claimed thee her domestic tree
> Storms came & shook thee many a weary hour
> Yet stedfast to thy home thy roots hath been
> (lines 15–20; *Middle Period*, III, 441)

This description may not be as literally accurate as Cowper's delineation of the changes wrought on the oak, but the distinction drawn is clear: it is the arbitrary hand of the owner of the land of the tree who is at fault, not the workings of nature itself. As Clare explained, 'The savage who owns them thinks [the trees] have done their best, and now he wants to make use of the benefits he can get from selling them.'[27] Nature stands outside of (and is implicitly opposed to) greed and self-interest, whereas in Cowper's vision of the old oak change is fused into the workings of worldly forces, so that blame is unspecified. Clare clearly identifies the chopping down of the tree as unnatural, to the point where the poem becomes what Goodridge calls a 'kind of honed political rant':[28]

> Thou owned a language by which hearts are stirred
> Deeper then by a feeling cloathed in words
> & speakest now whats known of every tongue
> Language of pity & the force of wrong
> (lines 31–4; *Middle Period*, III, 442)

The tree is a vessel of protest, rather than a passive repository and record of the necessary evils of change; its symbolic enunciation of what should be felt by all recalls Clare's description in his *Autobiography* of the unworldly innocence of his friend John Billings: 'he had never read Thomson or Cowper or Wordsworth or perhaps heard of their names yet nature gives everyone a natural simplicity of heart to read her language & the gross interferences of the world adulterate them'.[29]

The relationship between Clare and Cowper is a microcosm of Clare's use of earlier influence: it is enabling and inspiring, rather than anxious. Clare redefines the terms of the poetic relation to the world and nature in significant ways, particularly in his refusal to accept his marginalization from the social mainstream with the sort of sentimental fatalism that could be fetishized in Cowper. Tim Fulford has recently written sensitively of the detailed ways in which Clare's asylum manuscripts use quotations from him as a lead-in to his own poetry, and thus build upon 'the Cowperian need for refuge into the disclosure of a hidden path, shielded by nature from all but the observant, shared by poet and reader'.[30] The general aim is the same, but Clare's hidden path is different in degree from Cowper's, in his vision of unalienated pastoral.

This vision is often beleaguered, and represents hidden scenes of inspiration found amidst the apparent mundanity, or even ugliness, of the quotidian in nature, rather than the apparently sublime or overwhelming. 'To the Snipe', one of the most important poems of the Northborough upheaval of spring 1832, is as far from being a conventional descriptive nature lyric as is possible, choosing a drab, ungainly bird to underscore the spiritual value of the Snipe's marshy environment as an untameable place apart from humanity:

> In these thy haunts
> Ive gleaned habitual love
> From the vague world where pride & folly taunts
> I muse & look above
>
> Thy solitudes
> The unbounded heaven esteems
> & here my heart warms into higher moods
> & dignifying dreams
>
> I see the sky
> Smile on the meanest spot
> Giving to all that creep or walk or flye
> A calm & cordial lot

> Thine teaches me
> Right feelings to employ
> That in the dreariest places peace will be
> A dweller & a joy   (lines 73–88; *Middle Period*, IV, 576–7)

This sense of the divine in nature precisely where it is not expected, in the apparently desolate 'meanest spot', and the related communal feeling of peace as a lasting feeling is meant to convey both the unnatural route of modernity, and its psychic damage to the 'vague world'; here, the specificity of feeling and genuine spiritual replenishment of nature is founded upon an austere Biblical diction: as well as the allusion to Leviticus, there is Clare's debt to the Psalms, traced by Mina Gorji:

> the swamp is not portrayed in terms of Bible 'pictures', but it is nonetheless haunted by echoes from the Psalms which transform the landscape beyond the literal. Clare's recognition of a divine order beyond the temporal, natural world and his sense that the snipe could be an emblem of divine protection was a legacy of the Protestant imagination. Clare shared with Cowper and Bunyan, and with Daniel Defoe, a way of seeing visions on the roadside, and of domesticating the visionary into ordinary forms.[31]

This notion of domesticating the visionary, and concomitantly of finding imaginative release and reassurance in a sort of spiritual ecology, is the defining mark of Clare's unique aesthetic. The Protestant imagination too found the impression of divine wonder and purpose in nature and the everyday, but Clare did not just deify that nature, instead setting it apart and against the bourgeois encroachments of modernity, improvement, enclosure and other imaginatively and spiritually barren modes of thought. This sort of defiance is very different from Cowper's polite complaints, or even Goldsmith's paternalistic vision of pastoral in *The Deserted Village*, though Clare needed to draw upon such works to create his own ways of defining the significance of place and landscape in an increasingly unsympathetic environment.

Ultimately, it is Clare's sense of renewal and equality in nature, and of the need to place his hope in such renewal, that sets him apart from poets of a Cowperian sensibility. Like many of Clare's late asylum manuscript lyrics, 'O could I be as I have been' seeks to redress intolerance and moral ambiguity – especially as interfering with his understanding of nature – through syntactic clarity. It opens with a beseeching, Blakean appeal to childlike simplicity:

> O could I be as I have been
> And ne'er can be no more

> A harmless thing in meadows green
> Or on the wild sea shore
>
> (lines 1–4; *Later Poems*, I, 653)

It ends, though, after a list of former pleasures, on a more visionary note:

> To gaze upon the starry sky
> And higher fancies build
> And make in solitary joy
> Loves temple in the field
>
> (lines 29–32; *Later Poems*, I, 654)

There is an echo here of Byron's elegiac 'Stanzas for Music' (written in 1815) which starts 'There's not a joy the world can give like that it takes away', and concludes:

> Oh could I feel as I have felt, – or be what I have been,
> Or weep as I could once have wept, o'er many a vanished scene:
> As springs in deserts found seem sweet, all brackish though they be,
> So, midst the wither'd waste of life, those tears would flow to me.[32]

Byron's heartfelt, world-weary elegy may be one source behind Clare's sparse yearning, in plain language, for an uncomplicated return to a world of childish innocence, and instinctive, joyful interaction with nature. It can be noted, though, that even in this he moves away, slightly, from his predecessors: Cowper's last English poem famously concluded with the poet forsaken of all hope, and fearing a worse punishment: 'But I, beneath a rougher sea,/And whelm'd in deeper gulphs than he.'[33] Even at his most isolated, in poetry that seems to will almost an extinction of personality, Clare falls back on the imagination, and 'higher fancies', as well as the spiritual regeneration of nature, with the field as 'loves temple'. It is these sorts of differences in attitude that position him so uniquely within Romanticism, define his relationship with the poetry of the eighteenth-century, and make him both a natural inheritor of the poetic modes and styles of poets like Thomson and Cowper and immutably different from them, in practice and effect.

Notes

1. Francis Turner Palgrave, *The Golden Treasury of English Songs and Lyrics*, ed. Christopher Ricks (Harmondsworth: Penguin, 1991), p. 492.
2. Bridget Keegan, 'Broadsides, Ballads and Books: The Landscape of Cultural Literacy in *The Village Minstrel*', *JCSJ*, 15 (1996), 11–19 (11).

3. *Poems Descriptive of Rural Life and Scenery* (London: Taylor and Hessey, 1820), p. xi. For a suggestive reading of Clare's epiphanic purchase and furtive reading of Thomson, see John Goodridge and Kelsey Thornton, 'John Clare the Trespasser', in Haughton, pp. 87–129.
4. John Barrell, *Poetry, Language, and Politics* (Manchester: Manchester University Press, 1988), pp. 100–36 (p. 134).
5. James McKusick, 'Beyond the Visionary Company: John Clare's Resistance to Romanticism', in Haughton, 221–37, p. 224.
6. James Thomson, *The Seasons*, ed. James Sambrook (Oxford: Clarendon Press, 1981), p. 214.
7. Paul Chirico, *John Clare and the Imagination of the Reader* (Basingstoke: Palgrave, 2007), pp. 159, 20. 'Writing Misreading: Clare and the Real World', in *The Independent Spirit: John Clare and the Self-Taught Tradition*, ed. John Goodridge (Helpston: John Clare Society and Margaret Grainger Memorial Trust, 1994), pp. 125–38 (p. 126).
8. John Goodridge, *John Clare and Community* (Cambridge: Cambridge University Press, 2013), pp. 36, 37, 58. For his overview of Clare and the eighteenth century, see pp. 36–58.
9. Ibid., pp. 44–5.
10. For Goodridge's discussion of Pomfret, see pp. 36–40; for Cunningham, pp. 37–46; for Gray, pp. 47–58. Goodridge counters the negative influence of Cunningham perceived by Mark Storey, *The Poetry of John Clare* (New York: St Martin's, 1974), pp. 37–9. For Clare's reading, see also Greg Crossan, 'Clare's Debt to the Poets in his Library', *JCSJ*, 10 (1991), 27–41.
11. Goodridge, p. 40.
12. In a more secular age, it is easy to forget that Cowper did not view himself as in any way a professional writer, and that, for various reasons, he lived off other people for most of his adult life. See the useful discussion of Cowper from the innovative perspective of work (or its absence) by Sarah Jordan, in *The Anxieties of Idleness* (Lewisburg: Bucknell University Press, 2003), pp. 177–216. See James King, *William Cowper* (Durham, NC: Duke University Press, 1986), pp. 43–51 and 86–94, for outlines of his mental breakdowns.
13. *By Himself*, p. 135.
14. 'The Winter Evening' in *The Task*, Book IV. *Poems of William Cowper*, ed. John D. Baird and Charles Ryskamp, 3 vols. (Oxford: Clarendon Press, 1995) II, p. 190.
15. Richard Cronin, 'In Place and Out of Place: Clare in the *Midsummer Cushion*', in *New Approaches*, pp. 133–48 (p. 136).
16. Clare owned a copy of the *Divine Comedy* in Henry Cary's hugely influential 1819 translation, and had met Cary in 1820 through mutual London literary connections, and corresponded with him thereafter. See David Powell, *Catalogue of the John Clare Collection in the Northampton Public Library* (Northampton: Northampton Public Library Collection, 1964), p. 25, no. 151. *Bate*, pp. 169, 241.

17. *The Task*, Book V, 'The Winter Morning Walk', *The Poems of William Cowper*, II, p. 212.
18. John Milton, *Paradise Lost*, ed. Alastair Fowler, 2nd edn. (London: Longman, 1998), p. 105. The relevant passage is in Book I, lines 739–43:

    > and in Ausonian land
    > Men called him Mulciber; and how he fell
    > From Heaven, they fabled, thrown by angry Jove
    > Sheer over the crystal battlements: from morn
    > To noon he fell, from noon to dewy eve,

19. Dated around 1840, 'The Gipsy Camp' was one of the poems Clare gave to Cyrus Redding. These twenty poems were published with a supporting essay by Redding in his *English Journal*, 1.20 (15 May 1841): 305–9 and 1.22 (29 May 1841), 340–3.
20. Alan Vardy, *John Clare, Politics and Poetry* (Basingstoke: Palgrave, 2003), pp. 27, 26.
21. Tim Fulford, 'Cowper, Wordsworth, Clare: The Politics of Trees', *JCSJ*, 14 (1995), 47–59 (52–3), quoting from a letter to John Newton, 9 July 1785, *The Letters and Prose Writings of William Cowper*, ed. James King and Charles Ryskamp, 5 vols. (Oxford: Clarendon Press, 1979–86), II, pp. 362–3.
22. See *Poems of William Cowper*, II, pp. 317, 316.
23. Ibid., pp. 26–7. I have followed the text of the poem first published in the *Gentleman's Magazine* in January 1785, and printed in the footnotes by Baird and Ryskamp, rather than their text based on the manuscript, as the former was the version familiar to readers such as Tennyson, Palgrave and Clare.
24. Ibid., III, pp. 78, 79–80.
25. Fulford, 'Cowper, Wordsworth, Clare: The Politics of Trees', p. 55.
26. As well as Fulford's mapping of its connections, John Goodridge notes an obvious echo, in passing. *John Clare and Community*, pp. 116–17.
27. *The Village Minstrel and other Poems* (London, 1821), 'Introduction', p. xx.
28. *John Clare and Community*, p. 118. On Taylor's printing of this letter, and Clare's modifying his view somewhat as the letter progresses ('was People all to feel & think as I do the world coud not be carried on'), see Sarah M. Zimmerman, *Romanticism, Lyricism, and History* (Albany: State University of New York Press, 1999), p. 166.
29. *The Prose of John Clare*, ed. J. W. and Anne Tibble (London, 1970), p. 39.
30. Tim Fulford, 'Personating Poets on the Page: John Clare in his Asylum Notebooks', *JCSJ*, 32 (2013), 26–48 (32).
31. Mina Gorji, *John Clare and the Place of Poetry* (Liverpool: Liverpool University Press, 2008), p. 114. For the psalmic in the poem more generally, see pp. 103–14.
32. George Gordon Lord Byron, *The Complete Poetical Works*, ed. Jerome McGann, 7 vols. (Oxford: Clarendon Press, 1981), III, pp. 284, 286.
33. 'The Castaway', *The Poems of William Cowper*, III, p. 216.

CHAPTER 3

John Clare's conspiracy

Sarah M. Zimmerman

In a group of poems about birds and their nests, John Clare plots to protect the creatures' homes from predators: 'The Pettichaps Nest', 'The Yellow Hammers Nest', 'The Yellow Wagtails Nest', and 'The Nightingales Nest' share a conspiratorial poetics. In the fullest version of their common narrative, a speaker and a companion embark on a search for birds' nests, find them, and then pause to describe these vulnerable sites before walking away – agreeing to keep *schtum* and implicitly enlisting the reader's silence. Carefully crafted and laced with descriptive language, these poems have been praised as some of Clare's best work. They are dramatic poems – birds scared out of hiding, nests spotted, eggs discovered – and they are also playful, recalling the childhood game of 'birds-nesting' in which nests are sought and eggs stolen. These works nevertheless convey serious concerns about the birds' ability to raise their young and sing in peace, living what in human terms translates as 'private life'. As is often the case with Clare's poetry, his solicitude for the well-being of animals, plants and places also reflects concerns closer to home. In chronicling the birds' continual struggle to protect their nests, the locus of family and of song, these poems simultaneously address the consequences of the period's converging pressures on privacy for poetry and the poet.

Scholars have long recognized Clare's attraction to natural refuges, hiddenness and obscurity. That impulse has been interpreted as a response to particular historical circumstances, including the transformation of Clare's local environment by parliamentary enclosure. I argue that this drive towards seclusion should also be read in light of two significant pressures on privacy that intensified in the period of Clare's successful literary debut. First, renewed agitation for parliamentary reform in the post-war era prompted heightened governmental repression of political dissent, including what John Barrell has described as the 'politicization of private space'.[1] Second, the early nineteenth century witnessed the definitive emergence of a 'modern celebrity culture', in which Clare was caught up after the appearance of *Poems Descriptive of Rural Life and Scenery* (1820).[2] With his successful introduction by his publishers as 'a Northamptonshire peasant' in that volume, Clare became exposed to a celebrity culture that was, as Tom Mole puts it, expanding with 'the growth of a modern industry of production, promotion and distribution, and a modern audience – massive, anonymous, socially diverse and geographically distributed'.[3] The surfeit of attention that Clare received included curious readers who appeared at his door, eager to view the poet in his domestic circumstances. It also included patrons alert to any '*Radical* and *ungrateful* sentiments' in his verse, a surveilling impulse that carried ominous overtones in the fraught political climate of the post-war period.[4]

The convergence of these two very different pressures in early nineteenth-century England marks an important chapter in the history of private life.[5] As Patricia Meyer Spacks observes, 'Most scholars believe, at the very least ... that the concepts of public and private bear historical significance and that their nexus in the eighteenth century warrants special investigation.' I follow Spacks's lead in attending to privacy as a term that 'has received much less historicized attention' than scholars have given the 'public' in the aftermath of Jürgen Habermas's theorization of an eighteenth-century public sphere. I also share Spacks's desire to treat private experience beyond the terms set by that paradigm.[6] Her definition of privacy, drawn in part from the debates of legal scholars and philosophers, as 'freedom *from* – from watchers, judges, gossips, sensation-seekers' and 'freedom *to*: to explore possibilities without fear of external censure', suits Clare's concerns especially well.[7] His beleaguered birds are similarly impacted by these concerns. They aim to evade a variety of threats since, as John Goodridge observes, their nests are 'constantly vulnerable to being robbed or trampled, exposed or betrayed', and they seek the time and space necessary to build nests, raise their young and sing.[8]

Clare doesn't use the word 'privacy' in the birds-nesting poems, but their vocabulary makes clear the proximity of avian and human concerns. For instance, 'Birds Nests' (composed *c.*1832), conjures 'an hermitage/For secresy & shelter rightly made', and in 'The Wood Larks Nest' (also composed *c.*1832), the birds seek 'hidden homes' that are 'as safe as secrecy'. Birds don't keep 'secrets', but Clare recognized in their plight a need that they share with humans to find the time and space for private life. When eggs are stolen or nests destroyed in these poems, the birds fall into stricken silence or utter cries of distress that end their songs. Those songs are the poems' clearest link to the preoccupations of the poet, given the conventional and, for Clare, intuitive association of poetry and birdsong. In his birds-nesting poems, birdsong – and thus poetry – are closely related to two kinds of private experience: domestic intimacy and solitude.[9]

After sketching the historical circumstances that put increasing pressure on privacy in Clare's day, I turn to poems on the snipe, the sand martin and the nightingale. These three poems comprise a study in contrasts between a fantasy of masculine autonomy and a dread of feminized exposure. Clare's conspiratorial paradigm is gendered: while the birds' plight is feminized, both the threats to the birds and the speakers' protective responses are masculinized. His speakers draw on their own experience as birds-nesting boys, former predators who turn their expertise to their one-time victims' protection. After considering the snipe, sand martin, and nightingale as inhabitants of opposite ends of the spectrum of privacy, and glancing along the way at other birds who live between those poles, I turn to three poems whose conspiratorial plots lead to three different endings. Each of these turns on the movements of chance, which can spell opportunity or disaster for the birds and the conspirators who seek and protect them. In 'The Pettichaps Nest', Clare considers the necessity of handling, and the potential for exploiting, the unexpected; in 'The Yellow Hammers Nest', the element of risk leads to a vision of disaster; in 'The Yellow Wagtails Nest', the plot unravels into reverie. Once the metaphorical association between birds' nests and an endangered privacy was forged in these poems, it became indelible in Clare's work, and thus I conclude with two very late poems in which it persists as a figure for safe seclusion: 'To John Clare' and 'Birds Nests'.

Invasions of privacy: celebrity culture and political pressure

By 1824, when Clare began writing the bulk of his birds-nesting poems, he had been in the public eye for several years and would remain there, despite the diminishing sales of the three volumes that followed *Poems Descriptive*. While the history of celebrity begins before Clare's lifetime, he and his contemporaries witnessed what Jason Goldsmith terms the 'twinned phenomena of an expanding readership and the rise of mass media technologies, both of which reached unprecedented scale during the post-Revolutionary years'.[10] A desire to know the poet on the part of the reading public was spurred by a sense of increasing estrangement in an expanding cultural marketplace. This perceived distancing was partly countered by an accompanying phenomenon that Mole describes as a 'hermeneutic of intimacy': 'an impression of unmediated contact' that made it seem as if the celebrity's private self was 'hidden from the view of the undiscerning, but was also continually making itself legible, expressing itself in poems where its secrets could be read by the discerning few'.[11] This effect encouraged attention to celebrities' private lives and encouraged readerly intrusiveness. The consequences of these developments for Clare have been addressed by Goldsmith, who situates the poet within an important 'cultural shift in the terms of renown' in the Romantic period. Whereas in the eighteenth century celebrity was 'a quality one might possess', by the middle of the next it was 'something you were, a personality'.[12] Once Clare had been introduced as 'a Northamptonshire peasant' in *Poems Descriptive*, this 'branded identity' generated significant interest in how his humble circumstances could produce such appealing poetry.[13]

Clare describes how celebrity arrived at his cottage door, in carriages bearing literary tourists who interrupted his agricultural labour, costing him time and income. Some visitors posed intrusive questions, even subjecting him to scrutiny about his relationship with his wife. One man asked to take Clare's walking stick as a souvenir, and 'then asked me some insulting liberties respecting my first acquaintance with Patty and said he understood that in this country the lower orders made their courtships in barns and pigsties and asked whether I did'.[14] Thus Clare became acutely aware of the consequences of celebrity. In September 1821 he told his publisher John Taylor,

> I am sought after very much agen now 3 days scarcly pass off but sombody calls – some rather entertaining people & some d —— d knowing fools – surely the vanity woud have kill'd me 4 years ago if I had known then how I shoud have been hunted up – and extolld by personal flattery – but let me wait another year or two & t[he] peep show will be over –[15]

He felt like quarried prey, 'hunted' and then put on display. 'Clare sounds thoroughly modern decrying his loss of privacy', Goldsmith notes, in an era in which 'the individual has become the object of an anonymous, voyeuristic gaze'.[16] The experience may have played a role in undermining his physical and mental health. Jonathan Bate speculates that Clare suffered from bipolar disorder accompanied by delusions, but the sustained stress of his literary career may have contributed to his deterioration.[17] Matthew Allen, his doctor at the Northampton General Lunatic Asylum, where Clare was admitted in 1837, observed three years later that 'his mind did not appear so much lost and deranged as suspended in its movements by the oppressive and permanent state of anxiety, and fear, and vexation, produced by the excitement of excessive flattery at one time, and neglect at another, his extreme poverty and over-exertion of body and mind'.[18] Allen corroborates his patient's sense that the inconstancy of 'flattery' destabilized both Clare's finances and his equanimity.

Clare's domestic life might have served as emotional ballast amidst 'the vagaries of literary fame', but his home became a site of contest over how to manage his public profile.[19] By summer 1820, his publishers and patrons had established a trust fund to supplement his income, and talk had begun of finding a suitable home for the poet and his new family.[20] It wasn't until 1832, however, that Clare gained the rental of a 'well-furbished cottage and a substantial plot of land' in the village of Northborough, a little more than three miles from Helpston.[21] Clare's domestic life was to become a *tableau* of contentment that would counter any threat of upward mobility posed by his commercial success as a 'peasant poet'. The land included an orchard and a grazing pasture, and Taylor and his patron and friend Eliza Emmerson started a modest subscription to purchase a cow, two pigs and 'a few useful tools for husbandry'. Emmerson contributed money for the cow on the condition that it be named 'Rose, Blossom or May', a finishing touch in a pastoral scene featuring the grateful labourer poet.[22] The cow, however, turned out to be a poor milker, the pigs never arrived and the domestic experiment failed as Clare's psychological health declined. When details of Clare's new domestic circumstances were published in accounts that emphasized his status as the object of charity, he drafted annoyed responses, including one lamenting that 'I wish to live in quietness but they will not let me'.[23]

The monitoring of Clare's home life by his patrons and the reading public was in part a reflection of the heightened scrutiny of the private lives of the rural poor in a period of renewed anxiety about domestic unrest. In his account of the consequences for privacy of a governmental crackdown on political dissent in the 1790s, Barrell describes how, in the wake of the French Revolution, '[a]ctivities and spaces which had previously been thought to be private, in the sense not just that they were "outside" politics but were, by general agreement, positively insulated from it, suddenly no longer enjoyed that protection'.[24] Those spaces included the rural cottage. In popular eighteenth-century visual and poetic representations, it had provided 'a fantasy of retirement from the "world," from the rituals and routines of public and social life, into an unattainable privacy'. By the middle of the 1790s, however, 'the image of the cottage had become thoroughly politicized', suspected of housing political disaffection or even conspiratorial plots.[25] Thus, Clare's new cottage uneasily represented both the safe, protected space of nostalgia and a potential nest of radicalism. Although Barrell's account of the period's intense pressures on privacy addresses an acute moment of counter-revolutionary repression, it also speaks to the post-war resurgence of the movement for parliamentary reform, a period that included the suspension of Habeas Corpus for almost a year in 1817–18, the 1819 Peterloo massacre, and the Six Acts legislation, also of 1819, which limited freedoms of assembly, speech and the press.

Once Clare came to public attention, his life and his poetry were scrutinized for signs of what his patron Lord Radstock described as ingratitude. Although Clare was no Radical, Radstock objected to lines in 'Helpstone' and *The Village Minstrel*, including a damning apostrophe (in 'Helpstone') to 'Accursed wealth': o'erbounding human laws,/Of every evil thou remainst the cause'.[26] Demands from Radstock were relayed and seconded by Emmerson 'to expunge certain highly objectionable passages' that accuse 'the very persons, by whose truly generous and noble exertions [you have] been raised from misery and despondency' of 'pride, cruelty, vices, and ill-directed passions'. These demands carried weight in a period marked by several high profile trials of publishers for works deemed libellous or seditious. Clare's publishers, Taylor and James Hessey, defended Clare's authorial independence, but they could protect him from neither the consequences of celebrity nor his patrons' alertness to signs of rebellion. Both Clare's verse and his domestic life were to reflect one 'theme' of '*Gratitude*', as Emmerson told him.[27]

The metaphorical possibilities of birds' nests for addressing these threats to privacy and autonomy may have been suggested to Clare by a poem he loved, William Cowper's *The Task* (1785). Timothy Fulford observes that Clare strongly felt a 'Cowperian need for refuge' in natural environs, and in his birds-nesting poems Clare follows Cowper's lead in seeking 'a place of rural seclusion and peace'.[28] *The Task* makes the connection between the rural cottage and the bird's nest explicit. In Book I, the speaker discovers a 'cottage ... perch'd upon the green-hill top' and explains that it is 'so thick beset/With foliage of such dark redundant growth,/I call'd the low-roof'd lodge the *peasant's nest*'.[29] Although he eventually rejects the site's 'solitude' as making 'scant the means of life', which for him include 'Society', the place also inspires a fantasy of poetry-nurturing seclusion: 'Oft have I wish'd the peaceful covert mine', Cowper's speaker muses, so that he would 'possess/The poet's treasure, silence, and indulge/The dreams of fancy, tranquil and secure'.[30] Clare was under no illusion that cottages like his own were ideal havens, but *The Task* may have suggested the bird's nest as a figure for his own 'dream' of private life. Cowper's vignette of the 'peasant's nest' closely follows a passage describing birdsong, including 'Ten thousand warblers', 'cawing rooks, and kites that swim sublime/In still repeated circles, screaming loud,/The jay, the pie, and ev'n the boding owl'.[31] Clare develops Cowper's metaphorical association in poems that elaborate the fate of what Hugh Haughton describes as Clare's 'nesting instinct'.[32]

Birds were one of Clare's perennial subjects, but they gained a heightened significance in the mid-1820s. Margaret Grainger ventures that '[h]e probably wrote more about birds than about any other subject and probably more bird poems than any other British writer'.[33] We can nevertheless pinpoint when his treatment of birds intensifies to the point of becoming a subject in its own right, deserving of its own volume. Johanne Clare notes that although Clare wrote poems focusing on birds before 1824, in that year 'Clare began to take the subject of birds seriously enough to commit his energies to writing extended groups – one is tempted to say sequences – of bird poems'.[34] Although a proposed collection on 'Birds Nesting' never materialized, some of these poems were published in *The Rural Muse*.[35]

In a number of poems that detail their nesting behaviours, Clare studies the creatures' continual efforts to protect their homes, using what Michel de Certeau would call 'tactics', the only manoeuvres available to the vulnerable. In de Certeau's vocabulary, those who possess established power – 'a proprietor, an enterprise, a city, a scientific institution' – are able to exert their strength in full-blown 'strategies', while the 'weak' are 'always on the watch for opportunities that must be seized "on the wing"'. In elaborating his natural metaphor for the 'tactics' of the disenfranchised, de Certeau speculates that the 'models' for these everyday practices 'may go as far back as the age-old ruses of fishes and insects that disguise or transform themselves in order to survive'.[36] A number of Clare's poems on birds constitute a catalogue of their defensive moves. Some manage to scare predators away. Clare may admire most the tactics of the skylark, the object of a strong human impulse to anthropomorphize nature. In 'The Sky Lark' (composed *c*.1825–6), boys flush the bird out in hunting 'butter cups' and are enraptured with her flight: 'from their hurry up the skylark flies ... till in the clouds she sings' (lines 9, 12–14; *Middle Period*, III, 524).[37] Led astray by their own imaginations – 'neer dreaming then/That birds which flew so high – would drop agen/To nests upon the ground' – the boys fail to notice when she 'drops & drops till in her nest she lies' again (lines 17–19, 16). Clare's speaker relishes the skylark's escape, and these poems celebrate the birds' varied tactics of evasion, but the creatures remain fundamentally defensive, and defenceless. In many of his bird poems, Clare's speakers simply observe these efforts, but in the few that are my central focus they are instigators who conspire to protect the birds' homes. Combining elements of planning, action and secrecy, conspiracy represents a third way for those who do not possess the institutional power to deploy 'strategies' but do not wish to be limited to the spontaneous 'tactics' of the forever vulnerable.

Scholars have traced the roots of 'a Romanticism steeped in conspiracy' to the French Revolution – 'the embodiment of the conspiracy hermeneutic' – noting that in this period conservatives' 'fear of invasion and enemies abroad' was matched by 'an equal atmosphere of mistrust and suspicion [by] those on the English left'.[38] Those fears were revived in an economically and politically volatile post-war era punctuated by Peterloo and, in the year that followed, the event that became known as the Cato Street Conspiracy, when a plot (which included an *agent provocateur*) to murder the entire British Cabinet, along with the Prime Minister, Lord Liverpool, was intercepted and the accused were either hung or transported. In the 'very highly charged political environment' in which Clare wrote, 'conspiracy theories flourished'.[39] Orrin Wang makes the case that grasping 'the pervasiveness of conspiracy during the Romantic era ... means retrieving local instances of conspiratorial logic both at the material level of institutions, policies, and events and at the figural level of writings', including poetry.[40]

'Conspiracy' is a Keatsian word, and thus Nicholas Roe reads 'To Autumn', where the 'Season of mists and mellow fruitfulness' actively plots with the 'maturing sun', as a call for justice after Peterloo.[41] Without using the word, Clare's birds-nesting poems also reflect the period's heavy conspiratorial weather, as his speakers abandon his habitual stance of watchful interest to intervene in the birds' continual state of emergency and, indirectly, in their own. These speakers walk the line between passive observation and an intervention that is potentially predatory. Their tone is by turns intimate and urgent, suggesting that they are responding to a fear they share and a vulnerability they want to alleviate. Their plots risk discovery, but that danger is outweighed by another perceived to be greater and by the promise of what may be gained – in this case, the private time and space for family and song. In the game of birds-nesting in which Clare had participated, he found an apt figure for the threats to privacy that he himself experienced and a ready-made plot to protect it.

At the poles of privacy: snipes and nightingales

In two poems composed around 1832, Clare thinks through what it is like to live at the extremes of sociability, either completely alone or continually pursued. 1832 is the year in which Clare and his family moved to their new cottage in Northborough, and both texts speak to his acute concerns with privacy under pressure. By this point, Clare had written many birds-nesting poems, but 'To the Snipe' and 'The Nightingale's Nest' form an illustrative pair because they map Clare's poles of privacy in gendered terms and thereby make clear the costs of both real isolation and an attention-drawing fame.

In 'To the Snipe', Clare asks what it would be like to enjoy a solitude free from predators, and concludes that the terrain is barely habitable. The poem envisions a reprieve from the continual need for vigilance through a fantasy of masculine autonomy. The snipe is an unpoetic bird, with his bill 'Of rude unseemly length' made for searching the swamp's 'gelid mass for food' (lines 19–20; *Middle Period*, IV, 574). The poem is an ode to an unlikely figure of serenity: 'alone & mute', he 'Sitteth at rest/In safety' (lines 8–10). A fortress of time and space is required to foster his 'mystic nest': 'Lover of swamps/The quagmire over grown', he lives where 'Security pervades/From year to year' (lines 24, 1–2, 32–3). Bridget Keegan lucidly explains how the snipe's environment, 'both land and water, open and secure, unbounded and protected', is appropriate for Clare's theme of private experience: the 'fens in their extreme openness' are 'a paradoxical place of secrecy and seclusion'.[42] The cost of the snipe's 'solitudes' proves high, however (line 77). He has no mate, no eggs to protect, and does not sing. The silent snipe goes it alone, seemingly the only way to secure his 'calm & cordial lot' (line 84). Few birds possess such fortitude: the snipe must possess a 'power divine' to 'brave/The roughest tempest', but even his bravery affords only a limited range, a habitat too watery to withstand the press of human feet (lines 49–51). His 'instinct knows/Not safetys bounds – to shun', and indeed danger is nearby: beyond 'tepid springs/Scarcely one stride across' roams the 'staulking fowler' with 'searching dogs & gun' (lines 53–8). Clare's speaker relishes the snipe's remove from the 'vague world where pride & folly taunts', but implicitly acknowledges that the bird's untouchable status renders him almost antediluvian (line 75). The snipe's 'still & quiet home' is available only in a watery world 'untrodden' by humans (lines 72, 34). Thus, the snipe figures as a fantasy at the heart of modernity – a kind of privacy that is intensely wished for, and that may even be envisioned, even if it never actually existed, 'Mystic indeed' (line 25).

Although the snipe's autonomy is unavailable to the poem's speaker, the bird provides Clare with a vital sense of what an increasingly endangered privacy feels like, and thus enables his search for sites where it may still be found. Another poem from the same period that imagines that kind of freedom, 'Sand Martin' (composed *c.*1832), makes it clear that even though it is out of reach, airborne like the bird, it may briefly be vicariously experienced by tracking the bird's flight. The speaker watches the bird flying 'far away from all thy tribe' in the 'lonely glen' and 'unfrequented sky', and is strongly affected by 'a feeling that I cant describe/Of lone seclusion & a hermit joy' (lines 9, 1, 10–2; *Middle Period*, IV, 309–10).[43] He can't describe it because it is not within his realm of experience, but he can feel it in the sand martin's 'Flirting' flight (line 10). Like the snipe, however, the sand martin pays a price for being 'seldom by the nesting boy descried': it must 'labour undeterred/Drilling small holes along the quarrys side/More like the haunts of vermin than a bird' (lines 8, 5–7). Thus, the sand martin seems almost estranged from its own nature. As in 'To the Snipe', such extreme solitude seems silent, and although Clare doesn't explicitly gender the sand martin, it too has no eggs to protect.

The speakers in 'To the Snipe' and 'Sand Martin' assume a stance familiar in Clare's poems – that of the reflective observer. But in the cluster of birds-nesting poems to which I now turn, Clare's speakers become action figures, walking into the narrative frame to assume a direct, and even aggressive role in the birds' lives, doing for the creatures what they are unable to do for themselves: conspiring to protect their homes. In 'The Nightingale's Nest' (1832; *Middle Period*, III, 456–61), Clare treats a sought-after bird and imagines existence at the other end of the spectrum of privacy from the reclusive snipe and 'hermit' sand martin (line 1). While their nearly perfect solitude is apparently too 'lonely' for song ('Sand Martin', line 1), the nightingale has a 'home of love' that inspires a 'luscious strain' (lines 4, 33). That song's 'renown', in turn, threatens the domesticated solitude that seems necessary to it (line 19). In 'so famed a bird' (line 20), Clare finds a feathered figure for what Goldsmith calls 'the sense of spectacle by which modern celebrity has come to be characterized'.[44] In the course of the poem, one of 'solitudes deciples' who aim to 'spend their lives/Unseen' inspires a conspiratorial poetics to protect her home and her song (lines 85–6). Among a handful of birds-nesting poems that share a conspiratorial plot, 'The Nightingales Nest' most directly addresses the threat to poetry brought about by the loss of privacy and also provides the happiest resolution of that crisis.

'The Nightingale's Nest' is one of Clare's most studied poems for its reflections on poetry, fostered by the bird's association with the myth of Philomela. Clare's contemporaries readily spotted the poet in the poem. Emmerson penned her own verse in response to his. In 'On reading the Nightingale's Nest by John Clare', she exclaims '"Clare" and the "Nightingale" are one!'[45] Modern scholars have recognized that the poem addresses Clare's own literary career. Hugh Haughton suggests that it reflects Clare's awareness of his 'own problems as a writer', including 'his difficulties with his audience – with publishers, readers, critical interlocutors, social superiors and intellectual inferiors'.[46] One of those difficulties was the invasion of privacy he experienced: Simon Kövesi explains that 'the nightingale's world is the embodiment of an ideal for Clare' in that it is 'solitary, hidden, cut off from society with no path to encourage the encroachment of that private space by public others'.[47] Kövesi describes how Clare genders the invasion of privacy by feminizing the nightingale's vulnerability and, further, by sexualizing it, thereby heightening the sense of violated intimacy: 'Her wings would tremble in her extacy/& feathers stand on end as 't'were with joy/& mouth wide open to release her heart/ Of its out sobbing songs' (lines 22–5).[48] Clare understood the experience of being objectified and thereby feminized, having been subjected to intrusive questions about his sexual life by at least one prurient reader-tourist. Clare draws on the bird's ancient association with Philomela – turned into a nightingale by the gods after her rape and forcible silencing, her tongue cut out by her brother-in-law, the king – in order to emphasize the threat of a voyeuristic, masculinized aggression.

Clare's treatment of masculinity in the poem is complex, because both the threats to the nightingale's home (the 'rude boys') and its defenders (the speaker and his companion) are masculinized (line 52). Clare dissociates his speaker from the exploitation of the 'famed' bird by projecting the most destructive aspects of his predatory impulse onto the birds-nesting boys while preserving a measure of masculinized aggression for his autobiographical speaker as the nightingale's protector (line 20). It is the speaker who initiates the search, invades the bird's privacy, and plots to keep the nest's location secret. He is still a voyeur who watches the nightingale unawares, even though he knows that her song depends on privacy: 'if I touched a bush or scarcely stirred/All in a moment stopt' (lines 28–9). He nevertheless wishes to distinguish his behaviour on the bird's behalf from the destructiveness of those who would steal eggs and destroy nests.

He differentiates between these two kinds of aggression in an autobiographical narrative that distances temporally his childhood exploits of hunting the birds' eggs from his mature activity of protecting them. In 'The Nightingale's Nest', the speaker claims that his history as a predator has in fact given him the experience necessary to locate and defend the bird: 'There have I hunted like a very boy/Creeping on hands & knees through matted thorns/To find her nest & see her feed her young' (lines 12–14).[49]

The poem begins with Clare's speaker, at once *carpe diem* lover and ringleader, leading the way, having invited a companion – and, by implication, the reader – on 'another search today', entreating, 'Up this green wood land ride lets softly rove/& list the nightingale' (lines 47, 1–2). He knows where to find her and, as he is relaying the backstory that establishes his credentials as a hunter, catches the notes of the nightingale. The poem immediately shifts back into present tense to capture the moment of discovery: ' – Hark there she is as usual lets be hush/For in this black thorn clump if rightly guest/Her curious house is hidden' (lines 42–4). This a work of suspense in which the forward momentum of the hunt is abruptly suspended for a sustained exploration of a private world: 'Aye as I live her secret nest is here' the speaker declares, as the bird issues 'a plaintive note of danger' before falling 'Mute in her fears' so that she won't 'betray her home' (lines 53, 58, 65, 61). Then, while the bird remains frozen in terror, the speaker undertakes a meticulous inventory of her nest.

The poem defines privacy by first invading it and then meticulously documenting its spatial and temporal dimensions. The speaker arrests his story's progress to describe a nest made of 'dead oaken leaves', 'velvet moss' and 'little scraps of grass', containing 'curious eggs in number five/Of deadened green or rather olive brown' (lines 78–80, 89–90). Although Clare's nightingale inhabits a pastoral site – 'melody seems hid in every flower' – it is defined by these homely details (line 71). Haughton notes that as the examination commences, the poem's tone shifts from a high lyricism to an almost prosaic description of the nest's 'loose materials' and its location in a 'black thorn clump' (lines 77, 43). This extended passage of natural historical description is crucial to making the experience of a poetry-producing privacy seem tangible to the search party – the speaker, his companion and the reader – who spend time exploring the site together. When they, and the poem, start moving again, the speaker and his companion are motivated by this intimate knowledge of her home to protect the bird. 'We'll leave it as we found it', the speaker declares, promising 'We will not plunder music of its dower/Nor turn this spot of happiness to thrall' (lines 62, 69–70). Having demonstrated the bird's vulnerability by violating her privacy himself, he recognizes that all he can do to ensure her safety is utter a blessing and hope for the best: 'Sing on sweet bird may no worse hap befall/Thy visions then the fear that now deceives' (lines 67–8). The poem's final image is the pair walking away from a refuge that they know cannot be secured.

The nightingale perfectly figures the plight of the 'famed' poet, and, more broadly, the fate of privacy in Clare's day: it may be located in time and space, but it remains provisional, always subject to invasion. The nightingale nevertheless gets a happy, if tenuous, ending, with her eggs safe at the poem's close: '& here we'll leave them still unknown to wrong/ As the old wood lands legacy of song' (lines 92–3). In very different ways, then, 'To the Snipe' and 'The Nightingale's Nest' are poems of sheer wish fulfilment, fantasies of privacy preserved, if never entirely secure. Clare develops the conspiratorial plot that he employs to protect the nightingale in several birds-nesting poems composed in the mid-1820s. In 'The Pettichaps Nest', 'The Yellowhammers Nest' and 'The Yellow Wagtails Nest', Clare plays out that narrative's various possibilities, emphasizing the role that contingency plays in both the finding of nests and their fates once discovered.

Hatching plots: a conspiratorial poetics

Clare's conspiratorial poetics draws upon two distinctive impulses in his verse while avoiding their potential pitfalls: he employs both a richly detailed description that identifies beings and places, and a 'protective celebration of obscurity' that protects 'himself and his familiar world [from] certain forms of scrutiny'.[50] Scholars have assessed the costs and benefits of each mode. Adam Phillips notes that 'description may be redemptive – provide a voice for otherwise marginalized people and experiences – but it may also be predatory and encourage other predators'. Nicholas Birns explains how these competing impulses towards identification and evasion are at work in a crucial context for Clare – the transformation of his local environment by parliamentary enclosure between 1809 and 1820. In response to the 'rhetoric of efficiency and productivity' that defined the era's enthusiasm for agricultural 'improvement', Clare celebrated 'nature's elusiveness'.[51] The conspiratorial poetics that he develops shrewdly combines his habitual modes of evasion and lush empirical description. While the coordinates of the birds' private haunts are kept secret, those privy to the conspiracy – and this includes the reader – are treated to a full accounting of richly detailed natural spaces.

The speakers of 'The Pettichaps Nest', 'The Yellow Hammers Nest' and 'The Yellow Wagtails Nest' use inclusive pronouns – 'we', 'us' and 'you and I' – to form an intimate circle of those in the know. Each of these poems seeks to draw us into a transient experience of privacy, a here and now defined by Clare's detailed imagery (the 'here') and temporal shifts (the 'now'). These are action poems that seem to begin *in medias res*, both mid-stride and mid-utterance: 'Well in my many walks I rarely found/A place less likely for a bird to form/Its nest' ('The Pettichaps Nest', lines 1–3; *Middle Period*, III, 517). Thus 'The Pettichap's Nest' begins with an accidental sighting and goes on to examine the role of chance in the plot of birds-nesting, as both unexpected danger and unforeseen opportunity. The speaker and his companion nearly trample a nest that lies 'close by the rut gulled waggon road', directly in 'harms way' (lines 3, 7). But the speaker embraces this contingency: he marvels that 'you & I/Had surely passed it in our walk today/Had chance not led us by it' and 'had not the old bird ... fluttered out' (lines 9–13). Both the bird and the human pair are on the right side of chance 'today', although the bird's luck is limited. Having discovered the nest, the wanderers pause to conduct an extended examination of its construction and contents. We move from the backstory of almost overlooking it to a sustained invasion of the bird's privacy. The speaker describes 'outward walls', made of 'small bits of hay' and 'withered leaves', before exploring the interior manually: 'lined with feathers', it is 'Built like a oven with a little hole' and 'full of eggs scarce bigger e'en then peas'. The speaker then extracts a single egg by inserting 'two fingers' into its 'snug entrance' (lines 14–24). The moment is extraordinarily uncomfortable, both because of the gendered, sexualized violence of the imagery and because the terms of the implied conspiracy suddenly place the reader, along with the speaker, in the predatory role. This is what privacy is like for Clare – we all too frequently know it by its violation.

Viewed another way, the poem's ending could be said to stress the provisional nature of the bird's privacy. After the pair agree, 'We'll let them be', the poem shifts temporally again, to hopes for the future, by uttering a blessing. Before leaving the eggs in 'safety's lap' (line 35), however, another unexpected event occurs, and the pair and the poem are once again halted in mid-stride: ' – Stop heres the bird' (line 37) the speaker exclaims, a response to a surprise ('Well I declare it is the pettichaps' [line 39]) that solves a mystery (lines 27, 35–9). The speaker admits that although he had 'often found their nests in chances way ... never did I dream untill today/A spot like this would be her chosen

John Clare's conspiracy 71

home' (lines 41, 43–4). The poem's final lines thereby underscore the way in which conspirators must, like the birds whose domain they invade, take the opportunities they find 'on the wing' (as de Certeau puts it). Clare's conspiracy is full-blown in this poem: a suspenseful atmosphere, twists and turns, and a mystery solved.

In 'The Yellow Hammers Nest' and 'The Yellow Wagtails Nest', Clare's conspiratorial plot unravels in two different, telling ways – one emphasizing the fragility of any efforts to safeguard privacy, and the other insisting on the lasting benefits for the poet of fully experiencing that state, if only briefly. 'The Yellow Hammers Nest' (composed *c.* 1825–6) opens characteristically, in mid-stride and with a surprise: 'Just by the wooden brig a bird flew up'. Realizing that the bird's home must be nearby, the speaker suggests, 'let us stoop/& seek its nest' (lines 1, 3–4; *Middle Period*, III, 515). It is no sooner found than examined: ' – Aye here it is' (line 7), the speaker declares. He then offers one of these poems' most beautiful descriptions, underscoring the inseparability of a domesticated privacy and poetry: 'Five eggs pen-scribbled over lilac shells/Resembling writing scrawls which fancy reads/As natures poesy & pastoral spells' (lines 13–15). The eggs' loveliness heightens the horror of the poem's ending. Once again, the speaker begins to walk away from the nest and out of the poem, urging an agreement upon his companion: ' – so leave it still/A happy home of sunshine flowers & streams' (lines 21–2). This attempt at protective closure is thwarted, however, by the speaker's own inability to banish thoughts of the nest's vulnerability. 'Yet in the sweetest places cometh ill', he worries, 'For snakes are known with chill & deadly coil/To watch such nests & seize the helpless young' (lines 23–6). The poem ends with a vision of a devastated world, 'as though the plague became a guest' and the 'housless-home a ruined nest'. The final image is an avian portrait of inconsolability: the 'mournful' yellowhammer once 'woes hath rent its little breast' (lines 27–30). Thus, the speaker cannot prevent his own postlapsarian knowledge of a modernity in which privacy is under continual pressure – a state of exposure and vulnerability appropriately represented here by the menace of snakes – from spoiling an Edenic scene of seclusion.

In 'The Yellow Wagtails Nest', the speaker manages to linger in paradise lost, as the plot spirals into a recollection of having found the privacy necessary for poetry. The poem opens with a familiar pair pausing to document their progress: 'Upon an edding in a quiet nook/We double down choice places in a book' (lines 1–2). The speaker again begins with background, identifying the nook as one he had 'noted as a pleasant scene' when he once discovered 'A broken plough ... nestled like a thought forgot by toil' in 'clover grass' (lines 3, 4, 10, 5; *Middle Period*, III, 474). Instead of returning to a present moment of discovery, however, this poem dwells on what happened while he was sitting on the 'nestled' plough, a temporary 'place for rest' (line 11). He recalls reaching 'for a flower', a gesture that sets off a series of events before action stops altogether. 'A little bird cheeped loud & fluttered up', and in turning towards it the speaker spies 'a snug nest deep & dry' – a nest within a nest (lines 13–17). The bird had chosen her site carefully, 'From rain & wind & tempest comfort proof' (line 24). The glimpse of her 'six eggs sprinkled oer with spots of grey' launches a fantasy of being 'snug as comforts wishes ever lay' (lines 19–20). The speaker lingers in the recollection of a blissful, impermanent, solitude: '& I so happy then/Felt life still eden from the haunts of men' (lines 31–2). The reveries prompted by 'Such safety-places' are short-lived, but in the moment, he stresses, 'I almost felt the poets fables true' (lines 25, 36). Clare insists that the figure of what Haughton describes as 'inherently private, hidden' nests, can have a lasting effect that is almost tangible, since 'We feel such pleasures after many days' (line 44).[52] So, if the recollection of having briefly 'Felt life still eden' is all we have of such retreats, that visceral memory has a valuable afterlife for the poet.

Poets have repeatedly turned to birds as fellow singers in asking how to respond to moments of historical crisis and disruption. In 'Of Modern Poetry' (1940), Wallace Stevens describes the poet's task of 'finding/ What will suffice' (line 2). He explains that 'It has to be living, to learn the speech of the place', and in his day that means 'It has to think about war' (lines 6–8).[53] For Clare's contemporaries, one of the measures of modernity was increasing encroachments on privacy. In these birds-nesting poems, Clare answers his own version of a question that Robert Frost would pose in another wartime poem, 'The Oven Bird' (1916), of 'what to make of a diminished thing' (line 14).[54] In framing a song for 'mid-summer', once 'the early petal-fall is past' and 'the highway dust is over all' (lines 2, 6, 10), Frost's bird invokes 'that other fall we name the fall' (line 9). In his birds-nesting poems, Clare seeks a poetics suitable for the ruined aftermath of an idyllic time when he 'Felt life still eden from the haunts of men' ('The Yellow Wagtails Nest', line 32).

Two of Clare's very late poems offer his own view of 'what will suffice' in an era in which privacy seemed increasingly diminished. These verses were composed long after the close of Clare's active life on the public stage, once the historical pressures that threatened the bird's nest have seemingly fallen away, leaving only these undisturbed vignettes of poetry and privacy.[55]

These are poems with no need for conspiracy, because there is no longer an awareness of danger. 'To John Clare' creates a sonic microcosm of childhood experience in a sonnet of thickly woven rhymes and near rhymes. It begins with the same intimate address that opens the birds-nesting poems that I've been discussing: 'Well honest John how fare you now at home' (line 1; *Later Poems*, II, 1,102). Bate points out that 'John' may be the poet himself or his son. In either case, John's 'home' is a world in which 'birds are building nests' and a boy engages in three activities that are intimately related: birds-nesting, playing (with 'tops & tawes', line 11) and reading. In this sonnet, the literary consists only of 'lots of pictures & good stories too', and the only kind of fame is harmless: 'Jack the jiant killers high renown' (lines 13–14). In 'Birds Nests', possibly Clare's last poem, only the nest itself remains, its construction accompanied by birdsong that 'charms the poet' (line 4; *Later Poems*, II, 1,106). Poet and bird are suspended in the here-and-now of a moment of private experience: 'Tis Spring warm grows the South' (line 1). In that continuous present the 'Chaffinchs carry the moss in his mouth/To the filbert hedges all day long' while the poet listens to the 'beautifull song' as 'wind blows', 'warm the sunshines' and 'the old Cow at her leisure chews her cud' (lines 2–7). In these late lines, Clare has finally edited his poetic world down to a composite figure – the poet and a nest complete with singing bird – forged in the fires of political unrest and the public glare of celebrity, and surviving both in the long aftermath of his writing life.

Notes

1. John Barrell, *The Spirit of Despotism: Invasions of Privacy in the 1790s* (Oxford: Oxford University Press, 2006), p. 8.
2. Tom Mole, *Byron's Romantic Celebrity: Industrial Culture and the Hermeneutic of Intimacy* (Basingstoke: Palgrave Macmillan, 2007), p. 4.
3. Ibid., p. 10.
4. Eliza Emmerson is quoting Lord Radstock in a letter she wrote to Clare dated 11 May 1820; *Critical Heritage*, p. 61.
5. I borrow the phrase from Philippe Ariès, who nevertheless wonders whether it is 'possible to write a history of private life' since an understanding of privacy may 'refer in different periods to such different states and values that relations of continuity and difference among them cannot be established'. I address this legitimate concern by adopting the same approach taken by the multi-volume series by that name, of grounding accounts of private life as specifically as possible in particular times and places. Philippe Ariès, 'Introduction', *A History*

of Private Life, vol. 3: *Passions of the Renaissance*, ed. Roger Chartier, trans. Arthur Goldhammer (Cambridge, MA: Belknap Press, 1989), p. 1.
6. Patricia Meyer Spacks, *Privacy: Concealing the Eighteenth-Century Self* (Chicago: University of Chicago Press, 2003), pp. 3–4.
7. Ibid., p. 14.
8. Goodridge, *John Clare and Community* (Cambridge: Cambridge University Press, 2013), p. 135.
9. Ariès usefully locates privacy on a continuum of sociability that includes the intimacy of domesticity and a more complete solitude. 'Introduction', p. 9.
10. Jason N. Goldsmith, 'The Promiscuity of Print: John Clare's "Don Juan" and the Culture of Romantic Celebrity', *Studies in English Literature 1500–1900*, 46 (2006), 803–32 (821).
11. Mole, *Byron's Romantic Celebrity*, pp. 22, 25.
12. Goldsmith, 'Promiscuity of Print', p. 822.
13. Mole, *Byron's Romantic Celebrity*, p. 18.
14. Quoted in Bate, pp. 178–9.
15. Clare to Taylor, 6 September 1821, *Letters*, p. 215.
16. Goldsmith, 'Promiscuity of Print', p. 804.
17. I share Bate's view that '[p]osthumous psychiatric diagnosis' of any kind 'is a dubious activity' (p. 412); see also Bate, pp. 213–14, 518–19.
18. Allen's assessment is offered in his letter 'To The Editor' of *The Times* (London), published on 23 June 1840. Quoted in Goldsmith, 'Promiscuity of Print', p. 804.
19. Ibid., p. 804.
20. Bate, pp. 163, 175.
21. Ibid., p. 362.
22. Ibid., p. 393.
23. *Letters*, p. 590.
24. Barrell, *Spirit of Despotism*, p. 4.
25. Ibid., pp. 212–13, 220.
26. Radstock also objected to two love poems for their frankness about physicality, including sexuality. For accounts of these objections, see Bate, pp. 164–5, 197–203, 218–19.
27. *Critical Heritage*, p. 62.
28. Fulford, 'Personating Poets on the Page: John Clare in his Asylum Notebooks', *JCSJ*, 32 (2013), 26–48 (32).
29. *The Poems of William Cowper*, ed. John D. Baird and Charles Ryskamp, 3 vols. (Oxford: Oxford University Press, 1980), II, lines 221–2, 225–7. See Barrell, *Spirit of Despotism*, pp. 212–13.
30. Ibid., lines 248, 249, 233–6.
31. Ibid., lines 100, 203–5.
32. Haughton, p. 64.
33. *Natural History*, p. 123.
34. Johanne Clare, *John Clare and the Bounds of Circumstance* (Canada: McGill-Queens University Press, 1987), p. 205 n.

35. Of the poems discussed in this chapter, the following (with titles as printed) appeared in *The Rural Muse* (1835): 'The Nightingale's Nest', 'The Pettichap's Nest', 'The Yellow Hammer's Nest', 'The Skylark', 'The Thrush's Nest' and 'The Wryneck's Nest'. Eric Robinson and David Powell report that Clare 'intended a separate volume in which birds and their nests would be described in short poems of varying stanzas, the whole collection being called "Birds Nesting"'. See *Major Works*, p. 492 n.
36. Michel de Certeau, *The Practice of Everyday Life*, trans. Steven Rendall (Berkeley: California University Press, 1984), pp. xix, xi.
37. Eric Robinson, David Powell and P. M. S. Dawson suggest that a number of the poems I discuss – 'The Sky Lark', 'The Yellow Wagtails Nest', 'The Yellow Hammers Nest' and 'The Pettichaps Nest' – 'may be connected with the birds list he compiled in 1825–6'. I have suggested composition dates accordingly. See *Middle Period*, III, pp. 615, 618. I have used the (manuscript) versions of the titles instead of the titles of the printed volumes except when referring to those volumes.
38. Orrin N. C. Wang, 'Introduction: Romanticism and Conspiracy', *Romantic Circles Praxis Series* (August 1997). www.rc.umd.edu/praxis/conspiracy/wang/owint2.html. Accessed 26 October 2014.
39. Nicholas Roe describes this as the 'environment' in which Keats composed 'To Autumn'. See *John Keats and the Culture of Dissent* (Oxford: Oxford University Press, 1994), p. 254. Using a related metaphor to describe the 1790s, Barrell describes the pervasive influence of an 'atmosphere of suspicion'. See *Spirit of Despotism*, p. 5.
40. Jerome Christensen proposes 'a conspiratorial theory of Romantic poetry' that understands the 'Romantic poets as conspirators against the order of things' and Romanticism '[a]s a conspiracy against the given'. See *Romanticism at the End of History* (Baltimore: Johns Hopkins University Press, 2000), pp. 2–3.
41. Roe, *John Keats and the Culture of Dissent*, p. 261.
42. Bridget Keegan, *British Labouring-Class Nature Poetry* (Basingstoke: Palgrave Macmillan, 2008), p. 167.
43. Mina Gorji notes that the placement of 'Sand Martin' and 'To the Snipe' alongside religious lyrics in the manuscript Pet. A57 highlights shared 'preoccupations', which include a desire for 'the peace and comfort that can be found in solitary desolate places'. See *John Clare and the Place of Poetry*, pp. 100–2.
44. Goldsmith, 'Promiscuity of Print', p. 823.
45. Quoted in Bate, p. 368.
46. Haughton, p. 52.
47. Simon Kövesi, '"Her Curious House Is Hidden": Secrecy and Femininity in Clare's Nest Poems', *JCSJ*, 18 (July 1999), 51–63 (59).
48. Ibid., pp. 58–9.
49. As an adult, Clare continued the hunt as an amateur natural historian. The companions addressed in several birds-nesting poems are probably modelled

on the household steward at Milton Hall (until 1826), Edmund Tyrell Artis, an antiquarian and archaeologist, and Joseph Henderson, the head gardener for whom Clare collected birds' eggs. He also fulfilled other such requests, including Taylor's desire for 'a Nightingales nest & eggs'. After leaving Helpston in 1832, Clare also promised himself that he would return 'yearly' to 'hunt the nightingales nest in royce wood.' *Natural History*, pp. 67, 318.

50. Adam Phillips, 'The Exposure of John Clare', in Haughton, pp. 178–88 (pp. 180–1).
51. Nicholas Birns, 'The Riddle Nature Could Not Prove', in Haughton, pp. 202, 206.
52. Haughton, p. 64
53. Wallace Stevens, *The Collected Poems of Wallace Stevens* (1954. Reprinted New York: Vintage, 1990).
54. Robert Frost, *The Poetry of Robert Frost*, ed. Edward Connery Lathem (New York: Holt, Rinehart and Winston, 1969).
55. Eric Robinson and David Powell include them among 'The Last Six Poems' that Clare wrote; *Later Poems*, II, pp. 1,098–106.

PART II

Culture

CHAPTER 4

John Clare and the new varieties of enclosure: a polemic

John Burnside

> For poetry makes nothing happen: it survives
> In the valley of its making where executives
> Would never want to tamper[1]

July, 2013. I am walking with a friend on the trail that leads upwards from the Swiss village of Bräntschen to the Nivenalp. All week, the weather has been changeable; but for now the air is clear and slightly damp and the ground underfoot is teeming with insect life – so much so that, with each step I take, I struggle to plant my foot and do no harm. All around us, in the diverse grasses, meadow flowers abound, and an astonishing range and abundance of butterflies and other insects flit from blossom to blossom in the late morning sun. I can scarcely contain my pleasure at witnessing so much vivid confusion; and yet, at the back of my mind – or perhaps I should say, off to the side somewhere, like a bedraggled sailor at a wedding party – a hint of sorrow lingers. Sorrow, because it is a long time since I have encountered a meadow anywhere near as rich and diverse as this in Britain, and I cannot imagine seeing so many different butterfly species, in anything like these numbers, on agricultural land at home. Even the range of grasses is cause for delight. My friend, a Swiss doctor from further down the valley, walks here all the time, and she is accustomed to all this teeming life, even if she does not take it for granted, but I have to stop and be still for a moment, because I live in a land where agribusiness and 'development' has rendered such scenes defunct – a fond memory or a clichéd grandmother-story about the good old days when the garden was full of butterflies – a degraded state best described by E. J. Mishan, in *The Costs of Economic Growth*:

> Other disagreeable features may be mentioned in passing, many of them the result of either wide-eyed enterprise or of myopic municipalities, such as the post-war 'development' blight, the erosion of the countryside, the 'uglification' of coastal towns, the pollution of the air and of rivers with

chemical wastes, the accumulation of thick oils on our coastal waters, the sewage poisoning our beaches, the destruction of wildlife by indiscriminate use of pesticides, the change-over from animal farming to animal factories, and, visible to all who have eyes to see, a rich heritage of natural beauty being wantonly and systematically destroyed – a heritage that cannot be restored in our lifetime.[2]

Mishan wrote these lines in 1967 but, in spite of some (mostly cosmetic) 'greening' in areas where landowners' interests are not threatened, the condition of the British landscape, and the flora and fauna that live there, has worsened – and when I mention this to my friend, she assures me that the upper Valais, where we are now standing, is a special case, and that Britain is probably no more culpable than any other European nation. It is a dispiriting thought and, in an effort to avoid lingering over it, I look around again, my wonder increasing, if anything, the more I take it all in. For me, living where I live, and all too accustomed to the costs of economic growth, it is like looking into some remnant of an otherwise lost world – like the world John Clare knew, or had told to him, before his native ground was finally enclosed.

*

When I began writing this chapter, I was preoccupied with events that, in Mishan's terms, involved the wanton and systematic destruction of a wild bird habitat close to my home – a fact that I feel the need to mention here because it provoked in me a dismay somewhat akin (if less thoroughly tragic) to the dismay Clare must have felt at the height of enclosures. This is important, to my mind, because poets have to write, not only out of a sense of celebration of the land, but also in response to events that drive us to genuine despair. In reworking that first draft, I hope to have put aside my personal issues, but I have to confess that my main concern here remains polemical. Even when so great an authority as Auden declares it so, I find it impossible to accept that poetry makes nothing happen – and I read Clare not only for pleasure or for his keen observations of rural life, but also in the hope that his political concerns may still make a difference, one hundred and fifty years or so after his death.

So the question I want to ask in this chapter is both simple to state and impossible to answer, but, at its briefest, it is this: what kind of person (and writer) would John Clare be, if he were alive today? To my mind, it seems likely that he would also be engaged in some kind of polemic: as a poet whose life and work were deeply marked by the continuing agricultural enclosures visited upon his social class and home terrain, a resurrected

John Clare and the new varieties of enclosure: a polemic

Clare would surely be a trenchant critic of the myriad new enclosures to which we are presently being subjected: enclosures, not only of land and property, but also of the sky, the horizon, our means of communication, knowledge and ideas, the imagination and even our very senses. The enclosure of pleasure. The colonization of the Internet for motives of commerce and state security. The continuing enclosure of culture.

In school, I was taught that the gradual enclosure of the British Isles was a series of specific historical events, marked by Acts of Parliament and the occasional riot; I was even led to believe that, in its later, nineteenth-century manifestations, it represented a kind of progress, in which land was more efficiently and productively farmed – and it took some time, and a good deal of off-curriculum reading, to understand that *to enclose* is capitalism's central intention. My first alternative source was Marx (extremely non-curricular in my working-class, Catholic comprehensive school), who, having outlined the course of land enclosure from the late Middle Ages, through the Reformation and into the increasingly rapacious modern era, pointed out that, by the nineteenth century,

> the very memory of the connection between the agricultural labourer and communal property had, of course, vanished. To say nothing of more recent times – have the agricultural population received a farthing's compensation for the 3,511,770 acres of common land which between 1801 and 1831 were stolen from them and presented to the landlords by the landlords through the agency of Parliament?

He went on to conclude that,

> [t]he spoliation of the Church's property, the fraudulent alienation of the state domains, the theft of the common lands, the usurpation of feudal and clan property and its transformation into modern private property under circumstances of ruthless terrorism, all these things were just so many idyllic methods of primitive accumulation. They conquered the field for capitalistic agriculture, incorporated the soil into capital, and created for the urban industries the necessary supplies of free and rightless proletarians.[3]

Marx's analysis was slightly after the fact (*Capital* appeared three years after Clare's death), but Clare recorded what was being done to his class and his land as it happened, in a poetry that is not only finely attuned to the life-world he saw being degraded all around him, but is also instinctively dissident:

> On paths to freedom & to childhood dear
> A board sticks up to notice 'no road here'
> & on the tree with ivy over hung

> The hated sign by vulgar taste is hung
> As tho the very birds should learn to know
> When they go there they must no further go
> Thus with the poor scared freedom bade good bye
> & much the[y] feel it in the smothered sigh
> & birds & trees & flowers without a name
> All sighed when lawless laws enclosure came
> ('The Mores', lines 69–78; *Middle Period*, II, 349–50)

Yet, though these lines foreshadow *Capital*'s denunciation of enclosure, it would be simplistic to see Clare as some kind of proto-Marxist. Indeed, it is not difficult to find unsettlingly conservative and patriotic sentiments in his verse. I would argue, however, that these arose as a result of the socialization he underwent – a result, that is, of his place, class, and education – and I would venture to suggest that, given changes in the cultural climate and education system, our hypothetical twenty-first-century Clare would be highly critical not only of such predictable targets as agribusiness, chemical companies and the Common Agricultural Policy, but also of those who profit from, or collude with, today's less obvious and more controversial forms of enclosure. The most interesting question here, perhaps, is what form his poetry would take under present circumstances – which, for a politically and ecocritically motivated poet working now, is not just a fanciful way of asking what, if anything, one might learn from Clare's *oeuvre*, in the continuing project of critiquing and attempting to combat new instances of 'lawless law'. In short, my question here is: what can a contemporary poet learn from a predecessor who lived and worked before it was publicly pronounced that poetry makes nothing happen?

*

Whatever *actual* forms they take, enclosures are always *presented* as improvements – and, at times, they may even originate in ideas that are (at least theoretically) either beneficial or harmless. However, as the American painter Thomas Cole noted, 'what is sometimes called improvement in its march makes us fear that the bright and tender flowers of the imagination shall all be crushed beneath its iron tramp'.[4] Clare, arguably the only major Romantic to witness at first hand the human and environmental ravages of agricultural 'improvements', was more direct:

> By Langley bush I roam but the bush hath left its hill
> On cowper green I stray tis a desert strange & chill
> & spreading lea close oak ere decay had penned its will

> To the axe of the spoiler & self interest fell a prey
> & cross berry way & old round oaks narrow lane
> With its hollow trees like pulpits I shall never see again
> Inclosure like a Buonaparte let not a thing remain
> It levelled every bush & tree & levelled every hill
> & hung the moles for traitors—though the brook is running still
> It runs a naker brook cold & chill
> ('Remembrances', lines 61–70; *Middle Period*, IV, 133–4)

The likening of enclosure to Buonaparte here is both provocative and courageous, in the light of Clare's social position and his dependency on patronage. Even today, anyone dwelling in the British countryside is soon made keenly aware of the power, and the wilfulness, of his or her more prosperous, and politely ruthless, neighbours. Yet what is most noticeable in this poem – and what works so well as a countering value system to power – is the use of (and the assumed familiarity with) specific place names. Clare's system of imaginatively mapping the poem's terrain by reference to individual trees and geographical features recalls a near-magical intimacy with the land that was already being undermined by the agribusiness practices of his time. It actualizes specific phenomena as distinct, creaturely entities: they are no longer simply objects in the field of vision; they dwell in that field *with* us.

When such mental maps and place names are destroyed, however, spaces that were once dwelling grounds become what some aboriginal peoples call 'dead land', and this elimination of home terrain constantly finds new manifestations. Recently, for example, under the headline 'Ambitious renewable energy plan aims to provide power for the entire city', a *Peterborough Today* report described a new kind of enclosure in Clare's own backyard, claiming that:

> An energy self-sufficient [*sic*] Peterborough creating and delivering all the power needed by homes and businesses could be a reality in 20 years. This is the vision of civic leaders who want to create three renewable energy parks harnessing wind and solar power on farmland owned by Peterborough City Council at Newborough Farm, America Farm and Morris Fen. But standing in their way are some 22 farmers who have built their livelihoods on the same land for generations.[5]

Even in this short passage, several discrepancies stand out. First, it is deceptive for Peterborough City Council to claim energy self-sufficiency when its energy parks are to be sited well outside the city limits on what are, effectively, absentee landlord holdings. Notice, too, how the piece speaks of power '*needed* by homes and businesses' (my emphasis), as if this need were urgent and real and could be satisfied by an intermittent energy source such as wind.[6] The correspondent Paul Grinnell unfairly elevates the civic leaders' 'vision' over the perspective of the farmers, who are depicted as merely 'standing in the way' of that vision; then, having run through the usual wind industry flannel about the potential benefits of the plan, he finally gets to the key information: 'Funding would come from sources such as government grants and the private sector ... the scheme would generate a long-term net income to the council over 20 years of between £90 million and £137 million.'[7]

Yet, on reflection, it would not have taken much effort on *Peterborough Today*'s part to recognize this subsidy-grab project as one of the new forms of enclosure. When it comes to wind turbine planning issues, the powers-that-be have developed an ugly habit of trotting out lawless laws to suit themselves (or, as in Scotland, of simply wading in and overruling local decisions), not to mention misleading the public about costs and benefits, in order to allow larger landowners and developers to draw millions of pounds from tariffs and energy bills. That the illegality of this policy has now been exposed by the Christine Metcalfe UNECE ruling[8] is probably neither here nor there: too many rich people will get even richer from turbine installations for the process to be halted now[9]. Money, however, is only part of the problem. Even if the tariffs were operated on a fairer basis, and proper consultation were to be carried out, the impact of horizontal axis wind turbines on bird and bat life is finally beginning to be independently reported, after a long campaign (by government bodies, the power companies, and even certain media outlets) of deliberate misinformation and deceit – and the results are a matter for deep concern on the part of some environmentalists (though apparently only some). A 2012 study by the Spanish Ornithological Society, for example, points to bird and bat mortality estimates in the millions that, for some reason, have been persistently ignored, just as much by many mainstream 'greens' as by governments and the energy industry.[10] Perhaps the situation is best summed up by Clive Hambler, an Oxford University-based zoologist who specializes in species extinction:

> I think wind farms are potentially the biggest disaster for birds of prey since the days of persecution by gamekeepers, and I think wind farms are one of the biggest threats to European and North American bats since large-scale deforestation. The impacts are already becoming serious for white-tailed eagles in Europe, as is abundantly clear in Norway. A wind farm – built despite opposition from ornithologists – has decimated an important population, killing 40 white-tailed eagles in about 5 years and 11 of them in 2010.

The last great bustard in the Spanish province of Cadiz was killed by a wind development. In my experience, some 'greens' are in complete denial of these impacts, or hopefully imagine that these bats and birds can take big losses: they can't because they breed very slowly.

Birds of prey often soar where wind farms are best sited, and may be attracted to their deaths by the vegetation and prey around the turbines. A similar deadly ecological trap has been proposed for bats, with some species attracted by insect prey or noise around the turbines.

There are very serious suggestions of a cover-up of the scale of the problem, by some operatives hiding the corpses of birds, but you only have to look at the 'Save the Eagles' website to see the evidence accumulating despite scavengers or deception.

To my mind one of the worst problems is that wind farms will prevent the recovery of birds of prey, other threatened birds, and bats – denying them great swathes of the European and North American continent where they once dwelt. This flies in the face of the legally binding Convention on Biological Diversity, which encourages restoration of habitat and species whenever practicable. It makes a nonsense of the idea that wind is 'sustainable' energy – except in that it sustains and renews ecological damage.[11]

Yet, as much as these threats to the creaturely life of his home ground would horrify Clare, I think he would also appreciate a subtler point about the impact of turbines on the land – or, rather, on our sense of a horizon – that Frieda Hughes has pointed out:

> Knowing nothing about wind turbines, I used to imagine that they were a good idea. But while staying with relatives on the outskirts of Halifax a few years ago, I was dismayed to discover that the enormous picture window in their attic bedroom no longer framed the view over the unblemished Yorkshire hills that I was accustomed to, but a wind farm.
>
> It industrialised the horizon and was instantly depressing. No creative thought could wander that previously scenic vista; instead the turbines acted as anchors, preventing cognitive reasoning.[12]

This is a response with which Clare would surely have sympathized; few poets have his sense of the living space between land and sky, and the beauty of the horizons that are found in fen country. To return to 'The Mores':

> Far spread the moorey ground a level scene
> Bespread with rush & one eternal green
> That never felt the rage of blundering plough
> Though centurys wreathed springs blossoms on its brow
> Still meeting plains that stretched them far away
> In uncheckt shadows of green brown & grey

> Unbounded freedom ruled the wandering scene
> Nor fence of ownership crept in between
> To hide the prospect of the following eye
> Its only bondage was the circling sky
> One mighty flat undwarfed by bush & tree
> Spread its faint shadow of immensity
> & lost itself which seemed to eke its bounds
> In the blue mist the orisons edge surrounds
> Now this sweet vision of my boyish hours
> Free as spring clouds & wild as summer flowers
> Is faded all— ('The Mores', lines 1–17; *Middle Period*, II, 347–8)

This passage, with its invocation of the circling sky and the horizon's edge, echoes the sense of the sky and the air as a source of imaginative freedom that Bachelard has in mind when he says:

> Dans le règne de l'imagination, l'air nous libère des rêveries substantielles, intimes, digestives. Il nous libère de notre attachement aux matières: il est donc la matière de notre liberté [13]

> [In the realm of the imagination, the air frees us from substantial, internal, digestive reveries. It frees us from our attachment to matter: it is therefore the matter of freedom.]

It would be easy to make further points about the deployment of wind turbines as a process of enclosure, whether in terms of deliberate misinformation by government and developers, or in terms of the environmental damage done, or, in this subtler sense, as violations of the circling sky. Yet just as the sky and the horizon are being enclosed,[14] further inroads are being made elsewhere, undermining or polluting the ways in which we imagine, the ways in which we dream and the things we think we know. Before moving on to consider these new forms of enclosure, it might be worth reflecting a little on the poet's role – and his or her limitations – when faced with such attacks on space, human and environmental values, and the imaginative life.

*

In his Marxist approach to the work of the artist and his or her place in society, *The Necessity of Art*, Ernst Fischer notes that:

> In a class society the classes try to recruit art – that powerful voice of the collective – into serving their particular purposes ... On the one hand, we find the Apollonian glorification of power and the status quo – of kings, princes, and aristocratic families and the social order established by them and reflected in their ideology as a supposedly universal order. On the other

John Clare and the new varieties of enclosure: a polemic

> hand there was the Dionysian revolt from below, the voice of the ancient, broken collective which took refuge in secret associations and secret cults, protesting against the violation and fragmentation of society, against the *hubris* of private property and the wickedness of class rule, prophesying the return of the old order and the old gods, a coming age of commonwealth and justice. Contradictory elements were often combined within a single artist, particularly in those periods when the old collectivism was not yet too remote and still continued to exist in the consciousness of the people.[15]

That much of Clare's poetry emerges from 'the ancient, broken collective' is not surprising and, in his own time, the emotional and spiritual damage inflicted by private property and class rule cost him dear, arguably just as much as any physical privations. Even if we determine to avoid the old 'poet-madman-lover' clichés, there is no doubt that, in a predatory capitalist system – now, as then – those who value the land will suffer psychologically from what is done to its flora and fauna, its skies and waters, and its imaginative weather. Bearing in mind that aboriginal description of exploited terrain as dead land – land that, in a meaningful sense, can no longer be *intimately* named – and the demoralization of so many indigenous and rural peoples when that exploitation lays waste to their homes, we might choose to see what at first looks like madness as a natural response to unchecked external power. As Fischer points out:

> As human beings separated themselves more and more from nature, as the original tribal unity was gradually destroyed by division of labour and property ownership, so the equilibrium between the individual and the outside world became more and more disturbed. Lack of harmony with the outside world leads to hysteria, trances, fits of insanity.[16]

George Monbiot echoes this notion, with specific reference to Clare:

> What Clare suffered was the fate of indigenous peoples torn from their land and belonging everywhere. His identity crisis, descent into mental agony and alcohol abuse, are familiar blights in reservations and outback shanties the world over. His loss was surely enough to drive almost anyone mad; our loss surely enough to drive us all a little mad.[17]

However, we should be careful not to oversimplify Clare's madness. There are good reasons for seeing certain forms of insanity as *performance* – which is to say, as works of desperate art in which the supposed madman creatively (though often obliquely) enacts a rejection of those social forces (accepted by others as 'rational' or, at the very least, inevitable) that work to destroy his original sense of, and belonging with, the collective.[18] We are familiar with the notion of 'magical thinking' as fantasy, as a kind of superstitious rejection of 'reality' in favour of long-nurtured wishes; perhaps we also need to think of it, in relation to 'crazy', as a radical spiritual alternative to a denatured socio-political environment. In a real sense, this performed madness is an attempt to live according to some improvised, but meaningful, law in a social milieu where even the most fundamental laws have become corrupt, or 'lawless':

> Accursed wealth oer bounding human laws
> Of every evil thou remains the cause
> Victims of want those wretches such as me
> Too truly lay their wretchedness to thee
> Thou art the bar that keeps from being fed
> & thine our loss of labour & of bread
> Thou art the cause that levels every tree
> & woods bow down to clear a way for thee
> ('Helpstone', lines 127–34; *Early Poems*, I, 161)

By likening humankind to the natural world, and equating the damage done to 'human laws' with the despoliation of nature, Clare is making the point, familiar in contemporary ecocritical thinking, that social and environmental justice are not only linked, but continuous. As this is one of the key 'pillars' of the green movement that is most often compromised by political parties, it is worth recalling Edward Abbey's forceful expression of the continuity between humans and other life forms:

> The ugliest thing in America is greed, the lust for power and domination, the lunatic ideology of perpetual Growth . . . 'Progress' in our nation has for too long been confused with 'Growth'; I see the two as different, almost incompatible, since progress means, or should mean, change for the better – toward social justice, a livable and open world, equal opportunity and affirmative action for all forms of life. And I mean all forms, not merely the human. The grizzly, the wolf, the rattlesnake, the condor, the coyote, the crocodile, whatever, each and every species has as much right to be here as we do.[19]

Clare's critique of a wealth that becomes 'accursed' by 'oer bounding human laws' and Abbey's attack on greed should be familiar from the Biblical saying, gone into folk wisdom, that the love of money is the root of all evil.[20] Yet both writers go further and equate social injustice with environmental destruction – in each case, with a careful and cunning attention to the mores of his particular time. As Clare extends the indignity of bowing and scraping to the very trees themselves, so Abbey calls for an extension of affirmative action – normally associated with human victims of prejudice – to wolves and snakes and coyotes. Thus, for both, the continuity of social and environmental justice is not simply a maxim or a slogan, but an essential element of all morality. At the most fundamental level, their work takes as read the spirit of Ecclesiastes, in which the continuity of the human and other living things is set out in the starkest possible form:

> For that which befalleth the sons of men befalleth beasts; even one thing befalleth them: as the one dieth, so dieth the other; yea, they have all one breath; so that a man hath no pre-eminence above a beast.[21]

It comes as no surprise, then, that Clare extends his respect for other animals (and plants) to the land itself, a precursor of the land ethic best expressed in 'The Lament of Swordy Well':

> I am no man to whine & beg
> But fond of freedom still
> I hang no lies on pitys peg
> To bring a gris[t] to mill
> On pitys back I neednt jump
> My looks speak loud alone
> My only tree they've left a stump
> & nought remains my own
> (lines 121–8; *Middle Period*, V, 109)

The spoiling of Swordy Well parallels the destruction of the human collective: it is a piece of land that has 'fell upon the town' (lines 121–8; *Middle Period*, V, 111), like the men, women and children who, having been worked till they could not stand, were rapidly consigned, first to the poor house, and then to a pauper's grave. Swordy Well falls into parish hands and suffers the same degradation before losing the last vestiges of a specific identity: 'Of all the fields I am the last/That my own face can tell' (lines 251–2; *Middle Period*, V, 113). Yet both the success of the *entire* collective, and the sanity of *every* individual, depend upon, and are continuous with, an original tribal unity that constantly emerges out of intimate connection with the land and with the other creatures (living and dead) that dwell, or have dwelt, upon it. All life arises in the mixing of water with loam; spirit is breathed through the nascent clay by the wind; the origin, the continuing support and the final resting place of all living things is the earth. For this reason, as Fischer notes:

> The totemistic clan represented a totality. The clan totem was the symbol of the immortal clan itself, the ever-living collective from which the individual emerged and to which he returned. The uniform social structure was a

'model' of the surrounding world. The world order corresponded to the social order.[22]

This is a two-way exchange, of course: the 'perfect unity of man, animal, plant, stone, and source, of life and death, collective and individual' is a premise, not only of totemic magic, but of meaningful social existence. Harm the land, or the trees, or the totem spirits, and the social order collapses; but, by the same token, injustice within the social order leads to natural disaster in the outside world, thus threatening harm, in the longer term, to *all* members of the collective. Clare's description of Swordy Well, as it falls into the condition of 'dead land', both laments environmental destruction and, at the same time, cries out for the kind of land ethic that Aldo Leopold made explicit in the 1940s:

> There is as yet no ethic dealing with man's relation to land and to the animals and plants which grow upon it. Land, like Odysseus' slave-girls, is still property. The land-relation is still strictly economic, entailing privileges but no obligations.
> The extension of ethics to this third element in human environment is, if I read the evidence correctly, an evolutionary possibility and an ecological necessity. It is the third step in a sequence. The first two have already been taken. Individual thinkers since the days of Ezekiel and Isaiah have asserted that the despoliation of land is not only inexpedient but wrong. Society, however, has not yet affirmed their belief. I regard the present conservation movement as the embryo of such an affirmation.[23]

And he continues:

> All ethics so far evolved rest upon a single premise: that the individual is a member of a community of interdependent parts. His instincts prompt him to compete for his place in that community, but his ethics prompt him also to co-operate (perhaps in order that there may be a place to compete for).
> The land ethic simply enlarges the boundaries of the community to include soils, waters, plants, and animals, or collectively: the land.[24]

I do not think it is too much of a stretch to see in 'The Lament of Swordy Well' the outline of just such a land ethic in the making (or, at least, in a negative direction). When Clare speaks of the bees that 'flye round in feeble rings/& find no blossom bye/Then thrum their almost weary wings/Upon the moss & die' (lines 81–88; *Middle Period*, V, 107), we who live with the threat of honey bee colony collapse cannot help experiencing a chill; when we hear of the loss of the butterflies, and the beetles and of the 'dead tussocks' (line 112; *Middle Period*, V, 108), we are all too aware of the parallels between profit-driven enclosure and the image E. J. Mishan paints of 'a rich heritage of natural beauty being wantonly and systematically destroyed'. Nobody reading Clare today would deny that he is a precursor of our best ecocritical writers; however, the question a concerned contemporary still feels compelled to ask is: aside from the beauty and poignancy of the work, what difference does this actually make? How can the re-reading of a dead Northamptonshire peasant poet have any impact in a world where the greed and hypocrisy he identified not only continue, but multiply and mutate into new, ever more inventive and callous forms? How, in societies that still measure success by economic 'growth', can poetry of any kind help to provoke the necessary changes?

The answer, if there is one, lies in the reference to *re-reading*. Over the last several years, Clare has come to enjoy unexpected public recognition; now, the time is right to reconsider his vision and his warning, to point out the universal and ancient connection to the collective that his work embodies – a connection to folkways and values from which we can learn to recognize the subtle and varied nature of all of our present day enclosures, and the motives of those who would impose them. Re-reading Clare, we see the urgency of an ecocentric revaluation of how we use one another and the land we share, not just for environmental reasons, but also because our sanity, individual and collective, depends on right dwelling. For some years it was taken for granted in many circles that the Romantic project was over – that poetry about 'nature' was secondary and necessarily slight, if aesthetically pleasing. That this position has been reversed has as much to do with the re-assessment of Clare's writing and his importance as a naturalist over the last couple of decades as anything else. Now, the essential Romantic enterprise, the search for an *informed dwelling*, continues with ecocriticism, a discipline that begins with the recognition of our mutual creatureliness with all life and with the salvaging of a sense of wildness and spontaneity in ourselves – and without a doubt, one necessary forebear of this development is John Clare.

*

I have tried, as I said, to avoid portraying Clare as a proto-Marxist. It is tempting, however, to think of him as a forerunner of some of today's dissidents (some elements of the 'Occupy' movement, and of zero-growth theorists, for example), and I cannot help reading a poem like 'The Tramp' (as this poem is popularly known), for example, as a kind of thought experiment in ways of countering the capitalist state's 'ruthless terrorism', as Marx labels it:

> He eats a moments stoppage to his song
> The stolen turnip as he goes along
> & hops along & heeds with careless eye
> The passing crowded stage coach reeling bye
> He talks to none but wends his silent way
> & finds a hovel at the close of day
> Or under any hedge his house is made
> He has no calling & he owns no trade
> An old smoaked blanket arches oer his head
> A whisp of straw or stubble makes his bed
> He knows a lawless clan that claim no kin
> But meet & plunder on & feel no sin
> No matter where they go or where they dwell
> They dally with the winds & laugh at hell
>
> (*Middle Period*, V, 270)

The tramp's poverty is neither denied nor glamorized, but Clare also recognizes his vitality, his connection to the natural world through song (surely Dionysian in nature), and his dalliance with the winds and the 'lawless clan' that guides him (notice that Clare uses the term 'lawless law' for enclosure in 'The Mores' but, here, what the tramp 'knows' runs counter to that law: his 'lawless clan' is dissident, defiant and potentially insurgent). One immediately recognizes this figure as a member of Marx's proletariat, created by 'the forcible expropriation of the people from the soil ... turned in massive quantities into beggars, robbers and vagabonds, partly from inclination, in most cases from stress of circumstances ... chastised for their enforced transformation into vagabonds and paupers'.[25] That the tramp is not only poor and homeless, but also disenfranchised cannot be denied, but he also carries in his body the lineaments of an older knowledge of the world, a connection with song and the wind, and an ability to dwell in his own flesh and nervous system that the adherents of capitalism have sacrificed. His law disdains to locate all experience in the head: unlike the worthies in the 'passing crowded stage coach', he does not think in order to be, but experiences his environment with his entire body, for better or worse, out in the open and with no fixed abode or predetermined destination. For the time being, it is clear that he lacks a means by which to unite this soulful existence at the individual level with a collective, socio-political awareness, but there are hints, nevertheless, of meaningful dissidence.

This man owns nothing, but his ingenuity allows him, for the moment at least, to have the use of everything; because capitalism has taken away from him everything that *it* values, he is obliged to follow 'his silent way' and discover new, and potentially revolutionary, values of his own. In this, at the very least, he is exemplary for those currently faced with the new forms of enclosure and the latest fashions in cynical dispossession. A true child of Pierre-Joseph Proudhon, he reminds us that the limits and constraints of property outweigh its apparent benefits.

Naturally, it would be wrong to claim that Clare's tramp is a revolutionary, as such. What he provides, however, is a reminder of a now almost outmoded condition of openness to the world that is wholly consonant with what we have, in our tradition, sometimes called 'the soul' – a condition, one might say, that is entirely continuous with all being. As vulnerable as he is to contingency, the tramp no longer carries within him the garrison of a colonial force: he has, to some extent, overthrown the government in his head. His 'lawless clan', being true to nature and exigency, directly opposes the 'lawless law' of enclosure: for the moment, he is as free as it is possible to be under capitalism's aegis. Outlawed, he finds new allegiances. Talking to none, he enters into a silence that is full of potential for new and inventive ways of saying. With no calling, no trade and no kin, he is able to 'laugh at hell' and, in spite of his poverty and disenfranchised condition, he really does become a living exemplar of imaginative (if reactive) self-liberation. What makes him so is the quality of his refusal. His outsider status may not have been voluntarily adopted, but now that he is where he is, it seems unlikely that he would choose to return to a system that encloses the world and, so, denatures it. That refusal is the first step in constructing an alternative order, one that counters enclosure in all its forms with a truly inventive disdain.

The notion that poetry makes nothing happen, that it stands apart in its own privileged, and suspiciously ethereal-sounding, valley is one that I find deeply troubling. Such wise detachment may suit certain weathers, but in the current climate, the post-romantic, ecocritical project calls out for engagement. Looking around today, a contemporary Clare would quickly see that we live in an era of novel and insidious enclosures at every level: contemporary agribusiness, as Marx noted, 'is a progress in the art, not only of robbing the worker, but of robbing the soil; all progress in increasing the fertility of the soil for a given time is a progress towards ruining the more long-lasting sources of that fertility';[26] for many, a worldwide programme of enforced privatization, displacement and appropriation has placed the basics of life – water, fuel, medical care – in the hands of private companies whose first and overriding duty is to make money for their shareholders; concerted efforts are being made to control and commercialize the internet and rob the population as a whole of the beneficial changes it could offer;[27] gentrification is robbing the poor in many cities of what little of the built environment remains theirs; the horizon has been enclosed by tower blocks, pylons and wind turbines, the earth by monoculture and the frantic application of toxic chemicals; the entire biosphere is being genetically mapped and patented; imagination is enclosed by an endless tide of muzak, counterfeit history, product fetishization and infotainment – the list continues and, if we are not careful, despair can lead to the very quietism we most need to avoid. Considering his sensitivity to the enclosures of his own time, Clare would not only be aware of these dangers, but would also attack them with courage and wit, while lyrically celebrating the *real*, using his gift for precise yet tender observation to celebrate what endures – a meadow in the upper Valais, for example – as well as to lament what is endangered or lost.

Notes

1. W.H. Auden: 'In Memory of W.B. Yeats', in *Another Time* (New York: Random House, 1940), p. 108.
2. E. J. Mishan, *The Costs of Economic Growth* (London: Staples Press, 1967), pp. 6–7.
3. Karl Marx, *Capital*, trans. Ben Fowkes (London Pelican Books, 1976), p. 895.
4. Thomas Cole: *Essay on American Scenery*, in John Conron (ed.), *The American Landscape: A Critical Anthology of Prose and Poetry* (New York, Oxford University Press, 1973), pp. 577–8.
5. Paul Grinnell, 'Ambitious renewable energy plan aims to provide power for the entire city', *Peterborough Today*, 28 September 2013. Accessed 17 June 2014: www.peterboroughtoday.co.uk/news/latest-news/ambitious-renewable-energy-plan-aims-to-provide-power-for-the-entire-city-1-4312844.
6. To speak of 'need' here seems misleading, considering the fact that reports produced by DECC make clear that, on a climate-corrected basis 'the UK is a higher consumer of energy per dwelling than the EU27 average with two-thirds of countries having lower consumption per household in 2008. Since 2000 the UK has reduced energy consumption per dwelling by 4 per cent which places it in the top half of EU27 Member States but below neighbouring countries including France, Netherlands and Sweden where consumption reduced by at least 10 per cent over that period.' Anna Nikiel and Stephen Oxley, 'European Energy Efficiency trends – Household energy consumption', March 2011. Accessed 17 June 2014: www.gov.uk/government/uploads/system/uploads/attachment_data/file/65964/1524-eu-energy-efficiency-household-trends-art.pdf.

7. Grinnell, 'Ambitious renewable energy plan . . . '.
8. In August 2013, as reported by *The Independent*, the UN's Economic Commission Europe ruled that 'the UK Government acted illegally by denying the public decision-making powers over their approval and the "necessary information" over their benefits or adverse effects. The new ruling, agreed by a United Nations committee in Geneva, calls into question the legal validity of any further planning consent for all future wind-farm developments based on current policy, both onshore and offshore. The United Nations Economic Commission Europe has declared that the UK flouted Article 7 of the Aarhus Convention, which requires full and effective public participation on all environmental issues and demands that citizens are given the right to participate in the process.' Margaret Pagano, 'UN ruling puts future of UK wind farms in jeopardy', *The Independent*, 27 August 2013. Accessed 17 June 2014: www.independent.co.uk/news/uk/politics/exclusive-un-ruling-puts-future-of-uk-wind-farms-in-jeopardy-8786831.html.
9. According to Conservative MEP Struan Stevenson, 'it is estimated that a dozen or more of Scotland's wealthiest private landowners will pocket around £1bn in [turbine] rental fees over the next eight years'. See Struan Stevenson, *So Much Wind* (Edinburgh: Birlinn, 2013), p. 43.
10. When I asked a spokesperson for FoE Scotland why his organization was not concerned about bird and bat mortality rates in relation to turbines, he stated that the number of birds and bats killed was 'negligible'. When I asked where he got his figures, he said, with no apparent irony, that they came from the American Wind Energy Association.
11. Clive Hambler, quoted in Mark Lynas, 'Bats, birds and blades: wind turbines and biodiversity.' *Mark Lynas* (blog), 10 June 2011. Accessed 17 June 2014: www.marklynas.org/2011/06/bats-birds-and-blades-wind-turbines-and-biodiversity/. See also Clive Hambler, 'Wind farms vs wildlife: The shocking environmental cost of renewable energy', *The Spectator*, 5 January 2013. Accessed 17 June, 2014: www.spectator.co.uk/features/8807761/wind-farms-vs-wildlife/.
12. Frieda Hughes, 'Blowing ruin across the land', *Sunday Times*, 15 May 2011, p. 6.
13. Gaston Bachelard, *L'air et les songes* (Paris: José Corti, 1943), p. 195.
14. In spite of developer rhetoric, I believe the underlying reasons are commercial, just as they were with the enclosure of the land. It will be some time before the whole truth emerges, but I have come to this conclusion, partly from studying subsidy systems in other areas, partly because I have listened to engineers, ecologists, and economists who have studied the impacts of turbines in their own fields, and also, in no small measure, because such prodigious efforts have been made by developers and governments to deny the public the information it needs to make informed judgements about wind turbine planning issues.
15. Ernst Fischer, *Von der Notwendigkeit der Kunst* (orig. Dresden: Verlag der Kunst, 1959; this edition, trans. Anna Bostock, London: Penguin Books, 1963), pp. 40–1.

16. Ibid., pp. 40–1.
17. George Monbiot, 'John Clare, the poet of the environmental crisis – 200 years ago', *The Guardian*, 10 July 2012, p. 26. Accessed 17 June 2014: www.theguardian.com/commentisfree/2012/jul/09/john-clare-poetry.
18. One thinks here of Robert Walser who, when a visitor to the asylum asked what he was working on during his confinement, replied, 'I didn't come here to write, I came here to be crazy.'
19. Edward Abbey, *Postcards from Ed: Dispatches and Salvos from an American Iconoclast*, ed. David Petersen (Minneapolis: Milkweed Editions, 2007), p. 257.
20. 1 Timothy 6:10.
21. Ecclesiastes 3:19.
22. Fischer, p. 38–9.
23. Aldo Leopold, *A Sand County Almanac and Sketches Here and There* (Oxford University Press, New York, 1949), p. 203.
24. Ibid., p. 203–4.
25. Karl Marx: *Capital* (Pelican Books, London, 1976), vol. I, p. 897.
26. Ibid., vol. I, p. 638. To be blunt, we now have, and have for a long time endured, what a latter-day Eisenhower might call an agricultural-industrial complex.
27. R. U. Sirius interview with Douglas Rushkoff, 'Living in the Present is a Disorder':

> The early cyberpunk idea was that networked computers would let us do our work at home, as freelancers, and then transact directly with peers over networks. Digital technology would create tremendous slack, allow us to apply its asynchronous, decentralized qualities to our own work and lives. Instead of working for someone – as we had been doing since the dawn of the Industrial Age – we would be freed from the time-is-money rat race and get to be makers. Then business and marketing caught wind of this, and it shifted from a bottom-up people's renaissance to a top-down finance revolution.
>
> So instead of using digital technology to create more time and creative space for people, we used it to take more time from people. The technologies we developed became much more about retaining the attention of consumers, monitoring employees, and keeping people engaged 24/7.

Wired (8 April 2013). Accessed 20 June 2014: www.wired.com/2013/04/present-shock-rushkoff-r-u-sirius/.

CHAPTER 5

Ecology with religion: kinship in John Clare

Emma Mason

> the fields!
> our church
> – Stephen Collis, *The Commons* (2008)[1]
>
> we heard the bells chime but the fields was our church
> – John Clare, 'Autobiographical Fragments'[2]

In his essay 'Nature, Sound Art and the Sacred', the acoustic ecologist David Dunn argues that 'attentive listening to the sounds around us is one of the most venerable forms of meditative practice'. For Dunn, 'what we hear from other forms of life and the environment they reside in' make 'patterns of relationship' of which humans and nonhumans are part, and which in turn creates an 'experiential basis' from which to understand 'the sacred'.[3] The interconnectedness of all things – spiritual, material, divine and earthly – is key to John Clare's process of listening to the world, a venture that, this chapter argues, necessitates a religious response to ecological crisis. For Clare, the religious allows for a deep listening that counters empirical modes of knowing and classifying the world. Such empiricism engenders habits of mind that result in an overlooking of the poor, the isolation of species from one another, and a materially and emotionally destructive hierarchizing of the world. Deep listening, however, a sensual engagement that registers the presence of all beings, has the potential to occasion a state of thinking and acting that brings such beings into an intimate kinship rooted in religion.[4] By 'all beings' I mean both the natural and material as well as the supernatural and divine, the latter pertaining to that which Clare senses but which remains hidden and obscured, from gods to will-o'-the-wisps. Critics have addressed both the natural and supernatural in Clare, but the connections between religion and ecology within his poetry invite further attention.[5] I am not concerned here to align Clare with specific religious ideas and doctrines, nor do I wish to sentimentalize his 'nature' writing through ecological theory. I do suggest, however, that through an aural imagining of nature and the divine as cognate, Clare accesses, and is keen to communicate, a cosmic and non-dualist reading of kinship inclusive of all things. Clare finds himself as much 'within the imagined consciousness of a native animal, plant or waterway' as within a bird's song or the chime of a church bell.[6] Both of these sounds call Clare into a close listening and prayerful consciousness that merge his senses (he synaesthetically 'hears' the field become the church and the trees its spires) and also close the gap between himself, the landscape and the church. This poetic congruence is summed up in my epigraph from Stephen Collis's *The Commons* (2008) – 'the fields!/our church' – a part of his 'Clear as Clare' sequence and one that opens with Clare's familiar description of setting off to seek the end of the horizon at the edge of the world:[7]

> I had imagind that the worlds end was at the edge of the orison and that a days journey was able to find it so I went on with my heart full of hopes pleasures and discoverys expecting when I got to the brink of the world that I coud look down like looking into a large pit and see into its secrets the same as I believd I coud see heaven by looking into the water[8]

Rather than imagining a brink over which he might fall into nothingness, Clare hopes that the 'edge of the orison' will provide a threshold into what is hidden there, and associates these 'secrets' with a heaven reflected in water. As with his midnight walks over Baron parks, an ancient ruin where he kept 'a strict eye' out for 'ghosts and goblings', Clare here looks to 'secrets' as a way into the immaterial and mysterious.[9] It is this openness to 'beliefs', both orthodox and alternative, that some readers of Clare miss in their tendency to collapse categories like religion, Romanticism and nature into an undifferentiated affective mush. By taking seriously Clare's receptivity to a specifically religious form of mindfulness, I suggest that his writing materializes as a lived politics of religious ecology constitutive of care, interconnectivity and inclusivity.[10]

My discussion is in five parts. I begin with the strong relationship between ecocriticism and sound studies (specifically, whale song) and suggest that the field, aspiring to an objective and scientific status, has become increasingly uncomfortable with the subjective, seeking to prise any spiritual dimensions away from sensory experience. Part two follows with a reading of Timothy Morton's explicit ambition to replace 'religion' with a more 'scientific' account of interconnectedness that, in his work on ecology without nature, he calls the 'mesh'. I argue that Clare's religious ecology moves us beyond Morton's dualisms to embrace a cosmic experience of the world that reads and listens to it as a companionable space of sacred relations. Clare achieves this by reimagining Christianity, the religion with which he is most familiar, through the natural world so that church spires become trees and church bells call believers into the fields. Clare is not a pagan or a pantheist: rather, he engages an ecological consciousness in which being appears as an 'integrated fabric' of companionship and care.[11] Drawing on Donna Haraway's companion species theory of how to think of harmony between beings, part three also works with Heidegger's poetic thinking of care as a counter to an instrumental and scientized thinking of the planet as a consumable resource. Heidegger is not popular with Morton, who calls his 'environmentalism' a 'sad, fascist, stunted bonsai version, forced to grow in a tiny iron flowerpot by a cottage in the German Black Forest'.[12] Heidegger's essays on poetry, with their attentive focus on universal compassion and care, do nothing to redress the implicit connection between Nazism and anti-Semitism in the philosopher's questioning of being, home, language and history. And yet Heidegger's thinking on poetry does enable literary critics to step past readings of art as either aesthetics or ideology through an approach that finds in poetry a language of relationism and affection. Heidegger's notion of care (*Sorge*) and caring-for (*Fürsorge*) constitute 'the basic mode of the being of existence, and as such' determine 'every kind of being': care is the ground on which we understand ourselves and relate to others.'[13] Care is threatened, Heidegger argues, by a binarizing metaphysical thinking that dehumanizes us through a logic of production and manipulation inherent to a modernity that is conflict-, violence- and war-bound. Poetic thinking reinstates care by 'sheltering' it within a meditative 'saying' that guides us back to a feeling of 'home' and peacefulness that Heidegger calls 'dwelling' – a praxis of careful reading and listening.[14] Compassion and peace between beings 'happens' in poetry because it is a language that does not 'describe' or 'register' the world, but rather projects it as a coming together of the things that dwell within it. As I argue in parts four and five of this discussion, such thinking helps us to explore Clare's own relationship to the act of dwelling, with nature and with gods, and also to reflect on his poetic prose and verse as a way of vitalizing our being through habitual listening. By synthesizing his church and its panoply of bells with his natural landscape, Clare forges a space in which care might flourish as the foundation for kinship and communion.

All species are created equal

In 1967, the environmentalists Roger Payne and Scott McVay were among the first scientists to acknowledge that whales sing in rhythmic, complex and distinct repeated sequences, and in a style specific to context and place. 'All humpbacks in each area sing only the local song', Payne announced in 'Humpbacks: Their Mysterious Songs' (1979), written for the *National Geographic*: 'We have learned that all men are created equal, but the whales remind us that all species are created equal – that every organism on earth, whether large or small, has an inalienable right to life.'[15] Payne's 1970 recording, *Songs of the Humpback Whale*, spurred such renewed interest in the Save the Whales movement that the International Whaling Commission finally banned commercial whaling in 1986. Whale song has been extraordinarily significant as a context for the current study of ecocriticsm, as well as that of literature and the environment, associated with a political moment that produced many of the most influential founders of both fields.[16] As Harold Fromm argues, the literary movement known as 'ecocriticism' emerged in the early 1970s and was shaped at its inception by poets as well as environmentalists. Fromm also notes that the ecocritical language we now work with (deep ecology, eco-Marxism, eco-feminism and so on) is indebted to the poetic and musical traditions of pastoralism and Romanticism, as well as to literary critics and poets from Raymond Williams to Cecilia Vicuña, who have long made the connection between poetry and environmentalism.[17] He has less time, however, for the philosopher contemporaries of his 1970s history: Heidegger is dismissed (his philosophy is, apparently, 'desperately on life support'[18]), and thinkers such as Donna Haraway are excised from the account. Fromm briefly mentions Haraway in his earlier book, *The Nature of Being Human: From Environmentalism to Consciousness* (2009), but steers away from philosophers willing to countenance the immaterial to embrace instead Daniel Dennett and Richard Dawkins as his personal champions of earth's inherent 'wonder' and 'fantastic' realism.[19]

The use of whale songs and the development of ecocriticism provide two examples of how the immaterial is either ignored or violently translated into the material by many critics currently concerned with the environment. Despite the fact that humans eventually decided to save the whales because of their song, and that the ecological movement owes so much to the political environmentalism of poets, ecocritics are now keen to excise the subjective in favour of scientism and objectivity. Bioacoustics, for example, has turned the listening experience of birdsong into a gadget-lover's guide to recording techniques and homemade microphones that becomes more complex (and expensive) within the realms of the nature documentary industry.[20] The fashion for 'measuring' organic experience – of animals and plants (with blimps and hydrophones) as well as human 'being' (with magnetic resonance imaging) – avoids ways of thinking that value what cannot be measured (religion and Romanticism). Here are two agents provocateur in their controversial critiques of religion (Lynn White) and Romanticism (Timothy Morton). First, White on the 'huge burden of guilt' Christianity bears for validating an anthropocentric thinking in which science and technology flourish and we find ourselves superior in the world:

> Human ecology is deeply conditioned by beliefs about our nature and destiny – that is, by religion ... The victory of Christianity over paganism was the greatest psychic revolution in the history of our culture ... Christianity is the most anthropocentric religion the world has seen ... Our science and technology have grown out of Christian attitudes toward man's relation to nature which are almost universally held ... We are superior to nature, contemptuous of it, willing to use it for our slightest whim.[21]

Christianity is akin to fascism here, towering over other traditions and being allowed to do so because it elevates us, human beings, to power and predominance. Nothing of what Clare calls Christianity's 'beautiful instruction' of 'peace on earth & good will towards men' is acknowledged or even gestured towards, perhaps because such meaning is carried affectively rather than materially.[22] Morton takes a different route to a similarly reductive conclusion, arguing in *Ecology without Nature* that we are barred from true ecological thought by a dependence on a fetishized idea of 'Nature' as external landscape to be preserved and put 'on a pedestal' (as we used to do, he says, with 'the figure of Woman').[23] In reality, he asserts, 'Nature' is a 'transcendental term in a material mask', wavering

> in between the divine and the material. Far from being something 'natural' itself, nature hovers over things like a ghost. It slides over the infinite list of things that evoke it. Nature is thus not unlike 'the subject', a being who searches through the entire universe for its reflection, only to find none. If it is just another word for supreme authority, then why not just call it God? But if this God is nothing outside the material world, then why not just call it matter?[24]

In other words, whereas White locates the problem in a Christian anthropocentrism that denigrates nature, Morton sees us as prone to sanctify nature in vague, contradictory ways. For Morton, finding what exists 'between polarized terms such as God and matter, this and that, subject and object' opens us into an interconnected way of being that, paraphrasing Heidegger, reveals that we're part of the world we claim to look on and 'sustain'. Like White, Morton wants a connection to something, but it's not 'God': 'God' evokes conservatism, fascism, extremism, ego and so cannot be thought of in an 'interconnected' universe. And though he positions himself as being against binary paradigms, like so many critics of Christianity Morton dualistically rejects a cartoonish God of orthodoxy for his own exoticized reading of eastern spirituality as a philosophy of oneness he strips of its religion to make commensurate with a Dawkinsian 'wonder'.

Frozen religion

In his 'prequel' to *Ecology without Nature – The Ecological Thought* – Morton stages his discovery of Buddhism. Readers are treated to a holiday report from Morton's two-week trip to Tibet, where he camps under the Milky Way and realizes how much 'Tibetan culture and religion is all about space':

> The tantric teachings say there are 6,400,000 Tantras of Dzogchen (texts of a form of Tibetan Buddhism). On Earth we have seventeen. Up there, in the highly visible night sky, perhaps in other universes, there exist the remaining 6,399,983. Up there, someone is meditating.[25]

Dreaming under shooting stars, Morton considers Buddhism's 'ecological thought', one wherein 'our Universe, along with one billion universes like it, floats within a single pollen grain inside an anther on a lotus flower'. No wonder 'Tibetans' 'think big', Morton proclaims: 'Tibetans would arrive at the edge of the Solar System and declare, "Wow, what a great opportunity to learn more about emptiness"'. Discounting the possibility that someone like Clare would understand the orison – the edge of his own solar system – as a gateway to the secrets of heaven, Morton is determined to oppose 'Tibetans' ('outer space wouldn't undermine their "beliefs"') and Christians, who cower before science and the discovery of galaxies.[26] 'Good' Buddhism, presentist and peaceful, welcomes the beyond as part of its commitment to 'compassion', 'nonviolence' and 'restorative justice'; 'bad' 'Christian apocalypticism' looks only towards the end of times, knowing that, since 'the end of the world is nigh', there 'isn't much point in caring'.[27] Morton's limited reading of both Christianity and Buddhism continues through to the conclusion of *The Ecological Thought*, where he admits that 'There might be seeds of future ways of being together in religion, as there are in art', but stipulates that these hypothetical modes would require a new term.[28] Morton votes for the word 'mesh'. Not only is 'mesh' said to describe the 'interconnectedness of all living and non-living things', it also scores highly for him because it 'sounds' scientific ('it has uses in biology, mathematics, and engineering').[29] He also likes 'mesh' because it gets him around using holistic or sacred language, rejected because they connote warmth, fuzziness, brightness and optimism, and thus a naïve meaninglessness. Christianity is now condemned not simply for its cruel apocalypticism, but for its 'strongly affirmative, extraverted, and masculine' emphasis on health, heartiness and cosiness.[30] Only negativity is truly ecological, Morton argues, because it includes sickness, darkness, irony, fragmentation and the feminine, and also because it asserts our melancholic attachment to a mother earth wherein we experience loneliness as a 'sign of deep connection'.[31]

If negativity is more ecological than positivity, and the negative connotes the 'feminine' and the 'dark', then it might be argued that Morton contravenes the assessment of his earlier book by putting a feminized and introverted ecology on a pedestal over a positive and healthy one.[32] If we agree with Morton's initial statement in *Ecology without Nature* that such a move is 'a paradoxical act of sadistic admiration', then it follows that Morton's own project is itself potentially quasi-sadistic in its fetishizing of negativity, sickness and loneliness, and his cultural ignorance regarding both Christianity and Buddhism extraordinary (not to mention his self-appointed role as advisor to the 'Tibetans'). And yet it is not atypical within ecocriticism to parody Christianity while elevating a faux Buddhism, sneering at any idea associated with either transcendence or immanence. Thus, Morton denounces 'Romanticism', but excepts 'John Clare and William Blake' as 'outsiders' to 'mainstream Romanticism' without discussing why they were outsiders, or reviewing their unassailably canonical position within current literary studies, or thinking about their relationship to other 'non-mainstream' writers (Morton does not, for example, reference any Romantic women writers, possibly because, as already noted, he believes 'the figure of Woman' is no longer a problem).[33] At the same time, he hounds Heidegger out of the debate while simultaneously poaching from his work, and then condemns the influential phenomenologist, David Abram, for generating in his book *The Spell of the Sensuous* a 'fantasy-environment' dependent on 'silent reading'.[34] Morton especially dislikes Abram's book because it presents an 'image' of 'being embedded within a horizon, which establishes the *ersatz* primitivism of ecological writing in general ... the more embedded the narrator becomes, the less convincing he or she is as a spokesperson for the totality that he or she is trying to evoke'.[35] But Morton can only 'think' of Abram's horizon as illusory because of the dualistic approach in which his own thinking is caught: despite experiencing a joined-up sense of 'wonder' while star-gazing in the desert, he is left to bemoan his dependence on religious language and sacred joy to explain such an experience. Morton needs religion to evoke and describe his own sensitivity to ecological disaster, even though he's locked into thinking of it as merely ideological. All he can do is empty religion of its 'belief', replace its 'wonder' and hospitable inclusiveness with secular words like 'mesh', and then admit to his readers that his own thinking might just be 'too profound' for them and that it might be better to 'freeze' the mesh back 'into religion' anyway.[36] We are rescued from T. E. Hulme's spilt, treacly religion and given frozen religion instead.[37]

Cosmic companions

Clare's religious ecology is neither treacly nor frozen, but rather cosmic. Like 'Romanticism' and 'religion', the word 'cosmic' has a poor reputation in literary criticism as denoting abstract 'experience'. But its signification as *kosmikos*, meaning at once belonging to the world and relating to the universe, breaks the dualism between 'us' (the 'earth') and 'out there' (the 'universe'). Clare's cosmos is inclusive and communal, and is only threatened by a human will to stand outside of the world as if it is a scene from which we stand apart, the drama of which we grasp through our imposed reading of it in relation to ourselves.[38] Like Morton, I invoke Heidegger's essay on the world picture here, but, unlike Morton, find its language useful for conjuring Clare's vision of the human as part of 'that which is', in 'company with itself' and open to both 'oppositions' and 'discord'.[39] In Heidegger's reading, the Greeks are exemplary achievers of such openness to being, apprehending themselves as part of what 'is' – in contrast with us 'moderns', obsessed as we are with standing over and against 'being' as that which needs to be represented. Modern 'man' thus makes himself into an object in his own picture, and loses the ability to recognize what 'is' beyond stockpiled resources on which we can call for either consumption or production. For Heidegger, the truth (*a-letheia*) of being is withdrawn or hidden (unconcealed) from the moderns, not as mystery or enigma, but as a way of indicating that entities are always more than our experience of them.[40] What we can 'know' is that earth remains the 'ground' from which and into which living things emerge and withdraw. Humans override this by visualizing the world instrumentally as a resource we can exploit: we seek to systematize and classify the world into usable assets (trees make furniture) or aesthetic experiences (trees have 'intrinsic' beauty).[41] All things, all presences, become nothing more than a standing reserve to be used up and discarded. Against this, Heidegger asks us to engage with the interconnectedness (the 'gatheredness') of humans, earth, gods and sky, a 'simple oneness' of 'four' Heidegger calls the 'fourfold'. There is nothing cryptic or abstruse about this notion; rather, Heidegger points to an affective state of feeling 'with' rather than 'of' the earth, stating that we 'are in the fourfold by dwelling' and that 'dwelling' means 'to spare, to preserve ... Mortals dwell in that they save the earth'.[42] We 'dwell' poetically, Heidegger writes, because we belong through listening, a process that causes us to 'embrace' all persons and things, 'to love them, to favour them'.[43] Poetry teaches us to listen and attend to the world in words that 'opens to light' that which safekeeps and cares for us and then invites us into relation with it in a bond of 'intimate kinship'.[44] While productive and capitalizing thinking hems in (enframes) the world as a utility to expend and consume, poetry reveals, lights up and opens. Poetic thinking, then, should not 'depict' a world that readers aesthetically devour, but instead open into a 'questioning' and 'care' that brings us into kinship with all elements of the cosmos to which we belong.

That Clare is a poet who attends to even the smallest of these elements as part of the interconnectedness of things has been critically acknowledged. With his *John Clare: Flower Poems* (2001), Simon Kövesi drew readers to Clare by pointing out the poet's attention to natural detail and pattern as 'evidence of divinity, of a maker' that oversees a world 'of micro-cosmic ecosystems, and humanity's relationship with and effect upon them'.[45] Similarly, Tim Chilcott notes Clare's 'imaginative leaps from cosmos to cowslip' in his edition of Clare's 1841 poems; and Nicholas Birns records a 'chant of personal and even cosmic discovery' throughout his well-anthologized 'The Flitting'.[46] Jonathan Bate also invokes the 'cosmic situation' Clare's poetry captures by reflecting on Gaston Bachelard's reading of the 'cosmic implications' of bird nests.[47] For Bate, Bachelard's identification of 'the naïve wonder we used to feel when we found a nest' helps explain Clare's experience of it as 'an entire universe', its 'cosmic implications' producing at once child-like amazement and vulnerability.[48] Clare's nests are 'mystic' ('To the Snipe', lines 24, 25; *Middle Period*, IV, 575) spaces 'Of care' ('The Robins Nest', line 30; *Middle Period*, III, 533) that enable a secret 'joy' ('Sand Martin', line 12; *Middle Period*, IV, 310) held in place by 'modelled' moss, wood and clay ('The Thrushes Nest', lines 7–8; *Middle Period*, IV, 187).[49] Clare's 'poetic revealing' of the kinship he feels for birds and their nests really does 'shine forth' in the form of 'shining eggs as bright as flowers', 'like heath bells gilt with dew' ('The Thrushes Nest', lines 9–10). Yet these nest poems evoke more than an idealized world of shelter and care. They extend into what Haraway, predating Morton's 'mesh', calls a 'knot in motion', in which 'beings constitute each other and themselves' through 'their reaching into each other' as 'companion species'.[50] For Haraway, companion species are symbiotically interrelated, not just biologically or organically, but in terms of their 'significant otherness': the fact that we are different from other 'things' in the world, 'human and animal', makes the 'partial connections' we have with them even more significant.[51] An ethics that feels and intuits the nonhuman, Haraway argues, realizes difference with 'grace', joining creation in a kind of 'Real Presence' that exposes being as emotional experience. In Clare's case, again, the salient example is his being 'in company' with (or a companion species alongside) birds and their nests.[52] He protects that experience by calling on religious language to forge bonds of intimate kinship, not only between himself, birds and nests, but also between the living and the spiritual, the material and the immaterial. Even in the brief examples so far quoted, mystical nests bear golden eggs that synaesthetically shine like bells, objects Clare and his readers would have seen only inside church. As generic religious symbols – bells are found in churches of all denominations – Clare's 'heath bells' elucidate the crossover between the religious and the ecological. 'Gilt with dew', the flower bells appear spotlit within the mist, shimmering like gilt cups, but rooted in an uncultivated heath. Moreover, as similes – they are *like* the eggs sheltered in the thrush's nest – they forge an ideally interconnected image for Clare, gathering together the church, flowers, birds, heath and mist, as well as Clare as onlooker.

'We heard the bells chime'

The reach and euphony of church bells for Clare goes beyond their material status as ecclesiastical measures of everyday rhythm. Chiming out to indicate the beginning and end of workdays, births, weddings, deaths, funerals, as well as liturgical and ceremonial duties, bells called specifically to their local communities, their pealed content encoded from town to town. The church at Helpston, as historian Daniel Crowson tells us, rang a 'curfew bell' in the morning and evening, while its tower housed 'three mass bells' together with the bell that 'sounded the start of different village functions': the 'gleaners' bell and the 'pancake bell', the 'bell for the statice and the bullock fair' and 'the carriers' bell'.[53] Making clear the distinct tone of local bells, Clare notes hearing the 'Ufford bells chimeing for a funeral' while on a 'walk in the fields'; and bells were regularly sounded to guide lost travellers and shepherds through bad weather or kept noticeably silent during periods of mourning or reflection.[54] For Clare, however, the sound and rhythm of the bell accords with that of the poem, since both are living acoustic markers of 'the reflection and the remembrance of what has been'.[55] As Clare writes in 'Evening Bells' (*Early Poems*, II, 254–5), bells not only ring out the 'sweetest' (line 3) sound he can aurally imagine, but they also 'swell' into 'the music of the skies' (lines 7–8), breathing across the landscape's 'lonly dells' (line 12). Clare's synaesthetic world is transfigured by the 'rise' (line 6) of bells on 'this earthly ball', a phrase that exposes the vulnerability of the planet as much as 'the blue marble', the title of Apollo 17's famous 1972 photograph of the earth from space. The gentle pulse of Clare's evening bells is held buoyant in this poem by 'Zephers breathing' (line 16), as the wind carries the bells' ringing around the landscape like an invisible and permeable boundary. This 'ringing round' (line 48) is repeated in 'Sabbath Bells' (*Middle Period*, III, 573–5), where the range of the chimes establishes the security of borderlines without any of the malevolence of enclosure, while engendering at once a listening experience and trigger for verse. Here are the first and fifth stanzas:

> Ive often on a sabbath day
> Where pastoral quiet dwells
> Lay down among the new mown hay
> To listen distant bells
> That beautifully flung the sound
> Upon the quiet wind
> While beans in blossom breathed around
> A fragrance oer the mind . . .
>
> The ear it lost and caught the sound
> Swelled beautifully on
> A fitful melody around
> Of sweetness heard and gone
> I felt such thoughts I yearned to sing
> The humming airs delight
> That seemed to move the swallows wing
> Into a wilder flight
>
> (lines 1–8; 33–40)

As in 'Evening Bells' and the later 'The Chiming Bells' (*Later Poems*, II, 1,036), Clare sensualizes sound as something we can touch on the wind, smell in the blossom and echo through song: there is no break between the sonority of the bells within the landscape and those who listen to its knell. As R. Murray Schafer argues, the audile inclusivity of the church bell renders it an 'acoustic calendar', the 'most salient sound signal in the Christian community' and one that defines the parish as an 'acoustic space'.[56] Schafer also notes, recalling line 4 of Clare's 'Sabbath Bells', that church bells are most 'powerfully evocative' when listened to from afar: 'Perhaps no sound benefits more from distance and atmosphere. Church bells form a sound complement to distant hills, wrapped in blue-gray mist'.[57] Their hushed, far-off sounds open us into the world of which we are already part, rather than separating us from it by calling us elsewhere.

Church bells ring out again in Clare's 'Autobiographical Fragments', where they echo through the 'qu[i]et' of 'nature[s] presence' and into Clare's fellowship with shepherds and herd boys. In the following extract, Clare conjures his loving feelings towards the natural world as a space of gentle leisure (a place to throw marbles or go strawberry picking) and one that is significantly deepened by the chiming of church bells calling his community to prayer:

> I grew so much into the qu[i]et love of nature[s] presence that I was never easy but when I was in the fields passing my sabbaths and leisures with the shepherds and herd boys as fancys prompted somtimes playing at marbles on the smooth beaten sheep tracks or leap frog among the thimey molehills somtimes ranging among the corn to get the red and blue flowers for cockades to play at soldiers or runing into the woods to hunt strawberrys or stealing peas in church time when the owners was safe to boil at the gipseys fire who went half shares at our stolen luxury we heard the bells chime but the fields was our church and we seemd to feel a religious feeling in our haunts on the sabbath while some old shepherd sat on a mole hill reading aloud some favour[i]te chapter from an old fragment of a Bible which he carried in his pocket for the day a family relic[58]

The 'things' that populate Clare's world here – people, plants, animals, books – are presented as part of one interconnected space: moles and sheep are signified through their impact on the earth (molehills and sheep tracks), and flowers and berries become an unrestricted 'luxury' available to everyone once the landowners are in attendance at church. The bells signal 'safe' time for all that are called to God: Clare conveys a feeling of ease in the passage both because the landowners have temporarily disappeared into their church, and also because he is liberated into the sacred space of the fields with his friends. Resonating from the church but moving far beyond it, the bells call Clare and company not to the orthodoxy and doctrine of church ritual, but into a 'religious feeling' enhanced by the phonic power of an old shepherd reading from his battered family copy of the Bible.[59] For Clare, his sound perception of the bells, the Bible reading and the spiritual emotion each evoke is a psychoacoustic route into a profound 'religious feeling' that is rooted in the 'haunts' of a field and experienced on the 'sabbath'. The natural world is not external to the church: Clare speaks against John Wesley's 'all the world my parish' world picture, in which 'glad tidings of salvation' were universally painted, absorbed and instilled.[60] Rather, Clare experiences the fields as 'our church' ('the fields!/our church', writes Stephen Collis in his creative reading of Clare[61]), summoned by bells and materialized by everything he sees around him, from the Bible-reading shepherd to the raw stuff of a mole hill.

This non-dualist embrace of kinship holds that all things are related and equivalent, a communion that extends even to spirits and ghosts. In 'Autobiographical Fragments', Clare associates 'bells in churches ringing in the middle of the night' with 'spirits warning men when they was to dye', exposing his wider interest in superstitions, community rituals, communal tale-telling and folkloric festivals.[62] In her study of Clare's religion, Sarah Houghton-Walker devotes time to both Clare's 'alternative beliefs' and his orthodox religious reading, dispelling a secularist critical tendency to strip Clare of spiritual convictions. For Houghton-Walker, Clare's religious awareness is 'intellectual and experiential', inclusive of both spirits and orthodoxy, and informed as much by Anglicanism, Methodism and the Quakers as by religious freethinking and ghost stories.[63] At the same time, Houghton-Walker reveals that Clare's profound familiarity with theological literature and his commitment to the 'Mystery' of religious 'truth' makes sense within a Christian frame. As Clare himself states: 'No religion upon earth deserves the epithet of divine so well as the Christian'; it has 'nothing to record but prayers for mercy'; 'its beautiful instruction was peace on earth & good will towards men'; its 'founder' 'professed' what he 'pratised'; 'Religion properly defined is the grand aspiration to live well & die happy – Do unto others as ye would others should do unto you was the creed of the divine founder of christianity'.[64] While none of this identifies Clare as a Christian, it does affirm his deep affective connection with Christianity as an ecumenical and cosmic 'divinity' founded by a man who was, like Clare, on 'the side of poverty'.[65] That Christ was poor is a key driver behind Clare's anger at those who reduce religion to 'little more then cant/A cloak to hide what godliness may want' ('The Parish', lines 455–6; *Early Period*, II, 697–779), its churches populated by hypocrites who 'pa[y] religions once a week respects' (line 490). Clare recounts how such 'weekly church goers' attack him for 'forsaking the "church going bell"' for 'the religion of the fields', when in fact those very bells have called him into a profound religious feeling based on reflection over time. As a poet who professes to have 'thought seriosly of religion', he loathes those who have not: 'if every mans bosom had a glass in it so that its secret might be seen what a blotted page of christian profession and false pretentions woud the best of them display'.[66] Indeed, his commitment to the 'sacred design' and beneficial 'power' of an 'almighty' is continually plagued by an anxiety that 'the desird end' outlined in the 'New Testament' will be permanently obstructed 'while cant and hypocrisy is blasphemously allowd to make a mask of religion'.[67] Caught within the walls of the church and paralysed by the anechoic theology within them, the bells become a tocsin against the danger of institutionalized irreverence. Only when freed, as it were, to carillon out over the fields does Clare experience the religious feeling the bells orate, indicating that God is not only present in nature, but also heard through it: 'The voice of nature as the voice of God/Appeals to me in every tree & flower' ('This leaning tree with ivy overhung', lines 34–5; *Middle Period*, II, 212). The sound of God ap*peal*s to Clare in a verbal echo of a peal of bells, their 'peaceful sound' 'Calmly' reaching the ears of shepherds in an aural equivalent of the 'sweet' scent of the 'beanfields' ('The Chiming Bells', lines 1, 5, 9). Sound once more synaesthetically gathers Clare's other senses into a consonant experience of peace and joy.

'All our kin'

Like the sound of the bells, religious ideas flourish outside of the church for Clare. It is as if he wishes to return those New Testament ideas he most values – 'peace', 'good will towards men', care and kindness – to the natural desert world in which they were first preached. As David Jasper notes, Christ's ministry begins and ends in the desert, and that wilderness is a space we see Clare collapse into his local environment.[68] He envisions nature as a desert in 'The Request' ('the field's a desert grown', line 5; *Early Period*, I, 321), but, more ominously, invokes the desert as a space overridden by artificial 'Edens' in the name of empty fashions of style in

'Shadows of Taste' (lines 56, 171; *Middle Period*, III, 303–10). In 'Remembrances' (*Middle Period*, IV, 130–4) this logic is reversed, the 'cushion'-like 'hills of silken grass' 'leveled like a desert by the never weary plough' (lines 46–8) leaving particular locales, 'cowper green', for example, stark and barren like 'a desert strange and chill' (line 62). It is as if deserts are nature's endoskeleton for Clare, raw sacred ground protected and preserved by trees and foliage without which it stands defenceless, calling back to God for repair. In 'Prayer in the Desert' (*Later Poems*, I, 542–3), Clare calls on God as a non-denominational power that might revive the damage humans have effected:

> Almighty, ominpotent – dweller on high
> Protector of earth and its dwellers – thine eye
> Can look on this desert and bid it appear
> As green as fresh pastures at spring of the year
> And bid the earth's fatness bring food at command
> And refill the cruise that is dry as the sand
> Almighty omnipotent – dweller in bliss
> Thy will has the power – and thy power can do this   (lines 1–8)

We are in Heidegger's fourfold here, gods in the sky (Clare's god is at once the 'Almighty' and 'Alla' 'God of Mahomet', lines 18, 17), mortals on the ground, and all connected in a shared 'dwelling' that gathers everything into one. By the end of the poem, earth's 'desert of sand' is also God's 'dwelling place' (line 22), suggesting that despite our depletion of the earth's resources ('Our food is exhausted – the cruises are dry'; line 9), God's 'charity' might 'send/Supply to our wants' (lines 23–4) in return for a defended faith (line 21). Dwelling, for Heidegger as for Clare, means being 'at home' through a thinking and attending to the place where we are, one that embodies things living and spiritual.[69] Such faith in being where we are is free of 'fear' (line 19) and instead, he writes in 'Stanzas', inheres within 'endless joy', 'bliss' and 'kin' (lines 1–2, 8; *Later Poems*, I, 574–5). That 'all our kin' means 'Jews christian turks and gentle kind' (lines 8–9) leads Clare to imagine a 'place above/Redeemed by Gods unbiased mind/And everlasting love' (lines 10–2), a radically inclusive vision that hints at peace beyond earth. And yet Clare insists that this 'joy' is at once of 'spirits' and a material 'green' place (lines 21, 5): no wonder he conceives of trees as churches and churches as trees.

Despite Clare's reservations about the hypocrisy of church goers, he was not averse to attending worship on Sundays:

> like many more I have been to church [more] often then I have been seriously inclined to recieve benefit or put its wholsome and reasonable admonitions to practice – still I reverence the church and do from my soul as much as any one curse the hand thats lifted to undermine its constitution[70]

At the same time, he lists a string of characters in his prose whom he perceives to be 'religious' because they refuse to attend church – the Bible-reading shepherd, for example, as well as the father of his first love, Elizabeth Newbon, who read the Bible in search of interesting stories and 'thought him self a religious man tho he never went to church and he was so for he was happy and harmless'.[71] Revering the church while finding its members and espousals oppressive, Clare imagines physical church structures spread across the landscape and made of trees. Trees allow Clare to map the landscape, not just spatially, but phenomenologically; they are points of reference by which he can locate his physical position and emotional being.[72] He associates trees directly with churches, either using them as substitutes for places of worship ('On sundays I usd to feel a pleasure to hide in the woods instead of going to church to nestle among the leaves and lye upon a mossy bank were the fir like fern its under forest keeps'), or as analogies for them ('The arching groves of ancient lime/That into roofs like churches climb').[73] In his short piece, 'Autumn', Clare intimately describes the 'copses of reeds and oziers', willows and apple trees as a way of imagining the church and the tree as equally elevated, deliberately assimilating the 'jiant overtopping trees' with the 'church spire':

> and now the church spire looking rather large dimensions catches the eye like a jiant overtopping trees and houses and showing us his magnitude from half way up the tower to weathercock and looks noble above his willow woods nothing looks so noble among country landscapes as church steeples and castle towers[74]

Steeples, spires, towers, trees coalesce here in a cosmic union that threatens to collapse once any aspect of it is abused:

> there is the beautifull Spire of Glinton Church towering high over the grey willows and dark wallnuts still lingering in the church yard like the remains of a wreck telling where their fellows foundered on the ocean of time[75]

As we follow Clare's line of sight, we are moved from a thinking of kinship (the trees and churches as one) to a broken world picture (the trees a shipwreck and their kin drowned), and then back into a compensatory series of correspondences that engages all our senses: men 'cutting the weeds from the drains to make a water course for the autumn rains'; 'larks' and 'redcaps' flying in and out of hedges and grass; stone walls engraved with the names of lovers, 'houses churches and flowers – and sheep hooks and some times names cut in full'; crows nesting in willow trees; and tools that care for, rather than instrumentalize, an earth that is gathered into the local landscape as 'rustic implements and appendages of husbandry blend with nature and look pleasing in the fields'.[76]

Here is a poetic that invites us into a revealed world of shelter and care, where labour safekeeps and stones gladly bear our impress in time. It is a dream-like conjuring of connectedness, immediacy and relation in which all things are condensed into a scene of dependency. To close this discussion, I turn to Clare's feminizing of his model of religio-ecological kinship through his allusion to a female 'Guardian spirit' in 'A Remarkable Dream'.[77] The essay chronicles a series of dreams in which Clare describes being led through fields and crowds, first to a 'book sellers' displaying 'three vols lettered with' his name, and then on to a church where he is met by 'a loud humming as of the undertones of an organ and felt so affraid'. Only when Clare is led out of the church by his guardian 'lady-divinity' does he find a way to calm himself through a deep listening to the sounds of 'soft music' that fill the 'open air'. He is at once lulled by the sounds of nature and his spirit 'conductress', who 'uttered something as prophet of happiness I knew all was right'.[78] Through a listening to all the world – natural, spiritual, human, nonhuman – Clare is granted a way of conceptualizing and thinking about the world that he carries from his dream into his waking world, writing it 'down to prolong the happiness of my faith'.[79] Moreover, Clare's reveries are compassed by a musical diminuendo, the eerie blasts of the organ at the church door softening into the 'sound of soft music' to herald Clare's entry into a now spiritualized natural world. His reorienting of our attention – from trees to churches, kinship to shipwrecks, pipe organs to 'open air' music – enacts a synaesthetic gathering of dualisms into an ontology of universal kinship. As he writes in the fragment, 'Essay on Political Religion', our being is a 'revelation' of a 'providence who works by unknown means for the advancement of the earthly welfare & eternal happiness of mankind – giving to every human being an instinct of faith & a talisman of futurity'.[80] When Clare is called into the fields by church bells and feels before him an interconnected world, he is ecologizing through religion, freed to envision a mode of companionship and care that eclipses both denominational affiliation and secular pastoralism.

Notes

1. Stephen Collis, *The Commons* (Vancouver: Talonbooks, 2008), p. 32.
2. *By Himself*, p. 40.
3. David Dunn, 'Nature, Sound Art, and the Sacred', in *The Book of Music and Nature*, ed. David Rothenberg and Marta Ulvaeus (Middletown, CT: Wesleyan University Press, 2001), pp. 95–107 (p. 98).
4. Sam Ward notes Clare's fascination with sounds in '"To List the Song & Not to Start the Thrush": John Clare's Acoustic Ecologies', *JCSJ*, 29 (2010), 15–32.
5. On Clare's religion see Sarah Houghton-Walker, *John Clare's Religion* (Surrey: Ashgate, 2009). On his ecology, see, for example, Jonathan Bate, *Romantic Ecology: Wordsworth and the Environmental Tradition* (London and New York: Routledge, 1991) and *The Song of the Earth* (London: Picador, 2000); and Simon Kövesi, 'John Clare's "I" and "eye": Egotism and Ecologism', in *Green and Pleasant Land: English Culture and the Romantic Countryside*, ed. Amanda Gilroy (Leuven and Paris: Peeters, 2004), pp. 73–88.
6. James C. McKusick, *Green Writing: Romanticism and Ecology* (New York: St. Martin's Press. 2000), p. 78.
7. *The Commons* is part two of Collis's 'The Barricades Project', in which he aims to poetically obstruct the flow of capital in language by 'walking' through the 'the unownable' space of the 'commons' with Clare. See p. 139.
8. Collis, *The Commons*, p. 29; *By Himself*, p. 40.
9. *By Himself*, p. 45.
10. For a brilliant reading of interconnectivity in Clare through Deleuze and Guattari's 'rhizome', see Simon Kövesi, 'John Clare & ... & ... & ... Deleuze and Guattari's rhizome', in *Ecology and the Literature of the British Left: The Red and the Green*, ed. Valentine Cunningham, H. Gustav Klaus and John Rignall (Aldershot: Ashgate, 2012), pp. 75–88.
11. Gregory Bateson and Mary Catherine Bateson, *Angels Fear: Towards an Epistemology of the Sacred* (New York: Macmillan, 1987), p. 200.
12. Timothy Morton, *The Ecological Thought* (Cambridge: Harvard University Press, 2010), p. 27; on the current controversy surrounding Heidegger, see Peter Trawny's publication of Heidegger's *Schwarzen Hefte* (the black notebooks), in Martin Heidegger, *Gesamtausgabe*, IV: Abteilung: Hinweise und Aufzeichnungen, Band 94: Überlegungen II–VI, Schwarze Hefte 1931–1938 (Frankfurt am Main: Vittorio Klostermann, 2014); and Emmanuel Faye's *The Introduction of Nazism into Philosophy in Light of the Unpublished Seminars of 1933–1935*, trans. Michael B. Smith (New Haven: Yale University Press, 2009).
13. Martin Heidegger, *Logic: The Question of Truth*, trans. Thomas Sheehan (Bloomington and Indianapolis: Indiana University Press, 2010), p. 185.
14. See Martin Heidegger, *introduction to Philosophy: Thinking and Poetizing*, trans. Phillip Jacques Braunstein (Bloomington and Indianapolis: Indiana University Press, 2011), p. 5; and '... Poetically Man Dwells ...', in *Poetry, Language, Thought*, trans. Albert Hofstadter (London: HarperPerennial, 1971), pp. 209–27.

15. Roger Payne, 'Humpbacks: Their Mysterious Songs', *National Geographic*, 155 (January 1979), p. 24.
16. See, for example, Greg Gatenby, *Whale Sound: An Anthology of Poems about Whales and Dolphins* (Toronto: Dreadnaught, 1977).
17. Harold Fromm, 'Ecocriticism at Twenty-Five', *Hudson Review*, 66.1 (2013), 196–208 (207).
18. Ibid., p. 206.
19. Harold Fromm, *The Nature of Being Human: From Environmentalism and Consciousness* (Baltimore: Johns Hopkins University Press, 2009), p. 229.
20. See, for example, Wildlife Acoustics' '3rd Generation Song Meter Platform'. Accessed 15 March 2014. www.wildlifeacoustics.com/products/song-meter-sm3.
21. Lynn White, Jr. 'The Historical Roots of Our Ecological Crisis', *Science*, 155.3767 (10 March 1967), 1,203–7 (1,205–6).
22. Quoted in Houghton-Walker, *John Clare's Religion*, p. 204, from Pet. A46, vol. 2, p. 75; for a more thoughtful reconsideration of christofascism, see Dorothee Sölle, *Beyond Mere Obedience: Reflections on a Christian Ethic for the Future* (Minneapolis: Augsburg, 1970).
23. Timothy Morton, *Ecology without Nature: Rethinking Environmental Aesthetics* (Cambridge: Harvard University Press, 2007), p. 5.
24. Ibid., p. 15.
25. Timothy Morton, *The Ecological Thought* (Cambridge: Harvard University Press, 2010), p. 26.
26. Ibid., p. 27.
27. Ibid.
28. Ibid., p. 134.
29. Ibid., p. 28.
30. Ibid., p. 16.
31. Ibid.
32. Morton, *Ecology without Nature*, p. 5.
33. Ibid.
34. Ibid., p. 129; see also David Abram, *The Spell of the Sensuous: Perception and Language in a More-Than-Human World* (New York: Vintage Books, 1996).
35. Ibid., p. 133.
36. Ibid., p. 135.
37. Hulme writes, 'You don't believe in a God, so you begin to believe that man is a god. You don't believe in Heaven, so you begin to believe in a heaven on earth. In other words, you get romanticism ... It is like pouring a pot of treacle over the dinner table. Romanticism then, and this is the best definition I can give of it, is spilt religion', in 'Romanticism and Classicism', in *T. E. Hulme: Selected Writings*, ed. Patrick McGuinness (London: Routledge, 2008), pp. 68–83 (p. 71).
38. Martin Heidegger, 'The Age of the World Picture', in *The Question Concerning Technology and Other Essays*, trans. William Lovitt (New York: Harper Row, 1977), pp. 115–54 (p. 129).
39. Heidegger, 'Age of the World Picture', p. 131.

40. Bruce V. Foltz, 'Heidegger, Ethics and Animals', *Between the Species*, 9.2 (Spring 1993), 84–9 (85).
41. See, for example, Michael Jordan, *The Beauty of Trees* (London: Quercus, 2012), p. 6.
42. Heidegger, 'Building Dwelling Thinking', in *Poetry, Language, Thought*, pp. 141–60 (p. 148).
43. Martin Heidegger, 'Letter on "Humanism"', in *Pathmarks*, trans. Frank A. Capuzzi (Cambridge: Cambridge University Press, 1998), pp. 239–76 (p. 241); I note that Heidegger's 'listening' means an attending to rhythm that goes beyond the aural, and so embraces those who can, as well as cannot, hear; see David N. Smith, *Sounding/Silence* (New York: Fordham University Press, 2013), and Jennifer Esmail, *Reading Victorian Deafness: Signs and Sounds in Victorian Literature and Culture* (Athens: Ohio University Press, 2013).
44. Heidegger, 'The Question Concerning Technology', in *The Question Concerning Technology*, pp. 3–35 (pp. 25, 34–5).
45. Simon Kövesi, 'Introduction', *John Clare: Flower Poems* (Bangkok: M&C Services, 2001), pp. ix–xxii (pp. xviii, xxi).
46. Tim Chilcott (ed.), *John Clare: The Living Year 1841* (Nottingham: Trent Editions, 1999), p. xv; Nicholas Birns, '"The Riddle Nature Could not Prove": Hidden Landscapes in Clare's Poetry', in Haughton, pp. 189–220 (p. 199).
47. Gaston Bachelard, *The Poetics of Space*, trans. Maria Jolas (Boston: Beacon Press, 1964), pp. 237–39.
48. Bate, *Song of the Earth*, p. 158.
49. For further discussion of these interrelated depictions, see Simon Kövesi, '"Her Curious House is Hidden": Secrecy and Femininity in John Clare's Nest Poems', *JCSJ*, 18 (1999), 51–63.
50. Donna Haraway, *The Companion Species Manifesto: Dogs, People, and Significant Otherness* (Chicago: Prickly Paradigm Press), p. 6.
51. Haraway, *Companion Species Manifesto*, p. 25; Donna Haraway, *Simians, Cyborgs and Women: The Reinvention of Nature* (New York and Abingdon: Routledge, 1991), pp. 151–2.
52. Donna Haraway, *When Species Meet* (Minneapolis: University of Minnesota Press, 2008), p. 15; Haraway, *Companion Species Manifesto*, p. 15.
53. Daniel Crowson, *Helpston in the Time of the Poet John Clare*, printed by *The Peterborough Standard*, May 1964, pp. 6–7; my warm thanks to Guy Franks for generously giving me this reference.
54. *By Himself*, p. 210; see also John Steeple, 'About Bells', *The Aldine*, 9.4 (1878), 140–1; H. B. Walters, *Church Bells of England* (London: Oxford University Press, 1912); Alain Corbin, *Village Bells: Sound and Meaning in the Nineteenth-Century French Countryside* (New York: Columbia University Press, 1998); Shirley MacWilliam, 'The Sound of Bells and Bellies: Acoustic Authority and Sound Effects', *Circa*, 85 (1998), 22–7.
55. *By Himself*, p. 37.

56. R. Murray Schafer, *The Soundscape: Our Sonic Environment and the Tuning of the World* (Rochester: Destiny Books, 1977), pp. 53, 55.
57. Murray Schafer, *Soundscape*, p. 54.
58. *By Himself*, pp. 39–40.
59. Clare writes that 'the best poems on religion are those found in the Scriptures'; *By Himself*, p. 180.
60. John Wesley, *The Heart of John Wesley's Journal*, ed. Percy Livingstone Parker (New York: Fleming H Revelll, 1903), pp. 54, 56.
61. Collis, *The Commons*, p. 32.
62. *By Himself*, p. 53.
63. Houghton-Walker, *John Clare's Religion*, p. 1; while Clare was denominationally open, he shared his culture's prejudice against Roman Catholicism: 'The Catholics have lost their bill once more and its nothing but right they shoud when one beholds the following Sacred humbugs which their religion hurds up and sanctifys'; *By Himself*, pp. 229–30.
64. Quoted in Houghton-Walker, *John Clare's Religion*, pp. 204, 208, from Pet. A46, vol. 2, pp. 75, 68.
65. Ibid., p. 75.
66. *By Himself*, pp. 78, 133.
67. Ibid., p. 178.
68. David Jasper, *The Sacred Desert: Religion, Literature, Art, and Culture* (Oxford: Blackwell, 2007), p. 15.
69. See Heidegger, *Introduction to Philosophy*, p. 3; and 'Building Dwelling Thinking'.
70. *By Himself*, p. 30.
71. Ibid., p. 89.
72. See, for example, Clare 'Autobiographical Fragments', in *By Himself*, p. 69.
73. *By Himself*, p. 73; 'The Progress of Ryhme', lines 173–4.
74. *By Himself*, pp. 272–5 (p. 272).
75. Ibid., p. 273.
76. Ibid., pp. 273, 274, 275.
77. Ibid., pp. 253–5 (p. 253).
78. Ibid., p. 254.
79. Ibid., p. 255.
80. John Clare, 'Essay on Political Religion', in *A Champion for the Poor: Political Verse and Prose*, ed. P. M. S. Dawson, Eric Robinson and David Powell (Ashington and Manchester: MidNAG/Carcanet, 2000), pp. 281–2 (p. 282).

CHAPTER 6

The lives of Frederick Martin and the first Life of John Clare

Scott McEathron

This chapter examines the career of Frederick Martin, author of the first biography of the poet, *The Life of John Clare* (1865). It puts the biography's rhetorical emphases and polemical tendencies into context as extensions of Martin's unusual, and unusually conflicted, professional life. A German immigrant and self-made writer whose vocational journey was, in its way, every bit as remarkable as Clare's, Martin was virtually unknown at the time *The Life of John Clare* was published. Yet even as he was composing the *Life* in the months following Clare's death, Martin was also preparing the second edition of an ambitious new statistical annual, *The Statesman's Year-Book*, that sought to codify Victorian ideals of knowledge as 'a complete depository of facts bearing upon the political and social condition of the States of the civilized world, and the ever-varying forms which exhibit either the progress or the decline of nations'.[1] Martin's supervision of the *Year-Book*, continuing almost until his death in 1883, would gradually move him from the outermost periphery of Victorian print culture into the central orbit of London's political and cultural elite. In reviewing both *The Life of John Clare* and his broader career, I will show that even as Martin became a cultural authority in his own right, he manifested a continuing set of ambivalences towards literary authority and success that expressed themselves on a wide spectrum, from acute personal anxiety and resentment, to a more abstract, class-oriented scepticism towards hierarchy and bureaucracy. This chapter thus offers several perspectives on the ways in which Martin's evolving relationship to the field of literature, and the business of literary publishing, help us understand the dynamics underwriting *The Life of John Clare*.

Until recently there has been little discussion of the *Life*; the consensus has been that Martin was at once an opportunistic seeker of firm facts about Clare, and a willing fantasist – guilty of misrepresenting or even fabricating elements of Clare's story for aesthetic and rhetorical effect. Modern commentary begins with Eric Robinson and Geoffrey Summerfield's brief

The lives of Frederick Martin and the first Life of John Clare

'Introduction' to their 1965 edition, in which they commend Martin's lack of condescension in representing Clare's many difficulties, praise the frankness with which he treats matters of morality, especially those involving 'sex and drink', and argue that the biography's errors 'are probably no more than might be expected in any popular life written so soon after the death of its subject'.[2] Jonathan Bate defends Martin on somewhat different grounds, arguing that his tendency to 'inven[t] with all the gusto of a novelist' often leads to insights that more cautious later biographers, notably the Tibbles, failed to grasp: 'There is a structural, almost a mythic, truth to Martin's narrative that gives it value despite its factual inventions.'[3]

Juliette Atkinson's recent *Victorian Biography Reconsidered* offers the fullest critique to date of Martin's *Life*. Describing it as 'an examination of the public's relationship with, and responsibility towards, the nation's poets', Atkinson identifies an historical trend by which mid-century writers 'reconfigur[e] poetry as an extension of contemporary productivity', and says Clare is portrayed as benefitting from a 'healthy counterbalanc[ing]' of physical labour and poetry.[4] Atkinson underscores Martin's boiling indignation towards Clare's patrons, but also argues that even as Martin levels various assaults on John Taylor, Octavius Gilchrist and others who denied Clare his full artistic due, he fails to perceive the 'many parallels between patronage and biography' and 'ignores the complicity of his own biography in perpetuating the interest in Clare as a man rather than a poet'.[5]

On the question of Martin's identification with Clare, Atkinson is cautious: 'Like many of the biographers who took up obscure or neglected subjects, Frederick Martin expressed personal frustrations about his own career.' But while Atkinson hurries away from such 'tempting' speculation,[6] it is impossible to read the *Life* without perceiving that Martin appears to have had some powerful personal motivation to take Clare's battles as his own.

In this chapter, I suggest that several of these themes – Martin's populism; his personal identification with Clare; his status as a Victorian writer; the 'national disgrace'[7] that is England's treatment of its poets – can be enriched by a more comprehensive discussion of Martin's career. After establishing his ongoing labour on the *Statesman's Year-Book* as a necessary backdrop, I turn to Martin's early employment as an amanuensis for Thomas Carlyle; then to the Clare biography; and then to his 1869 novel *Alec Drummond*, whose motifs and social commentaries may be viewed as illustrative outgrowths of those in the *Life*. Finally, I turn to Martin's late correspondence and his crisis-ridden final years with the *Year-Book* in an attempt to understand his persistently conflicted attitudes towards bureaucracy, hierarchy, class and the individual talent.

Martin's career trajectory

The brief extant accounts of Martin's life (1830–83) imply a smooth arc from early struggle to later success, culminating in his receipt of a Civil List pension, a defining marker of achievement and cultural entrenchment. The outlines of this narrative cast Martin as a type of Victorian industriousness and earnestness, who, à la Matthew Arnold, began adulthood with a strong literary focus but later moved into professional realms associated with educational, material and commercial productivity. Martin's early years are shrouded in mystery, and we do not know for certain whether he was born in Geneva or in Berlin.[8] He resided in Wolverhampton, in the West Midlands of England, in the mid-1850s, where he was employed at a boarding school, and in 1856 moved to London to serve as the '*famulus* and factotum' of Thomas Carlyle.[9] The relationship quickly grew strained, however, and Carlyle 'banished' him after only five months. For the next several years Martin struggled to support his wife and young family while cultivating contacts in publishing, literature and journalism. In 1862 he contracted with Alexander Macmillan to compile the *Statesman's Year-Book*, envisioned as a yearly compilation of vital global statistics. This arrangement brought a decisive shift in Martin's professional standing, and he exploited his emergent authority as a statistical maven by publishing a remarkable array of books. In just a dozen years he produced *Stories of Banks and Bankers* (1865); *Commercial Handbook of France* (1867); *Handbook of Contemporary Biography* (1870); *The National History of England* (vol. 2; 1873); *The History of Lloyd's and of Marine Insurance in Great Britain* (1876); and *The Property and Revenues of the English Church Establishment* (1877).[10] Meanwhile Martin continued, single-handedly, to publish the *Year-Book*.

A review of the *Year-Book* in the *Standard* is telling for the terms by which it declares the centrality of Martin's endeavours to the business of the nation:

> Everybody who knows this work is aware that it is a book that is indispensable to writers, financiers, politicians, statesmen, and all who are directly or indirectly interested in the political, social, industrial, commercial, and financial condition of their fellow-creatures at home and abroad. Mr. Martin deserves warm commendation for the care he takes in making 'The Statesman's Year Book' complete and correct.[11]

New editions of the *Year-Book* were regularly reviewed in the national press throughout the 1870s,[12] and the perceived importance of Martin's unique contribution to national development was recognized in 1879 by Disraeli with a Civil List pension in the amount of £100 per annum. Thus, Martin's journey from struggling immigrant to cultural insider was complete.

In this narrative Martin appears to embody the Victorian ideals of industriousness and progress, almost stereotypically. The titles of his published books glory in the structures of civil society and in the organizational mania that lies behind it – in the enabling systems of finance and commerce, committees and associations. Together they express the 'conviction most Victorians shared that knowledge, despite its modular character, should and would be united'.[13] Within this view the humanizing virtues of literature were granted a legitimate, even fundamental role – so that it was not an absurd paradox, after Martin's death, for one of his obituaries to note that 'Amongst his most permanent work was a '"History of Lloyds" and a life of John Clare, the poet'.[14]

Martin's literary publications – the biography of Clare (1865), an edition of Chatterton's poetry (1865), and the novel *Alec Drummond* (1869) – are clustered at an early point along this arc. *Alec Drummond*, it should be noted, features a first-person narrator who also has a dual-life in Victorian print culture, working under remorseless journalistic deadlines by day and nurturing his manuscript of Burnsian poems by night. The main action of the novel begins when the protagonist exchanges the corrupt commercial world of London newspaper publishing for a life of military adventure, eventually becoming a soldier in the Crimean War. For Martin, publication of *Alec Drummond* marked a similar if less dramatic transition: this was to be his last foray into *belles lettres*, as he increasingly devoted his professional energies to his statistical work. The gradual receding of Martin's literary ambitions appears to have been a necessary corollary to his increasing worldly success – not a formal abandonment, perhaps, but an inevitable impact of his expanding franchise of statistical volumes.

For all its seeming coherence, this story of a career conceals a wellspring of angst and existential frustration. It is this sense of conflict, more than Martin's apparent successes, that should steer our understanding of his life relative to the *Life of Clare*. Martin's career is not quite representable as a gradual rebalancing of literature relative to utility, or art relative to profit. Even within a culture that encouraged ambitious career building, Martin was peculiarly swept up in the drama of trying to make a respectable living while finding a suitable outlet for his abilities and, in a broader sense, his sensibility. Clearly he wished to make money, and in quantities he felt commensurate with his talents: as he put it to Macmillan, he hoped the *Year-Book* would not only provide him 'a small return in money, but [would] lead to my name becoming more known that it is at present, so as to lift me from that dreary sphere of labour, paid by the day or week, in which literature is a mere trade'.[15] Yet these seemingly mild, conventionally Victorian aspirations existed as a kind of overlay, or uncertain counterpart, to a persistent strain of populist radicalism and advocacy that drives both the *Life of Clare* and *Alec Drummond*. For years we see Martin aggressively seeking insider status even as he denounces the dulling amorality of bureaucracy. And there is a further complication. As the *Life* makes clear, Martin was especially consumed with the torments of class liminality, of the oppressiveness of social rank for persons whose abilities were unconventional and multi-valent. In his own life, these same torments led Martin towards crises of humiliation and desperate action that were as fully and unsettlingly dramatic as those he imagined for John Clare.

Martin and Carlyle

In 1856, unhappily employed in Wolverhampton, Martin accepted the post of research assistant for Carlyle's *Life of Frederick the Great*. The record surrounding Martin's dismissal, just five months later, does credit to neither party – but Carlyle's behavior, by his own account, was harassing if not abusive. Even before meeting Martin, Carlyle tested his tolerance for servitude by proffering the example of a previous assistant, 'a scholar like yourself . . . who had been cheated out of his money in this big City', and who served Carlyle assiduously for a pittance. 'One sovereign a week was all I could afford him', Carlyle declares, yet somehow this 'thrifty and wise' paragon supported a wife and child for two years 'and was gradually looking towards better prospects, had longer life been granted him. But he died, to my sorrow in more ways than one'.

The terms of this introductory letter are hardly enticing, yet Carlyle seems certain that Martin, likewise supporting a wife and child, is in no position to refuse:

> If you now like to try a similar function with me on the same terms, – as I take it for granted you will . . . the experiment can begin as soon as you please . . . Judging that you will certainly accept . . . I inclose you a

Post-Office Order for £1 (your name is "*Frederick* Martin," not Friedrich); – if you wish to stay a week or two longer in W*n*, you can do it: but I rather expect to see you in few days.[16]

In the event, the high-handed Carlyle and the fastidious, doleful Martin did not mix; Carlyle delighted in baiting Martin with nicknames and diagnostic labels, including 'Peesweep', a reference to the shrill-voiced bird. The account Carlyle gives his brother of terminating Martin is positively gleeful:

> I have put away "Peesweep," – such was the title of unfortunate Wagner-Martin in late weeks; title rather descriptive of him. He was unhappy, and the cause of more unhappiness. Like to drive me distracted, sometimes, with his hysterical futilities, – poor soul. The 'whistling thro' the nose' (in breathing in cold weather) made me send him home "to work"; at home or at the Museum, he was futile, *chaotic* not cosmic: "too weak for the place." I got on perceptibly better since his unbeautiful face was veiled from me. Poor soul, we shall have a bout still before there can be some new outlet found for him. But his "help" I will have no more of, whatever come.[17]

Even after Martin's departure, it was more of the same. When Martin sought Carlyle's support for a proposed translation of the *Memoirs of Wilhelmina*, Carlyle instead reiterated an earlier offer to try to secure him something 'In the direction of [a British] Museum Clerkship', and ridiculed Martin's aspirations to scholarly work: 'for *annotating*, rectifying and elucidating ... you appear to me to be (rather *eminently*) destitute of the indispensable qualifications'.[18]

In citing these letters, I might seem to be making the case that the rage against literary snobbery that permeates *The Life of John Clare* was incubated in the poisonous environment that Carlyle fostered at Cheyne Row – that Martin chafed against Carlyle's hierarchical, Great-Man theory of history, and became bent on proving that neither he nor Clare were 'destitute of the indispensable qualifications' for literary achievement. But the full truth appears more complicated. There is evidence from early and late that Martin existed in a perpetual state of grievance vis-à-vis all of his employers and that he contributed to the tensions that inevitably arose. The strange brew of exaggerated humility and aggressive ambition marking Martin's professional behaviour suggests that he was a psychologically complex and contradictory figure whose resentments towards authority never vanished, even as his social status improved.

Still, Martin's resentments towards Carlyle did take a shocking form: nothing less than criminal theft. It is now accepted by Carlyle scholars that during his brief period of employ, Martin systematically stole from Cheyne Row a group of Carlyle's private papers and manuscripts. The precise scope of this activity is unknown. Fred Kaplan names only 'the unpublished draft of [the novel] "Wotton Reinfred", which Carlyle thought he had thrown into the fire', but Alexander Carlyle asserted in 1914 that the 'sneak-thief' probably also 'stuff[ed] into his satchel... the *Tour in Ireland*, the *Excursion to Paris, The Guises*', as well as 'many of Carlyle's Letters to his wife, mother, etc., many of Emerson's Letters to Carlyle' and finally some 'Love Letters from Miss Welsh'.[19] There is no sense that Carlyle ever knew of the thefts, and neither can we know whether Martin was driven most by opportunism, revenge or a twisted sort of admiration. Events from the last few months of Martin's life, twenty-five years after the theft, suggest that Martin may indeed have had a very fluid conception of his own motives. I describe these events below; it is important first to recount how Martin transitioned from the Carlyle residency to *The Life of Clare*.

The Statesman's Year-Book and *The Life of John Clare*

By the early 1860s Martin had begun working with Alexander Macmillan to produce a new kind of statistical almanac, having been introduced either by Gladstone or by Joseph Whitaker, the founder of *Whitaker's Almanac* and the sponsor of Martin's 1864 application for British citizenship.[20] A letter from Martin to Macmillan dated 17 February 1862 suggests that preliminary work on the *Year-Book* had been underway for some time:

> I beg to ensure you that I work as hard at the "year book" as I [possibly] can; so hard, in fact, as to have fallen ill lately from sheer over-work. The task, I confess, is a much more laborious one than I supposed in the first place... but as accuracy, in a work of this kind, is of even greater moment than time of publication, I think you ought not to blame me in this matter.[21]

The letter is notable both for its indication of the difficulties involved in developing the project and for its defensiveness of tone – a rhetorical posture of self-justification that would permeate Martin's correspondence with Macmillan for the following two decades.

It was not until December 1862 that a contract was formalized, and not until the beginning of 1864 that the first edition of the *Year-Book* finally appeared. There was clearly a great deal of anxiety associated with getting it to press: 'I have been fighting the battle of life in rather a rough manner', Martin wrote to Macmillan, 'and, often, wounded and trod under foot, am sore all over'.[22] Awareness of this overhanging burden is important in contextualizing Martin's commitment in taking on the Clare biography. Clare died in May 1864, and within twelve months *The Life of John Clare* had been written and published, even as Martin had also prepared, and seen to press, the second volume of the *Year-Book*. His edition of Chatterton's poems was immediately to follow. How did Martin manage this?

An intuitive explanation is that, having striven for years to secure a quasi-professional position, Martin was simply determined to exploit all opportunities. His ability to rebound from the Carlyle disaster and the impoverishment that must have followed is suggestive at once of self-discipline, ambition and a remorseless drive to labour. The schedule required to get work to market became a career-long habit that would make possible Martin's avalanche of statistical volumes, but there was an inevitable tension between the behind-the-scenes frenzy of his research life and the aura of sober reliability with which he sought to imbue these volumes, especially the *Year-Book*.

Relatedly, the most striking feature of Martin's professional correspondence is its extraordinary tonal bipolarity. At first glance, Martin appears effortlessly to play the educated Victorian gentleman, employing genteel deference and polished charm. Many of his letters betray not the slightest sense of anxiety – neither the immediate pressure of an impending deadline, nor broader impatience with the requisite forms of polite professional discourse. Yet there are individual letters in which Martin positively explodes with rage and frustration, and in ways that suggest that the physical toll of his literary labours, when combined with the psychological toll of always writing as the beggar – approaching his correspondents hat-in-hand, seeking information or an opportunity – was just about killing him. Here is an illuminating description of Martin's *Year-Book* correspondence with Macmillan.

> The incoherence, contradictions, vagueness and rudeness of his letters, his alternation between black despair and assertive optimism, his forgetfulness of vital statements written 24 hours earlier, his constant threats of bringing Macmillans into court immediately followed by abject protestations of his devotion (and requests for further advance payments)—all these are suggestive of an instability of mind which may be either the cause or the effect of his chronic but undefined ailments.[23]

The commentator here, writing on the occasion of the *Year-Book*'s centenary in 1965, is Sigfrid Henry Steinberg, who served as the *Year-Book*'s fourth editor from 1946 to 1969. Steinberg's reading of Martin is caustic; he focuses on Martin's manic reversals of tone, and, even more, on what he sees as Martin's absurd misjudgement of his expertise.

> His amazing naïveté in money matters and his complete ignorance of every aspect of publishing, contrasting with his undoubted efficiency as an editor, were at the route of his incessant quarrels with the Macmillans ... He never ceased to tell the Macmillans how to run their business more profitably, what discounts to give to wholesalers and retailers, how to make the Statesman's Year-Book pay (by 'stopping altogether the American sale'!).[24]

Acknowledging the elements of truth in Steinberg's summary – and also noting that Martin's pace of work truly was endangering his health – I think it important to understand that at least some of Martin's frustration emerged from a kind of existential confusion he was able to diagnose but not quell. The question was one of social location. Did Martin fundamentally understand himself as an insider or an outsider – and, relatedly, did he understand his own special competencies as primarily entrepreneurial or primarily aesthetic? In the Macmillan correspondence, Martin alternates, painfully, between self-assertion and obsequiousness, seemingly unable to project a self-image that satisfies himself, or that enables his progress in the world. This grounding tension informs Martin's rhetoric in the *Life of Clare*, especially in two competing refrains: one decrying patrons' failure to nurture an impoverished and chronically ill man, and the other working to combat booksellers' characterization of Clare as a naïve rustic and victim of circumstance. To put the question in the kind of language Martin favoured: was Clare constitutionally weak or nobly virile? A sacrificial lamb or a caged lion?

It is both partially accurate and too simple to say that Martin expressed his personal sense of professional neglect through his portrayal of Clare as victim. It is more useful to think of the *Life's* account of Clare's professional suffering as voicing Martin's own half-conscious confusion about the relative worth of individual artistic merit and professional literary competency – about the value of spontaneity and instinctual 'genius' relative to that of hard work and pragmatism. In choosing an epigraph for the front matter of the *Year-Book*, Martin confronted this dilemma and seemed to come down on one side of this debate, via a memorable Goethe quotation: 'It is often said: Figures rule the world. But this is certain, figures show how it is governed.'[25]

The lives of Frederick Martin and the first Life of John Clare 127

But *The Life of Clare* plays it differently. For the most part in the *Life* commerce is pitted directly against art, and the publishing establishment is portrayed as a soul-deadening force; the machinery of literary London cannot support the talents of a provincial singularity like Clare. One example of this machinery is the mass production of gift-books and annuals, which Martin ridicules as a debasing, modern quicksand Clare keeps getting pushed towards. Annuals represent, for Martin, the kitschy commodification of writers and writing – 'gold-edged toy books' soliciting 'poetry by the yard', but with capricious editorial and payment policies, as Clare discovers on at least two occasions.[26] Fighting for attention with the flashy annuals, Clare's *Shepherd's Calendar*, Martin argues, was doomed to failure by its cheap, even 'clownish' binding – and even more so through 'the negligent manner in which it was published', by which he means John Taylor's failure to control distribution:

> Books, like all other earthly objects requiring to be bought and sold, must undergo certain preparations, and run through prescribed channels of trade in their way from the producer to the consumer, and it is well known that the regulation and management of this process may either greatly retard or accelerate the sale of a work ... [R]eally valuable works have met with very little success, owing to want of energy or thought on the part of the publishers; while, on the other hand, not a few bad or paltry books, utterly unworthy of public patronage, have, through active commercial management, met with a considerable demand, and brought both profit and fame to the writers.[27]

Even in this short space, we can see dramatic fluctuations in Martin's tone. His cynically despairing description of books as commodities 'requiring to be bought and sold' quickly gives way to the sort of earnest marketing lecture that prompted Steinberg to offer a scoffing account of Martin's business dealings with Macmillan. Such tonal vacillation pervades the *Life*, but is especially evident when art and commerce are facing off, as in Martin's account of Clare's compositional practices. In one such sequence, Martin first rhapsodizes over Clare's insular process of poetic invention:

> There were some favourite places where he delighted to sit, and where the hallowed vein of poetry seemed to him to flow more freely than at any others. The chief of these spots was the hollow of an old oak, on the borders of Helpston Heath, called Lea Close Oak – now ruthlessly cut down by 'enclosure' progress – where he had formed himself something like a table in front. Few human beings ever came near this place, except now and then some wandering gypsies, the sight of whom was not unpleasing to the poet.

> Inside this old oak Clare used to sit in silent meditation, for many hours together, forgetting everything about him, and unmindful even of the waning day and mantle of darkness falling over the earth.[28]

A monastic purity of poetic composition makes Clare Clare. Yet in going on to describe the transfer of the manuscript poems to John Taylor and Clare's accompanying determination not to 'allow any change, save orthographical and grammatical corrections', Martin's attitude changes radically. For all Clare's genius, Martin ruefully suggests, he made a solipsistic mistake in viewing all copy-editing of his work as a violation of his poetic vision:

> There was at this time an impression on Clare's mind that the songs came floating from his lips and pen as music from the throat of birds. So he held his own orthodoxy more orthodox than that of the schools. In which view poor John Clare was decidedly wrong, seeing that his music was not offered gratis like that of the skylark and nightingale, but was looking out for the pounds, shillings, and pence of a most discerning public.[29]

Martin's sarcasm towards the culture-industry comes ringing through, but so does his wish that Clare had recognized his financial dependency on consumer demand. Later, when discussing Clare's decision to buy Taylor's unsold copies of *The Shepherd's Calendar* for independent resale, Martin is similarly torn. He understands both Clare's panicked commitment (in the heat of which, Martin says, Clare forgot to pursue Allan Cunningham's advice of demanding a full reckoning from Taylor) and the tantalizing idea of direct-marketing of his own goods, even at the personal cost of becoming a 'pedlar' or 'hawker'.[30] But he is frustrated by Clare's ineptitude in enlisting others' help: Mrs Marsh of Peterborough, for instance, the socializing wife of the bishop, was a well-meaning if eccentric resource, and Martin rues Clare's failure to understand that 'Mrs. Marsh would have assisted him in selling ten times as many books as he could ever hope to do in his whole life'.[31] All in all, the episode causes Martin to reflect that 'It was strange how little John Clare understood the world in which he lived.'[32]

This final phrase crystallizes the ambiguity of Martin's editorial perspective. Though he does present Clare as a victim of circumstances and cultural attitudes beyond his control, it is surprising how often Martin criticizes Clare's lack of social and business acumen. Such modulations permeate Martin's account of Clare's failed 1823 plan to acquire the property known as 'Bachelor's Hall', an episode that he describes as 'the turning period of the poet's life'. Seeking outside financing in the amount of two hundred pounds, Clare finds 'all doors resolutely closed against him':

> The explanation was that Lord Radstock, like most of Clare's other patrons, was entirely ignorant of the poet's character, regarding him in the light of a genial infant, full of intellect, but without strength of character. What chiefly produced this impression on his lordship, otherwise decidedly the truest friend of the poet, was that Clare, notwithstanding repeated advice to that effect, had neglected to make a good arrangement, or, in fact, any arrangement at all, with his publishers, so that he stood to them in the position of a helpless client.[33]

Clare's fantasies of land ownership are naïve in one sense, justifiable in another; Radstock's rejection is similarly layered – at once a product of class bias and an understandable response to Clare's stumbling. Martin presents the whole episode as the sorry revelation of a 'great truth': Clare grasps that class is indeed destiny, and that his fate is to be that of a hack-poet for elites – 'something better than a clown, and something less than a lackey in uniform'.[34]

These competing emphases are perhaps resolvable along the following lines: in a better, more egalitarian world, Martin implies, Clare's basic human failings would not have brought him so much pain. For all Martin's fury against the shoddy treatment and neglect that Clare faced – the failure of even his supporters to perceive 'the noble and manly, nay lofty heart that beat under the ragged lime-burner's dress'[35] – one could argue that his grand theme is the conflict between the individual personality and the institutional apparatus, a conflict that is merely focused through the story of John Clare and the historical world of London publishing. This may explain why Martin's embedded mini-biography of Octavius Gilchrist, whose 1820 *London Magazine* piece first brought Clare to public attention, is so complex. Martin is unsure where to place Gilchrist along the class and educational axis, and whether to make his provinciality register humility or self-delusion. His initial sketch of Gilchrist, which establishes his Oxford education and his clear preference for poetry over and against his inherited Stamford grocery business, ends by condemning Gilchrist's *London* piece for employing a 'tone in which a *parvenu* might speak of a pauper', and for its fawning account of the business risk Taylor had undertaken on Clare's behalf. 'Though perhaps well-meant in the first instance', Martin argues, '[Gilchrist's] patronizing manner in speaking of Clare, and attracting public attention to him, less as a poetical genius, but as happening to be a poor man, did infinite mischief in the end. It did more than this – it killed John Clare.'[36]

Seemingly disregarding his opening account of Gilchrist's literary sensitivity, Martin drifts into portraying him as a puffed-up Stamford burgher. Martin later claims that it was William Gifford of the *Quarterly Review*, not Gilchrist, who produced a clear-eyed, class-conscious appreciation of Clare in that magazine and who later gave Clare a wise warning 'against booksellers and publishers', which Gilchrist immediately and 'somewhat maliciously' flouted.[37]

More confusingly, though, Gilchrist is given the final word in a lengthy anecdote recalling how a misguided attempt to gain the favour of Walter Scott resulted in Clare's 'mortification'.[38] Offering Clare a consoling parable after Scott has snubbed him, Gilchrist wryly recalls that 'simple Mr. Walter Scott', before becoming famous, had thanked him profusely for a brief magazine review, and he tells Clare that, with hard work, he too may expect that 'the great baronet in his high path will be the first to shake hands'. Martin closes the anecdote with a flourish: 'Thus spoke Octavius Gilchrist, grocer of Stamford, and contributor to the "Quarterly Review". And his speech set John Clare musing for some time to come.'[39] Martin clearly intends his penultimate 'grocer and contributor' line as a satiric *coup de grâce*, but what, precisely, does it mean? To make the anecdote cogent requires an elaborate interpretation – that Gilchrist is somehow a vessel of wisdom despite himself, and that his words give Clare an even clearer insight into the vagaries of fame than he consciously intends. Martin is always poised to spring at the slightest hint of self-importance, but his scorn is so instinctive, and so directly tied to his sense of his authorial voice, that it leads him to forced reversals.

Thus, when Martin rehabilitates Gilchrist he makes him the agent of the biography's crucial claims about Clare's relationship to charity, first explaining to the reader the nature of Clare's reluctance to accept gifts ('The high manliness of Clare now struck [Gilchrist] for the first time, and he deeply admired it') and then having Gilchrist explain to Clare why this reluctance was sometimes misplaced ('He even remonstrated [to Clare] about his ... coldness in receiving gifts offered by real lovers and admirers of his genius').[40] Further, in his account of Gilchrist's decline Martin establishes a series of parallels between the two men, as each hides from the other the extent of his physical and emotional suffering. Clare's seeking-out of Gilchrist after the crushing failure of the land scheme is effectively staged twice – once after the ailing Gilchrist has beat his last retreat from London and 'journalistic controversy', and again after Clare's own health has suddenly improved. Walking to Stamford 'along the sunny path ... reveling in golden day-dreams, in none of which the image of his dear friend Gilchrist was wanting', Clare arrives at the peak of renewed hope and happiness, only to find that Gilchrist has died an hour before.[41] Martin tacitly equates the two men as pummelled and discarded by the literary establishment. The point seems finally to emerge with some clarity: that class was destiny for Gilchrist as surely as it was for Clare – and, Martin implies, as it was for countless, nameless others.

The Story of Alec Drummond

The wishing-away of this bitter truth is one of the central motives behind Martin's next major work and sole venture into fiction, the 1869 novel *The Story of Alec Drummond, of the 17th Lancers*. Here Martin's canvas is bigger: the 'national disgrace' of England's failure to support its poets is expanded into an exposé of the failings of British imperial warfare. Martin gives his protagonist Alec Drummond all the attributes that John Clare lacked: self-confidence, physical strength, clarity of mind, and an instinctive, unpretentious savoir-faire that allows him to move effectively across class boundaries. In the harsh social milieu of the *Life*, Clare's weaknesses always lead to privation and humiliation; in the harsh social milieu of *Alec Drummond*, Alec's strengths are always enough to overcome physical threats and bureaucratic bungling.

In this regard, and in the romance plot that is ladled onto the narrative, the fantasy elements of the novel could hardly be plainer. Even so, the social protest of *Alec Drummond*, grounded in close renderings of military mismanagement, is even more clamorous than that of the *Life*. Contemporary reviewers were confounded by its juxtapositions: '[A] more curious combination of minute realism in detail, and violent romanticism in the outline of the story, can scarcely be found than in Mr. Martin's account of the adventures of his imaginary private', wrote the *Spectator*, while the *Westminster Review* wondered 'what could have induced Mr. Martin to throw his admirable pictures of a war ... into the form of a three volume novel? As a novel the book is poor, but as a descriptive history of the Crimean war excellent'.[42] If *Alec Drummond*'s satiric warrant mainly offers depictions of Britons abroad, it shares with *The Life of Clare* Martin's Victorian treatment of poverty, illness and the failure of social safety nets: we again see the plight of the subsistence wage-earner, whether agrarian, military, or, as in his own case, clerical. *Alec Drummond* clarifies that Martin's animus was aimed not just at a callous gentry, but also at an ideological blindness to workers – both their welfare and their distinctive talents.

We first see Alec as a young Scot in London, seeking a literary career but working as an assistant sub-editor for a financial weekly. Shocked to learn that the paper's proprietor is a tyrant who extorts bribes in exchange for favourable coverage, Alec quickly loses his job and residence, taking refuge in the army. Almost instantly on his absorption into the Scottish Lancers, Alec is reconstituted as a skilled equestrian and urbane social observer, his own class stock slowly rising even as he sleeps in the mud and faces perpetual dangers. In effect, Martin has exchanged a single worker's view of localized graft for a global view of 'disgrace' relative to whole populations of workers.

The pattern thenceforward, once the regiment arrives in Turkey for an amphibious journey to the Crimea, is that at each stage Martin shows Alec befriending locals on both sides of the conflict, learning enough of their language and colonial history to mediate between these people and his colleagues in the Lancers. At the same time, Martin shows the abject squalor and suffering inflicted upon 'common soldiers' by a logistically incompetent British army, whose leaders seem surprised but unmoved by recurring waves of cholera. The back-and-forth between travelogue and muckraking modes gives unexpected depth to statements such as that of Alec's friend Brown, who calls one sortie a 'wild-goose chase, planned for some mystic object by our political rulers at home', or like that of Alec himself, who views a grotesque blend of 'goods and chattels, live and dead things' on a beachhead and wonders at the sufferings of his fellow soldiers, 'children of the so-called richest nation on earth'.[43] Indeed, Martin seems more concerned with officers' general class chauvinism than with close tactical analysis, to the extent that when he arrives at the novel's grand set-piece – the suicidal mission at Balaclava that Tennyson had memorialized fifteen years earlier in 'The Charge of the Light Brigade' (1854) – he muddies the account of a benighted chain-of-command with an alternate theory of multinational espionage.

We might be tempted to downplay the class-protest connection between this novel and *The Life of John Clare*, because *Alec Drummond* seems in many ways a wish-fulfilling antidote to all that Martin found haunting in Clare's story. Alec's social and professional liminality is constantly foregrounded, but represented as a virtue rather than an unshakeable albatross. As a Scot, Alec feels like a foreigner among Englishmen, but in ways that reinforce his self-esteem and social ease. His literary, professional and equestrian education is vaguely outlined yet clearly sufficient. His fascination with a nameless blue-eyed woman he rescues from the sea at Dover takes on a Petrarchan fervour, but unlike for Clare (the Petrarchanism of whose obsession with Mary Joyce is stressed by Martin), the vision proves real, and the lady finally rejects a Russian count in favour of Alec. By no means hostile to all aristocrats, Alec enjoys the protection of some, while noting the frivolity of others. Then, too, Alec forms bonds with working men, smiling occasionally at their rusticity but valuing their mettle and good sense. Knocked about a good deal – concussed, wounded, ambushed and abducted – he always recovers quickly, aided by the medicinal liquor that he accepts in strict, self-imposed moderation.

Yet Alec's heroic equipoise throws into relief Martin's larger rhetorical project of describing the failed logistics of British military transport, billeting and supply lines. '[A]s for the physical incidents of the Varna encampment, and the first month of the Crimean expedition', wrote the *Spectator*, 'no description of them so telling and graphic and effective in every way has yet appeared ... [since] Russell's Crimean letters to the *Times*'.[44] Alec and his peers are repeatedly made to start or stop – to break or make camp – to prepare needlessly for a battle that doesn't come – with a randomness that bewilders, alienates and infuriates them. They are privy to no larger view or understanding of the ostensible purpose behind their movements. Martin opens volume II with an extended account of the bleak aftermath of the Battle of Alma, from 20 September 1854, traditionally understood as the first major battle of the Crimean War. The disorganization of the British side is contrasted, pitifully, with the relative orderliness of their French allies:

> While the French had removed the whole of their wounded and dead from the field the day before, not leaving the former even a night to their sufferings, both officers and men going forth to assist them immediately after the fight, our troops, on the other hand, had not completed one-half of the same sad duty at the end of thirty-six hours, and on the morning of Friday, the 22nd September, the hill-side was still strewn with corpses in British uniforms, and men groaning in the agonies of death.
>
> There seemed to be with us an utter want of organisation for relieving and remedying, as far as lay in human power, the casualties of the battle, just as if a combat with the Russians, and the possibility of our soldiers being killed and wounded, was something unnatural, and altogether out of the common order of things, and as such had never been thought of by our generals ... Thus our poor soldiers, hit by Russian bullets or swords, but, to their misfortune, not fatally, were laid down on the cold earth, to perish like dogs, with a mere mockery of medical care and attention.[45]

In contrast to such horrid visions are tantalizing glimpses of health and pastoral wholesomeness, suggesting the possibility of restoration through contact with an Edenic nature. Indeed, Martin makes it clear that for Alec, as it had been for Clare, a life 'out of doors' is preferable to an indoors one, even in such circumstances.[46]

In both books, Martin takes pains to associate the outdoor life with a paradoxical blend of native wit and worldly perspective – in the novel, the associations are advanced through depictions of Alec's horsemanship and Scottishness – and it becomes clear that for Martin healthy manliness emerges from the connection with the *genius loci*. The related idea of homesickness furthers the argument: recall that Martin supplies for Clare the dying words 'I want to go home', and insinuates that Clare was unmanned as much by his removals from Helpston as by his illness.[47] Homesickness in the two books is again a sign of right-thinking. At Balaclava, the last shout of a charging Lancer – 'Scotland for ever!' – is at first readable as one more example of useless glory-seeking naïveté: 'He repeated it thrice; but the cry had no sooner escaped his lips for the third time when he was struck by a cannon-ball through the head, and fell from his steed as if lifted off by invisible hands'.[48] But one realizes that his battle cry is actually an expression of personal autonomy and a reproach to the general 'disorganization' that has been described at length over the previous hundred pages.

Alec is always both resolutely Scottish and a citizen of the world, and Martin is eager to connect this duality with successful self-fashioning. Alec's superhuman linguistic facility – by novel's end he is fluent in Turkish, French, German and Russian – places him first among several expatriates with similar talents, and Martin habitually uses Scotland as a metonym for demographic fluidity and social mobility through language.[49] One cannot but help think here of Martin's own personal and cultural transition in coming to England – but also, from the other side, of Clare's difficulty in negotiating the relationship between Helpston and London, and also of his struggle to exploit his poetic voice, and his experiments with genre, in ways that would move him beyond the peripheral literary category to which he had been assigned.

Five years earlier, in the first volume of the *Statesman's Year-Book* – 'An Account of the Existing Sovereigns, Governments, Armaments, Education, Population, Religion, &c., of every Nation in the World'[50] – Martin had invoked a metaphor of nations-as-individuals, and claimed that his new publication would provide an accurate guide to these biographies of states:

> 'France,' 'Italy,' 'Russia,' 'Australia,' 'Germany,' are constantly referred to as living entities, possessed of a certain amount of force, strength, and volition,

the quality and quantity of which is supposed to be generally known. But . . .
the subject is far from being generally known, and . . . is at least environed
with a large amount of complexity.[51]

Martin had here embraced the basic validity of the metaphor, but suggested it was often employed in ignorance. If in *Alec Drummond* Martin also sometimes hedges on the question of a readily discernible 'national character', he is nonetheless intent on using the novel to parade his own burgeoning knowledge of world geographies, economies and languages. With the growing authority of the *Year-Book* behind him, Martin is determined to expose the novel-reading public to a less Anglocentric world, and to advance, through a popular literary genre, his authority regarding international affairs.

If Martin reads darkly the operations of 'Sovereigns, Governments, [and] Armaments', the novel's most interesting expression of worldliness may well lie in its unreconciled chasm between realism and romance. For the *Spectator* reviewer, the novel's 'startling' display of romance elements was so excessive that 'we suspect our author *intended* to make something of a satire on English novel-readers' tastes' – and, similarly, the review argued that, through his presentation of Alec's physical strength and powers of recovery, 'Mr. Martin is laughing in his sleeve at his reader, whom he is determined to sate with the wonderful achievements of his hero'.[52] This toying manipulation of novelistic form, evidently designed with sales in mind, can thus be registered as a meta-critical display of sophistication on Martin's part: the calculating exploitation of the same flawed marketplace that had so badly victimized Clare.

The final decade

The urbanity Martin projected in *Alec Drummond* was not, in practice, something he could maintain in his own working life. Despite the continued appearance of new book volumes and the regular issuance of the *Year-Book*, the last decade of Martin's life was marked by worry and a growing sense of failure. Even as he appeared steadily to consolidate the brand of Frederick Martin – the repository of all information, the man who knew it all – he remained haunted by his self-image as an outsider and a disrespected underdog. Even the conferral of the Civil List pension in 1879, a vital source of financial relief and an unquestionable mark of prestige, did not fully repair his finances or his self-esteem.

Our best window into these strains is Martin's ongoing *Year-Book* correspondence with Alexander Macmillan. As indicated earlier, this correspondence is characterized by violent swings between proud self-assertion and apologetic self-abasement. While Martin's emotional crises were often catalyzed by financial anxiety, they seem to have been rooted in his sense that, despite his unceasing efforts, he remained, like Clare, a subaltern within an elitist literary establishment. I focus below on a single, six-month sequence of letters as illustrative of Martin's conflicting self-conceptions as underling and one-man franchise.

In April 1870, Martin threatened to quit the *Year-Book*. Seeking a new written contract that would formalize a longstanding verbal agreement under which he had been operating, Martin was shocked when Macmillan instead referred him back to their initial document of 1862. The terms of that contract were 'entirely unfavourable', wrote Martin, and he noted that even the more generous verbal contract – which had set his annual salary at £100, established that he was to receive half the *Year-Book*'s profits, and instituted a set price for the volume – was barely sufficient. 'Though what I have received under these verbal arrangements has not by any means paid me', he wrote, 'yet without it I must have broken down years ago, and the undertaking would have dropped'.[53]

Martin's negotiation was not merely a matter of long-term prudence: an unpleasant dispute concerning his responsibilities on the forthcoming *Handbook of Contemporary Biography* had brought to a head enveloping feelings of persecution:

> I expected thanks from you, and not abuse, and when, last Friday, you addressed me in a way I consider utterly cruel and unjust, it came upon me like thunder from a blue sky. In all my dealings with you, I have been the very opposite from mercenary, and it is on this account mainly that I deeply feel the injustice of your reproaches.[54]

There were more details as well, including claims of deteriorating health and fears for his family's financial future. (Martin's worry was doubtless increased by the fact that, though he did not say so, his wife was three months pregnant with their seventh child.)[55]

Rather than engaging the details of either protest, however, Macmillan simply refused to answer. This is a telling insight into his understanding of Martin's volatility – and, indeed, when Martin wrote again in two weeks' time, his self-justification was wrapped in a mantle of apology:

> Are you displeased with my previous letter, asking for a written agreement concerning the 'Statesman's Year-book'? If anything in my note has given offense to you, I am sincerely sorry for it, though, at the same time, I cannot regret having made the demand I did ... It is an old story, and a sad story,

that there are few things that do so much mischief, as <u>verbal</u> agreements in separating men, and destroying mutual confidence ... Please let me have a line to tell me whether you are angry with me, or merely prevented answering my former note. I am truly anxious to be on the old friendly terms with you, and it is anxiety which dictates these lines.[56]

Macmillan's patient silence seemed justified, for within three months we find Martin excitedly discussing a plan for a new, nationally focused, publication to be called *The Parliamentary Year-Book*. Describing it as an independent undertaking for which he will not ask Macmillan's support ('I was thinking of a venture on my own hook'), he ends by implying that he would welcome another agreement with Macmillan – and that, implicitly, all is forgiven: 'Now for my great question. Do you agree with what Mr. Walters said at the Statistical dinner that "the publication of such a book cannot fail to be commercially successful"?'[57]

But just as Martin's upset had not lasted, neither did this renewal of optimism. When Macmillan wrote in November to say that there were no profits to be shared from the 1870 *Year-Book*, Martin plunged into despair:

My dear Sir

Your note, which I received late last night, has made me feel utterly wretched. I hoped the tide of ill-success of my Year-book had turned last year, and hearing that there is again nothing to divide, I feel more miserable then I can tell you. It is now ten years since I commenced the Statesman's Year-book, and ever since I have toiled at it as few literary men toil. Now it has ruined me in income, and ruined me in health, and I can go no further. Sitting up night after night to add together, correct and correct again, long rows of figures has made my eyes so weak that I am at times almost blind. And when I think of my wife and seven children, who have to suffer, and are suffering already, from the ill-success of this most wretched of all undertakings I ever began and carried on, I feel as if my life is lost.

Yours in sorrow
Fred Martin[58]

This remarkable cry of futility seems as if it must be totalizing and permanent. Yet by the very next day Martin had recovered considerably, offering a detailed proposal to Macmillan's partner George Craik that would allow him to continue with an endeavour that only a few hours earlier he had described as 'this most wretched of all undertakings'.

So the *Year-Book* went on,[59] and so did Martin, playing out his characteristic pendulum-swings of ambition and desolation. Between these poles were sour expressions of truculence. A letter to Macmillan of November 1874 begins:

> Your question as to "whether I am taking any steps about the New Year-Book" I cannot understand. By "New Year Book" you mean, I suppose, the issue for 1875; but I am doing nothing special as regards it. The course followed by me in all the issues, eleven in number, that have appeared, has been to begin working at the new issue from the moment of publication of the preceding one – in fact all the year round.[60]

Two of Martin's new schemes were for periodicals; the failure of the first of these, *The Brighton Magazine*, resulted in a net loss of £150 and led him to promise 'Never more shall I venture upon publishing', though he also explained, 'The speculation would have been a safe one, had I not, ignorant of commercial undertakings, been compelled to lean upon others, who proved rogues.'[61] The second, *The Biographical Magazine*, met a similar fate.[62] Opening its inaugural issue in 1877 with the first of a promised multi-issue account of the life of Carlyle, the whole enterprise was scrapped after the family objected to its continuation and Carlyle printed a note in the *Athenaeum* reading 'Mr. Frederick Martin has no authority to concern himself with my life, of which he knows nothing'.[63]

It is difficult to ascertain Martin's precise financial situation in the 1870s.[64] Steinberg is profoundly sceptical – his unsympathetic reading is that, in effect, Martin was a bounder, unhappy not because he was truly needy but because he misconstrued his social standing. Summarizing Martin's correspondence following the 1879 pension award, Steinberg writes:

> [P]hrases such as "I am literally penniless" occur with monotonous regularity, and–the depth of Victorian penury–his daughters, "brought up as ladies," had to do all the housework as the servant had to be discharged. Martin's creditors were pressing him–he assessed his debts at "over £2,000;" he himself and his wife were ailing ... In fact, Martin's will, proved on 10th February, 1883, reveals a less disconsolate state of affairs: his widow Susan, née Styles, received his personal estate of £1,962 3s. 1d.[65]

Steinberg is surely cherry-picking the evidence here, as will become clear below – but in any case Martin's sense of injury was never reducible to a number in his account book. It seemed to him that his incisive understanding of social condescension and establishment politics, ably demonstrated in the *Life of Clare* and *Alec Drummond*, had gotten him nowhere. Even with a raft of publications, a public name, and a Civil List pension that Alexander Macmillan and other prominent figures had secured for him,[66] he was convinced he couldn't outflank a system that still classed him as a drudge and a glorified clerk.

This tangle of resentment, wounded pride, real financial worry and perceived literary marginality had its expression in a final, incredible sequence. In January 1882 Martin wrote to Macmillan that he was 'hard pressed by creditors', and pleaded for an immediate advance of £100, which he received that day.[67] Even so, the walls continued to close in. Perceiving Martin's snowballing distraction, Macmillan suggested in June that he receive help in preparing the 1883 *Year-Book*. Though Martin strenuously resisted, at the beginning of July he admitted that he was 'overwhelmed with debts now and scarcely know how to extricate myself'.[68] By early October his threatened bankruptcy had become a legal matter: 'by orders of my creditors I must go into liquidation'.[69] And then that same month, in kind of a closing, tragicomic flourish, Martin left the *Year-Book* proofs in a railway carriage, jeopardizing its publication. The volume's rescue mission was handed over to John Scott-Keltie – who the next year would assume full-time editorship of the *Year-Book* – and Martin's tenure with the *Year-Book* was over.

A month later, frantic for money, Martin determined that he would sell his Carlyle manuscripts on the black market – the manuscripts stolen twenty-five years earlier. Our knowledge of this turn of events derives mainly from the 1904 *Autobiography* of the American-born religious reformer Moncure Daniel Conway, who in 1882 was living in London and working for the publisher Harper. While in America Conway had been a friend of Ralph Waldo Emerson, and had recently been informed by the family that Emerson's letters to Carlyle had gone missing. Thus, he was immediately suspicious on being introduced to 'a small middle-aged man who was trying to sell an important manuscript of Carlyle'. Following the man's instructions, Conway went to 'a miserable house' in Kentish Town where, he says, 'I was met at the door by the same man ... He began saying he admired and loved me, thereby placing me on my guard. He then brought out the manuscript he wished to sell to the Harpers, – Carlyle's autograph journal of his tour in Ireland.'[70]

Conway knew something was very wrong, especially because at about the same time the *Athenaeum* published four of the missing Emerson letters. Conway set about making inquiries – his full account, too long to recapitulate here, provides many important details – and soon enough 'discovered that the man who offered me the manuscript had been for a time an amanuensis for Carlyle'. (The seller used an alias, and Conway 'suppress[es]' Martin's name 'because I believe he has children', but his identity is made clear.) Eventually learning that the letters had passed to a dealer, Conway visited the shop, and the next day (20 November 1882) Martin's wife appeared at Conway's residence in Bedford Park.

'The woman was middle-aged, crafty, and very timorous', writes Conway:

> As she had come all the way from Kentish Town ... my wife hastened to refresh her with tea, and treated her like a lady. Finding that she had brought only four of the letters, I agreed to her price, ten pounds for the four, on condition that next day I might bring them to her and examine others, until I could select the four preferred.

By gradual extension of this contrivance, Conway and his wife were able, over a series of days, surreptitiously to copy the entire cache of twenty-seven letters before 'unfold[ing] the whole matter to Sir James Stephen, – coexecutor with Froude of Carlyle's papers'.[71]

If there is still detective work to be done to track the dispersal of these papers and the full extent of Martin's involvement, the general contours are clear enough: Martin had quietly held them for a quarter-century, and then – under the cover of a mysterious German pseudonym ('Beckerwaise')[72] – attempted to sell them covertly. Perhaps unsurprisingly, given the utter desperation implied by this context, only two months later Martin was dead, aged fifty-three.

Granting the harsh realities of Martin's financial plight and failing health, the symbolic dimensions of this last act are nonetheless extraordinary. If not precisely the public slaying of a literary father, it certainly reads as the assumption of power and control, a retributory claim of lasting authority. But there is a bloodless aspect to it as well – Martin systematically jobbing a literary marketplace that had failed to adequately reward him. His use of the pseudonym 'Beckerwaise' – not a common German name, but an improvised compound that amalgamates the family name 'Becker' with the word for 'orphan' – is perhaps the clearest indication that Martin himself viewed the activity in richly figurative terms. We can imagine Martin implying that the papers themselves are somehow orphans, and then declaring, cynically, that he is seeking only to find them a proper home. The more obvious interpretation, however, is the better one: that Martin sees himself as a literary orphan or refugee – someone who remains, after all these years, a man without a place.

While we cannot know if John Clare's poverty led directly to his madness, as Martin had hypothesized in the *Life*, so much of Martin's own troubled behaviour seems to have been driven by his internalizing a series of pressures that, in the *Life*, he had identified as damaging to Clare. There was more to this than reflective self-pity. In the *Life* he had written about the mainly 'just' – but in Clare's case hurtful – idea that 'genius and talent are self-supporting, and that he who cannot live by the exercise of his own hand or brain, does not altogether deserve success'.[73] Martin's success in speaking in several cultural registers indicates a fluency – a blend of 'genius and talent' – that he was never able fully to leverage, just as he was unable to embrace his own belief, as stated in the *Life*, that 'real happiness is found distributed with tolerable equality among all ranks and classes'.[74] If Martin's final unwindings seem sadly to undercut the literary stature he sought for so long, they remind us of the real power of those cultural expectations that, in his presentation, had governed the life of John Clare.

Notes

1. *The Statesman's Year-Book*, II (1865), p. viii.
2. Frederick Martin, *The Life of John Clare*, ed. Eric Robinson and Geoffrey Summerfield, 2nd edn. (New York: Barnes and Noble, 1964), pp. xvii, xvi. All further references to the *Life* are to this edition.
3. Jonathan Bate, 'John Clare: Prologue to a New Life', in John Goodridge and Simon Kövesi (eds.), *John Clare: New Approaches* (Helpston: John Clare Society, 2000), pp. 1–16 (pp. 7, 9). Bate is thinking here of Martin's account of Clare's grandfather, John Parker Clare. Later, however, recounting Martin's description of an episode from 1823 to 1824 when Clare 'sank for the first time into a deep and prolonged depression' (p. 11), Bate suggests that Martin may have been working 'from a documentary record and not just his own lively imagination', such that 'one of the most romantic, fictionalised-sounding images of Clare which we possess might actually have a basis in fact' (p. 15). In two essays in the *JCSJ*, Bate corrects a series of errors made by earlier biographers, including Martin. See 'New Light on the Life of Clare', *JCSJ*, 20 (2001), 41–54; and 'New Clare Documents', *JCSJ*, 21 (2002), 5–18.
4. Juliette Atkinson, *Victorian Biography Reconsidered: A Study of Nineteenth-Century 'Hidden' Lives* (Oxford: Oxford University Press, 2010), pp. 205, 208, 210.
5. Ibid., p. 211.
6. Ibid., p. 206.
7. *Life*, p. 263.
8. According to both the original and updated entries in the *Dictionary of National Biography*, Martin was born in Geneva in 1830 and subsequently

educated in Heidelberg. Atkinson follows this account, but Robinson and Summerfield say straightforwardly that Martin was German. S. H. Steinberg, a twentieth-century editor of the *Statesman's Year-Book*, calls the *DNB* account 'completely bogus' and cites Martin's 1864 application for British citizenship as stating that he was born in Berlin and had come to England in 1855 at around age thirty. Steinberg adds, however, that these claims were 'vouchsafed only by Martin himself and not substantiated by any official documents'. S. H. Steinberg, 'Statesman's Year-Book: Martin to Epstein', *Journal of Library History*, 1.3 (1966), 153–66 (158).

9. Francis Espinasse, *Literary Recollections and Sketches* (London: Hodder and Stoughton, 1893), p. 260.
10. *Stories of Banks and Bankers* (London: Macmillan, 1865); *Commercial Handbook of France* (London: Longmans, Green and Co., 1867); *Handbook of Contemporary Biography* (London: Macmillan, 1870); *The National History of England*, vol. 2 (London: William Collins, 1873); *The History of Lloyd's and of Marine Insurance in Great Britain* (London: Macmillan, 1876); and *The Property and Revenues of the English Church Establishment* (London: Society for the liberation of religion from State-patronage and control, 1877).
11. Quoted in *Athenaeum*, 2472 (13 March 1875), 347.
12. See, for example, the following numbers of the *Times*: 26663 (2 February 1870), p. 7; 29195 (6 March 1878), p. 4; 30143 (16 March 1881), p. 4.
13. Thomas Richards, *The Imperial Archive: Knowledge and the Fantasy of Empire* (London: Verso, 1993). p. 7.
14. 'Death of Frederick Martin', *Royal Gazette* 56.12 (Hamilton, Bermuda; 20 March 1883), p. 1.
15. Martin to Alexander Macmillan, 25 February 1865. © The British Library Board, Add MS 55042. Unless otherwise noted, all further references to Martin's letters are © The British Library Board.
16. Thomas Carlyle to Frederick Martin, 15 October 1856. *The Collected Letters of Thomas and Jane Welsh Carlyle*, vol. 32, ed. Ian Campbell, Aileen Christianson, Sheila McIntosh, David Sorenson, and Kenneth J. Fielding (Durham: Duke University Press, 2004), pp. 12–13.
17. Ibid., p. 106. Thomas Carlyle to John A. Carlyle, 21 March 1857.
18. Ibid., p. 161. Carlyle to Frederick Martin, 7 June 1857.
19. Fred Kaplan, *Thomas Carlyle: A Biography* (Ithaca: Cornell University Press, 1983), p. 545; Alexander Carlyle, 'Eight new love letters of Jane Welsh', *The Nineteenth Century and After*, 75 (1914), 86–113 (87).
20. Steinberg, p. 159.
21. Martin to Alexander Macmillan. 17 February 1862. Berg Collection of English and American Literature, New York Public Library. I thank Elizabeth James, former curator of the nineteenth-century British Collection at the British Library, for alerting me to this letter and for additional help on the Macmillan papers.
22. Martin to Alexander Macmillan, 27 February 1864. BL Add MS 55042.
23. Steinberg, p. 160.

24. Ibid., p. 159.
25. *The Statesman's Year-Book*, II (1865), p. iv, prints the Goethe in the original German: 'Man sagt oft: Zahlen regieren die Welt. Das aber ist gewiss, Zahlen zeigen *wie* sie regiert wird.'
26. *Life*, pp. 202, 232–3.
27. Ibid., p. 205.
28. Ibid., p. 133.
29. Ibid., p. 134. This is a dramatically reductive account of Clare's feelings about editorial intervention. See Zachary Leader, *Revision and Romantic Authorship* (Oxford: Clarendon, 1996), pp. 206–61.
30. Ibid., pp. 221, 227.
31. Ibid., p. 226.
32. Ibid., p. 231.
33. Ibid., pp. 164–5.
34. Ibid., p. 167.
35. Ibid., p. 87.
36. Ibid., p. 88.
37. Ibid., pp. 103, 157–8.
38. Ibid., p. 129.
39. Ibid., p. 131.
40. Ibid., p. 127.
41. Ibid., pp. 168, 171.
42. 'Alec Drummond', *Spectator*, 42 (23 January 1869), 111–12 (111); 'Belles Lettres', *Westminster Review*, 91 (1869), 570–2 (571).
43. Frederick Martin, *The Story of Alec Drummond, of the 17th Lancers*, 3 vols. (London: Chapman and Hall, 1869), I, pp. 185, 242, 244; hereafter *Alec Drummond*.
44. *Spectator*, 42, p. 112.
45. *Alec Drummond*, II, pp. 1–3.
46. See, for example, *Life*, p. 8 and Martin's account of Granny Bains.
47. *Life*, p. 295.
48. *Alec Drummond*, II, pp. 122–3.
49. An example of the elaborate synthesis of these ideals is conveyed in a courtship episode involving Alec's hard-drinking friend Mike. Alec awakens from several days' illness to find his abrasive friend 'an altered being', earnestly helping a German girl in the fields and supplementing her English with a Sir Walter Scott novel (III, pp. 179–81). Alec helps Mike acquire some German in ensuing weeks, yet Mike remains too awestruck to propose marriage; the solution is to have Mike memorize 'a German translation of one of Burns's ballads' (III, p. 187). Readers know from Martin's chapter epigraph that this will be 'My luve's like a red, red rose'. Accordingly, a Christmas party is capped by the singing of 'old German ballads', Mike's recitation of the Burns poem (provided for us in German), and the long-awaited marriage proposal. Mike's rehabilitation from rowdy soldier to

pastoral homebody is thus certified by the Scottish acid-test of cross-cultural and cross-class literacy.
50. *Bookseller*, 72 (31 December 1863), p. 993.
51. 'Preface to the First Edition', *Statesman's Year-Book*, II (1865), p. v.
52. *Spectator*, 42, p. 112.
53. Martin to Macmillan, 6 April 1870. BL Add MS 55042. Implicit here and elsewhere is that Martin had to shoulder various clerical and administrative costs in exchange for a share of *Year-Book* profits.
54. Ibid., Martin to Macmillan, 6 April 1870.
55. Ibid., Martin to Macmillan, 11 October 1870.
56. Ibid., Martin to Macmillan, 20 April 1870.
57. Ibid., Martin to Macmillan, 11 July 1870.
58. Ibid., Martin to Macmillan, 26 November 1870.
59. Surviving letters indicate that Martin eventually signed a new contract, probably in early 1872. This guaranteed him £150, rather than £100, but by 1874 he was again questioning its terms in argumentative letters with Craik and claiming that he was being denied large amounts of salary due him. See Martin to Craik, 19 November 1874. BL Add MS 55042.
60. Martin to Macmillan, 2 November 1874. BL Add MS 55042.
61. Ibid., Martin to Macmillan, 30 October 1874.
62. Information on the *Brighton Magazine* is scarce; for possible bibliographic detail see *Catalogue of the Printed Books in the Library of the British Museum*, vol. 38, pt. 1 (London: British Museum, 1885). The single issue of *The Biographical Magazine* was published in June 1877 by Trübner and Co., London.
63. Quoted in Kaplan, *Thomas Carlyle*, p. 546. Kaplan notes that Carlyle's niece Mary 'admitted that she could "see that the article ... is written in no malicious spirit"' (p. 545).
64. For discussion of Martin's attempt to raise cash in the 1870s by selling William Hilton's portrait of Clare, which he had bought at auction in 1865, see my 'John Clare, William Hilton, and the National Portrait Gallery', *JCSJ*, 32 (2013), 5–25.
65. Steinberg, p. 160.
66. The evidence indicates that Macmillan had directly enlisted William Henry Smith, then first Lord of the Admiralty, to lobby Disraeli on the pension. Smith is famously remembered as the founder of the W. H. Smith bookseller business. See the Macmillan letters of 31 January and 10 April, 1879 in BL Add MS 55042.
67. Martin to Macmillan, 12 January 1882. BL Add MS 55042. The transcription here and in the two references immediately following have been generously provided by Alysoun Sanders, archivist of Palgrave Macmillan, and are taken from the notes of S. H. Steinberg housed in the Macmillan archive.
68. Ibid., Martin to Macmillan, 4 July 1882.
69. Ibid., Martin to Macmillan, 12 October 1882.

70. *Autobiography: Memories and Experiences of Moncure Daniel Conway*, 2 vols. (Boston: Houghton, Mifflin and Co., 1904), II, pp. 407–8. Martin lived at 22 Lady Margaret Road, Kentish Town.
71. Ibid., pp. 408–9.
72. Conway, II, p. 408.
73. *Life*, p. 137.
74. Ibid., p. 160.

CHAPTER 7

John Clare's deaths: poverty, education and poetry

Simon Kövesi

John Clare's access to education was dependent on the death of two of his siblings. By his own account, that his parents had a 'small family' of four children meant that Clare's mother could sustain her 'hopfull ambition ... of being able to make me a good scholar'.[1] From birth, Clare was marked out as the child most likely to die:

> in my early years I was of a waukly constitution, so much so that my mother often told me she never coud have dreamed I shoud live to make a man, while the sister that was born with me being a twin was as much to the contrary a fine livley bonny wench whose turn it was to die first for she livd but a few weeks[2]

It is no surprise that two of Clare's siblings died in infancy; Clare grew up in a period when 'up to two out of every five infants died before they reached their fifth year', as Roy Porter surmises.[3] If the death of a twin sister and another sibling freed the Clare family enough to support the boy's learning, poverty stymied such plans and meant that Clare repeatedly had to work alongside his father in the fields. Yet Clare would have it that the persistence of his mother to invest in her boy's education won out even if, paradoxically, she is described by her son as having 'beleved the higher parts of learning was the blackest arts of witchcraft and that no other means coud attain them'.[4] Suspicion of education is characteristic of inhabitants of Helpston, Clare implies. Many thought Clare's learning a 'folly', and his scholarly habits 'crazd' or even 'criminal'.[5] In his 'Sketches', Clare reinforces the precariousness of his education's existence, in the context of rural poverty, with its perennial threats of deprivation, destitution and death. Clare's health is a constant problem too:

> I my self was of a week const[i]tution and a severe indisposition keeping me from work for a twelvemonthe ran us in debt   we had back rents to make up, shoe bills, and Bakers etc etc   my fathers asistance was now disabled and the whole weight fell upon myself ... my indisposition, (for I cannot

call it illness) origionated in fainting fits, the cause of which I always imagined came from seeing when I was younger a man name Thomas Drake after he had fell off a load of hay and broke his neck the gastly palness of death struck such a terror on me that I coud not forget it for years and my dreams was constantly wanderings in church yards, digging graves, seeing spirits in charnel houses etc etc   in my fits I swooned away without a struggle and felt nothing more then if I'd been in a dreamless sleep after I came to my self but I was always warnd of their coming by a chillness and dithering that seemd to creep from ones toe ends till it got up to ones head, when I turnd sensless and fell; sparks as if fire often flashd from my eyes or seemd to do so when I dropt, which I layd to the fall – these fits was stopt by a M[r] Arnold M.D. of Stamford ... tho every spring and autum since the accident happend my fears are agitated to an extreem degree and the dread of death involves me in a stupor of chilling indisposition as usual[6]

This gothic tale provides dramatic origins for Clare's psychological problems, compounded by ongoing physiological issues and their impact on his ability to earn money. Jonathan Bate considers this a fanciful passage,[7] yet its manner of presentation is central to Clare's understanding of his own psychological development: it is as if his subsequent mental life was blighted by post-traumatic stress disorder. This is the birth story of a prophet–poet, fire flashing from his eyes; he is a wild visionary, a super-sensitized madman whose gift of perception is born of trauma, and the macabre. Clare formulates a similar transformation in the poem 'First Love'. At a deathly moment, when the natural world is inverted as love overwhelms, poetry pours out: 'I could not see a single thing/Words from my eyes did start' (*Later Poems*, II, 677). The speaker is never the same again: shocked and transfigured. Clare extrapolates this experience beyond himself in an early poem, 'Lines Written While Viewing Some Remains of an Human Body in Lolham Lane' (*Early Poems*, I, 17–18), which speculates that the 'mangled remains' to which the poem bears witness might have been those of a genius poet, whom Clare worries might be forgotten. Fanciful indeed, visionary certainly, gothic perhaps – this is nevertheless a poetic journey founded in a gruesome, upsetting spectacle. In his 'Sketches' Clare says that being witness to this death at a formative age precipitated thoughts of monetising his secret poetic scribblings. Even at his most prophetic moments, even when thrown or disturbed, Clare exhibits a practicality, born of sheer material need.

Adulthood brings with it another bodily threat to Clare's existence, in which death is corporeally bound up with sexual desire. Displaying the impetuous honesty of a latter-day Rousseau, the 'Sketches' confess:

temptations were things that I rarely resisted   when the partiallity of the moment gave no time for reflection I was sure to seize it what ever might be the consequence . . . my easy nature, either in drinking or any thing else, was always ready to submit to persuasions of profligate companions who often led me into snares and laughd at me in the bargain when they had done so.   such times as at fairs, coaxed about to bad houses, those painted pills of poison, by whom many ungarded youths are hurried to destruction, like the ox to the slaughter house without knowing the danger that awaits them in the end – here not only my health but my life has often been on the eve of its sacrafice by an illness too well known, and to[o] disgusting to mention.[8]

Socialized into venereal disease, a holy fool led astray by the corruptions of male desire, Clare is brought close to death because of straightforward carnality. Whether Clare's self-diagnosis was right, or whether this story of brothel visits is the exaggerated product of a guilt-ridden hypochondriac, we might never know. Either way, Clare evidently considered such sexual experiences pivotal in determining his development.

To summarize, this prose autobiography locates two deathly contexts as being the catalysts for the poetic career of Clare – both of them traumatic: first, a reduced number of siblings frees up the money and the parental attention to provide him with foundational learning. Second, being witness to a corpse which had suffered a violent end leads to a 'dread of death' that stimulates a visionary capacity. The impairment of the fainting fits that follow in turn give practicable impetus to his desire to be a published poet, while uncontrolled sexual desire threatens to mortally and morally wound all of his plans for a public life. The poet's efforts are impelled by a desire to relieve the poverty of all around him, not least his parents, for whom his literary money (as he happily estimated it in 1821 at least) would act 'as recompense for the rough beginnings of life bid their tottering steps decline in peaceful tranquillity to their long home, the grave'.[9] Graves bookend this presentation of a fledgling literary life: from birth of a womb shared with a soon-dead twin, to poetry providing solace to the final destination of his parents. This frame of morbidity stuck with Clare; in the 1840s, for example, he wrote 'Infants are but cradles for the grave/& death the nurse as soon as life begins'.[10]

The 'Sketches' were sent to his publisher, John Taylor, on 3 April 1821 – though possibly not for publication.[11] At this time Clare anticipated that publishing would provide relief from the poverty he and his family had always endured. As it turned out, he was naïve in the extreme about how much money could be made from poetry. He could not know then that having peaked in 1820 – his first year on the London literary scene – poetry

John Clare's deaths: poverty, education and poetry 149

publishing was about to suffer a precipitous decline in fortunes.[12] It was the wrong time to start out as a poor poet.

Partly because none of his subsequent works sold better than the first of 1820, Clare's 'dread of death' would have good cause to stick with him for the rest of his life, leading to restless 'night fears'[13] and, possibly, to more serious debilitations in later years. As I have suggested, some of these deathly hauntings seem to be extensions of Clare's intense, even violent, apprehension of the world around him. But other manifestations of the threat of death are impersonal, imposed on Clare by a literary culture that – whether for commercial positioning or moralistic instruction – makes death the overriding context for the labouring-class poet. The desire to be a poet was meant to be fatal for someone like Clare, and so his story was readily and variously deployed as warning or rallying call for those who might follow him. This chapter will consider such responses to Clare from the beginnings of his career, through the stages of his impoverished obscurity, on to his presumed death, and, finally, to his actual death.

Clare's position as a poetic phenomenon became so overcast by the shadow of death that it seemed to negate the possibility of a literary estate or posthumous legacy. Indeed, if Romantic poetry is characterized by writers who gnaw away at their future reputations, at their posthumous remains, and at the transitory nature of fame, then, in this regard at least, Clare is quite typical.[14] But there are specific social and economic dimensions to Clare's situation which marked him out as being part of a distinct tradition. With hindsight, it is as if the doomed morbidity which grips the speaker of 'Resolution and Independence' leads directly to the social–poetic position of Clare, via the wobbly stepping stones of Chatterton, Burns, and, now, a trepidatious Wordsworth:

> I thought of Chatterton, the marvellous Boy,
> The sleepless Soul that perish'd in its pride;
> Of Him who walk'd in glory and in joy
> Behind his plough, upon the mountain side:
> By our own spirits are we deified;
> We Poets in our youth begin in gladness;
> But thereof comes in the end despondency and madness.[15]

Clare was deliberately pitched at this succession of poets which serves as a route map pre-determining how his work was to be received. From before Clare's time through to our own, poets and critics have loved a tale or backdrop of doom and death, of disparagement, failure and neglect,[16] as do publishers promoting their charges. And so it was for the way Clare was presented at the outset of his career. Here Taylor introduces Clare's first collection in 1820:

> [T]hough Poets in this country have seldom been fortunate men, yet he is, perhaps, the least favoured by circumstances, and the most destitute of friends, of any that ever existed ... One of our poets has gained great credit by his exterior delineations of what the poor man suffers; but in the reality of wretchedness, when "the iron enters into the soul," there is a tone which cannot be imitated. CLARE has here an unhappy advantage over other poets. The most miserable of them were not always wretched. Penury and disease were not constantly at their heels, nor was pauperism their only prospect. But he has no other, for the lot which has befallen his father, may, with too much reason, be looked forward to as his own portion.[17]

The poet who has been successful in his 'exterior delineations of what the poor man suffers' is Wordsworth. Poverty poetry is en vogue, and Taylor hopes this book will latch on to it. Yet even at this early stage, Clare is contradistinguished from the forerunner of rurally situated poetry about the poor: Clare is someone who lived the sort of impoverished life of the fields that other poets could describe only through 'exterior', if sympathetic, observations. Clare is said to live in depths and qualities of impoverishment that Wordsworth and his ilk – including Taylor's anticipated readership – simply could not fathom. It is almost as if Clare writes out of a different species of deprivation. He is a superman of poverty, being *'least favoured* by circumstances, and the *most destitute* of friends, *of any that ever existed*' (my italicized emphasis). Clare is *the* human abject, the *ur-*pauper, the poorest poet that ever did exist, sui generis. If other poets follow Thomas Gray to churchyards touristically to meditate on mortality and death, but then head off for a good dinner and a warm bath, here a pauper's grave is already dug for Clare. It is only a matter of time. The type of isolating threat that Taylor builds here will frame Clare's career, from the cradle of this first publication in 1820 to the graveyard of newspaper notices in 1864.

It would be a mistake to see this as a mere imposition – as Taylor tailoring Clare to fit a perceived market hunger for the rural original, for a 'genuine' voice of poverty. Taylor's sensitized sympathy for Clare's lot is a motivation which Taylor seems desperate to have replicated in the readership. Taylor's superlatives suggest that he is overwhelmed by Clare's circumstances – not that he is cold to them, or exploitative of them, as other critics and editors have variously implied.[18] If ravaging poverty and looming death together form a marketing construction Taylor deliberately intended, it is not without a rich source in Clare's own verse. Clare was fully aware that poverty threatened to shorten life brutally, abruptly. He frequently drew on the threat of death in his verse, in poems ranging from the paradoxical ('Invite to Eternity'), to the strangely celebratory ('The Soldiers Grave'), to the purely apocalyptic ('Song Last Day').

Even when he is idealizing his dream home in his youth, the ever-present pains of labour mean that Clare cannot entirely shake off dire portents.[19] 'The Wish' (*Early Poems*, I, 43–50) is structured around a conditional fantasy where the speaker considers the ideal dwelling that would 'free' him 'from all labouring strife' (line 3). Salivating over full cupboards, beneath a roof framed by 'british oak' (line 15), and topped with stone rather than thatch, '[b]ecause slate roofs will not so easily fire' (line 18), the speaker builds for himself a safe, warm, snug cottage, with 'books in eightvo size or more' (line 48), shelves to sit them on, shiny kitchenware, good views and an expansive garden described luxuriously here. Years later Clare would reduce woman to an emotional thing and exclude her from his posthumous green garden, imagining a heavenly world, 'where woman never smiled or wept' (*Later Poems*, I, 397, line 14) in the ever-prominent poem 'I Am'. Similarly, the young Clare cannot imagine a peaceful, labour-free home with a wife:

> With trifling in the garden now and then
> Which finds employment for the greatest men
> Each coming day the labour should renew
> And this is all the labour I would do,
> The other hours I'd spend in letterd ease
> To read or study just as that might please,
> This is the way my plan of life should be
> Unmaried Happy in Contentment free.
> For he that's pester'd with a noisey wife
> Can neer enjoy that quietnes of life
> That does to life belong—Therefore I'd ne'er
> Let Hymen's torch within my cot appear.
> For all domestic needs that did require
> Womans assistance—I'd a servant hire
>
> (*Early Poems*, I, 49, lines 208–21)

This is a poem all about a desire to avoid labour: even the effort of a domestic relationship seems a ludicrous and irrational burden for someone with serious writerly aspirations. But this is no monk's cell, no ascetic hermit's retreat. He knows well that literary pursuits depend upon a writer's domestic security – so he furnishes his home with a female servant.

Before we laugh, let's remember that the fantasy is not idle. This is a boy looking at his most likely future: a life of rural labour. 'The Wish' is driven by a desperate desire to escape the seeming doom, the certain pains, of a labourer's life which, other than poetry, is all he can see before him:

> My eyes shall wander oer
> A Pleasant prospect, Acres just threescore,
> And this the measure of my whole domains
> Should be divided into woods and plains,
> O'er the fair plains should roam a single cow
> For not one foot should ever want the plough
> This would be toiling so I'd never crave
> One single thing where labour makes a slave.
> Tho health from exercise is said to spring
> Foolhardy toil that health will never bring.
> But 'stead of health—dire ills a numerous train
> Will shed their torments with afflictive pain.
> Be as it will I hold in spite of strife
> That health ne'er rises from a labouring life ...
>
> (*Early Poems*, I, 48, lines 189–202)

This is as close as Clare gets to adopting the mantle of estate ownership in his work, to easing himself into the cosy position of a middle-class gentleman, albeit of modest means. And though modest, this dream was completely unrealizable. The capitalized 'Pleasant prospect' has the ring of a phrase lifted straight out of popular travel writing, or theorizations of the picturesque. The view afforded by the position of his 'domains' is to be a controlling one. But this project is explicit that its ambition is not aesthetic, but pragmatic: to secure his existence against the blunt realities of a labouring life – a future that intrudes suddenly here and throws the speaker back to a leaden mortality. In an early untitled stanza Clare talks of taking his 'corpse to work', and continues:

> Deuce take a labourers life thought I
>   They talk o slaves els where
> I sees much choice in foreighn parts
>   As I do in Slavery here   (*Early Poems*, I, 352, lines 5–8)

Similarly, a labouring life for the speaker of 'The Wish' means a miserable and painful route to an early death. He hopes instead for a 'single cow' and a female servant to milk it, while he watches from his perfectly positioned 'chamber window' (line 79). The jarring combination of poetry with labour is too painfully paradoxical to contemplate. There will be no ploughing here, and no plough-boy poets either.

John Clare's deaths: poverty, education and poetry

We now move two decades forward, to a less hopeful time for Clare. In 1840, Clare died, in the press at least.[20] His public career had begun dying long before, from 1827's sales failure of *The Shepherd's Calendar* through to the reduced appearance of *The Rural Muse* in 1835, his final book. With few facts to hand, the press took Clare's absence from the public scene to its next natural stage. Starting in the *Halifax Express*, and repeated in *The Times*, news of the poet's death rapidly spread across the nation in June of 1840. The curt line in *The Times* ran 'The poet Clare died some months ago at the Lunatic Asylum at York – *Halifax Express*'. This was repeated, often verbatim, in papers such as *The Morning Post, The Standard, The Northern Star and Leeds General Advertiser*, the *Hampshire Advertiser and Salisbury Guardian, The Examiner, The Belfast News-Letter, The Derby Mercury* and *Trewman's Exeter Flying Post or Plymouth and Cornish Advertiser*.[21] Clare's name still had enough currency to be reported across Britain.

Matthew Allen corrected the error in *The Times* and again, news spread nationally and rapidly.[22] Clare was alive, though poverty remained a threat, as Allen's letter attests:

> The Northamptonshire peasant poet, John Clare, is a patient in my establishment at Highbeach, and has been so since July, 1837. He is at present in excellent health, and looks very well, and is in mind, though full of very strange delusions, in a much more comfortable and happy state than he was when he first came. He was then exceedingly miserable, every instant bemoaning his poverty, and his mind did not appear so much lost and deranged as suspended in its movements by the oppressive and permanent state of anxiety, and fear, and vexation, produced by the excitement of excessive flattery at one time, and neglect at another, his extreme poverty and over exertion of body and mind, and no wonder that his feeble bodily frame, with his wonderful native powers of mind, was overcome.
>
> I had then not the slightest hesitation in saying that if a small pension could be obtained for him, he would have recovered instantly, and most probably remained well for life. I did all I could to obtain it for him, but without the slightest success. Indeed, some noblemen have withdrawn the pittance they allowed him, his wife, and family, and most are in arrears.

Allen grasped the opportunity to bring Clare back to the public consciousness, and at the end of the letter asks readers to donate to the poet's cause. Either we can think kindly, that Allen did this to help Clare find the financial stability that he thought was undermining the poet's mental health and that, previous to his admittance, had led to an incapacitating malnourishment; or we can think cynically, that Allen did this to help pay Clare's trustees' outstanding residential fees.[23] Clare's time with Allen has been considered widely,[24] so for our current purposes we will focus upon the manner in which the doctor repeatedly ties Clare's health to his dire poverty. What Allen wants to see is bills paid, and Clare in that same worry-free position he fantasized about when young in 'The Wish', albeit with the addition of a wife and seven children.

Allen's corrective note garnered widespread attention and led to the first substantial publication of Clare's work since 1835. An essay about Clare, including twenty new poems, appeared across two issues of the *English Journal* in May 1841.[25] The author Cyrus Redding, owner and editor of this Saturday weekly, set out his stall on the opening page of his first issue in January of the same year:

> Our object now is to mount a step higher, still catering for rich and poor alike, – for all who desire to store their minds with facts, and awaken the imagination to agreeable associations ... As the empire of letters under which the mind is cultivated constitutes a republic, so should its benefits belong to all and its fruits be equally and universally attainable. Knowledge is no heritage of a condition, but the certain reward of those who seriously labour in its pursuit ... It remains now that we become an intellectual and a thinking people, and that can only happen through the general cultivation of the intellect ... Those who are born to toil, may still find time to exercise thought, if their pursuits are merely mechanical, by employing the mind upon agreeable and useful subjects during the time of labour. Bloomfield was a remarkable instance of this, for he composed his "Farmer's Boy" while working at his trade with six or seven others.[26]

With social inclusiveness foremost of his aspirations, the first writer Redding mentions in his new publication is the shoemaker poet Bloomfield – the most significant English figure in shaping Clare's sense of a labouring-class poetic tradition.[27] The moderate yet progressive Redding leapt at the chance to interview a living Bloomfield in John Clare. It is not the aim here to consider Redding's account of his visit to High Beach, as this story has been told many times, and has even been novelized and dramatized.[28] Instead, working towards the theme of death, I will focus on a writer who knew Redding, who wrote to Bloomfield, whose work appears in the *English Journal*, and who might well have visited Epping Forest to see Clare, but who has mostly slipped under the radar of Clare scholars, receiving just a brief mention in the Tibbles' biography.[29]

Inspired by Redding's call to readers to donate generously to Clare, James Dacres Devlin published a poem in the *English Journal* in June 1841, which I reproduce with its footnote in full:

A REFLECTION

ON READING THE APPEAL IN BEHALF OF THE POET CLARE
IN THE " ENGLISH JOURNAL," MAY 15.
BY JAMES DEVLIN.

> ALAS, poor CLARE! and so it still hath been;
> And thou seem'st but another with the rest—
> A BURNS, a BLOOMFIELD, and the Boy unblessed,
> Who sought in Redcliffe's aisles his fears to screen,
> Doubtful to let the clever truth be seen,
> So played the fame-prank of a ghostly guest!
> And they, the spell-cursed of the Island Green;
> And he, with life and love alike oppressed:*
> These—aye, these—and others, through all times,
> And every place, have felt the trying doom—
> The want of solace—bread! the tear that grimes,
> The cruel fate, denying living room!
> We build the palace gaol to hold our crimes;
> At best, we give to Genius but a tomb!

* The cases of BURNS, BLOOMFIELD, and CHATTERTON, are of the familiar misfortunes of our knowledge. The world has already rung of the "Inspired ploughman," and of WORDSWORTH's "Sleepless Boy," and may yet hear more of the "Gentle GILES". BOYCE was of Ireland, and fell a victim to the bad taste of the age, when the flashes of intellect were constrained to administer to the destructive applause of the midnight wine-bibber: and DERMODY, also of Ireland—even in his childhood a prodigy—was thrown into the same desperate fascination. He lies buried at Lewisham, near Deptford, a plaintive verse, of his own composition, being scratched over the stone slab that covers the remains of the "Poet." The story of TANNAHILL, a native of Cumberland, is more isolated. The conjoined sweetness and earnest power of many of his lyrics have great interest. He was one of those, who, too sensitive and fervent for the many cares which gathered around him, felt the madness of the mind batter down his hopes; and, in a moment of melancholy desperation, drowned himself. The immediate cause, it is said, was love-disappointment. However gratifying it was to be sung of, as he sang of his charmer, still it was perilous to unite herself, inextricably, with the unsevering curse of poetry and poverty. She refused her hand, and *that* broke his heart. But CLARE! *he* still lives; and, what is more, there are those in his divided home, who alone live for him! and, if money can help, shall it not be given? Aye, even to the "penny of the poor!" At least, he shall have mine.[30]

Devlin the shoemaker reaches out to a fellow traveller, another 'hand-producer' as he labels himself,[31] in much the same way that Bloomfield did to Clare, and as Clare did to Allan Cunningham in turn.[32] Devlin follows

Wordsworth in building a succession of famous poets who have suffered for their art. In his footnote, Devlin extends Wordsworth's tradition with a number of other case studies of impoverished poets and details their neglect and deaths. Along with other poems, Devlin published a startling two-part essay on the poor in the *English Journal*, which is rare in its moving detail about how the poor lived, and in its quiet rage.[33] Under his pseudonym 'The Trialist' Devlin published a collection of poetry and prose in the late 1830s, while publications under his own name made him the foremost reformist voice in shoemaking.[34] Eric Hobsbawm and Joan Wallach Scott consider Devlin to have been 'the best craftsman in the London trade'.[35] Shoemaking was the most politically active of all trades in the nineteenth century and Devlin was a substantial figure at a crucial moment in Chartism.[36] Clare would have read Devlin's co-authored letter and poem to Bloomfield as it was included in an appendix of correspondence in the posthumously published *Remains* of 1824.[37]

Devlin wrote the first and only book-length poem dedicated to Clare published during his lifetime.[38] His imperatively entitled *Go to Epping!* was produced by the pre-eminent radical publisher in London, Effingham Wilson, a 'determined champion of a free press', leading publisher of the reformists, and pillar of the 'popular education movement'.[39] For the title, Devlin plays on the notoriety of the 'Epping Hunt' as having been an attractive 1820s pursuit for all manner of riff-raff from London – 'famous in the annals of *cockneyism*', as Pierce Egan puts it.[40] Indeed, so snootily downgraded did the Epping Hunt become, that in 1829 Thomas Hood published a popular, teasing account of it, his comic verse illustrated by George Cruikshank.[41] Hood had been central in the *London Magazine* scene, and Clare met him at Taylor's dinners.[42] Epping Forest had also been a location for boxing matches, a fact that cannot have been lost on Clare, who was reaching for masculine empowerment in 1841 through fantasies of prize-fighting as a Regency-period champion, Jack Randall, and through writing as one of the Fancy's most famous followers, Byron.[43] Randall served in the corner for a fight in Epping Forest during the Fancy's heyday.[44] By 1841, both hunting and boxing had long departed, leaving Devlin to play with cultural traces of Epping Forest's significance as a socially inclusive entertainment destination.

No longer extant in full, Devlin's poem surfaces only as fragments quoted in a review in the Chartist weekly *Cleave's Penny Gazette* in June 1841.[45] The reviewer feels sympathy for Clare, and, while charmed by the poem overall, is perturbed by Devlin's politicization of poverty:

It is of no great length, but there are many passages very far above average merit, possessing strength with sweetness, thought with melody, within its compass. Yet, as an exponent of the worldliness that pervades society, we would fain not wholly accord with its truthfulness in some particulars. We hope—trust earnestly, that the light of Poesy has yet power amid the "reckless money rout," and the thronged battle-field of Politics. We will quote lines, that for *their own sakes*, as poetry, are to us pleasing and forcible.

>   "Go to Epping! will you go?
>   Are you deaf, or blind, or lame?
>   There the forest trophies grow,
>   There abides the son of Fame!
>   Would you hear the blithe birds' gladness,
>   Would you see the Poet's sadness
>   Falling—fallen into madness!
>   Go—I bid you go!"

The reviewer quotes only this stanza and the following two which, together, at least give a sense of Devlin's political rage at what Clare's suffering symbolizes:

>   'Tis a feeling coarse, as cold
>   That nor worth nor beauty sees,
>   But as the hand may actual hold,
>   And never in these reveries.
>   Most mistaken—most deceiving,
>   Is this profitless believing;
>   There are truths of Fancy's weaving,
>   Firm as e'er was told!
>
>   Oh! If ever thou hast dwelt
>   On the wrong the Poet grieves;
>   Oh! If thou hast ever felt
>   What it is that so deceives;
>   If, like him, thou hast hope-striven,
>   Dreamt the dream that seem'd of Heaven,
>   Be the holy fault forgiven,
>   And in kindness melt!

This might not amount to memorable poetry in itself, though to give Devlin the benefit of the doubt, it is possible that the reviewer – given the gestures towards issues of taste – omits the most intriguing stanzas. I quote Devlin at length to illustrate just what Clare could mean to a fellow 'hand-producer' poet. Devlin wants 'the son of Fame', surrounded by 'forest trophies' (echoing the departed sports, perhaps?), to be a celebrated *living* tourist attraction; not a grave or sepulchre to visit, or literary curio, but instead a figure at the centre of a call for socio-economic change. Devlin uses his example – and the tradition of labouring-class poets' suffering – for a wider cause of improving the lot of the poor, though Clare never became an icon for the Chartists.[46] Pressingly, and more personally, Devlin is desperate to ensure that Clare does not succumb to the weight of poverty and deprivation, as had so many poor poets.

There is no record of Devlin visiting Clare at High Beach, nor of Clare reading the shoemaker's pamphlet poem. This was an especially complicated time for Clare, as he had Byron, Mary Joyce, Randall and escape on his mind. If anyone had followed up on Devlin's call, and had visited Epping Forest to meet Clare, they probably would have missed him. The pamphlet was published just a few weeks before Clare took leave of Allen's asylum, and left Epping for good, on his 'Journey Out of Essex', in July of that summer.[47]

From December 1841 until his death in 1864, Clare was committed to the Northampton General Lunatic Asylum. The successful writing partnership of husband and wife William and Mary Howitt visited him twice in the early 1840s.[48] While neither appears to have written about these visits, William did talk of it with dramatist, rural writer, and poet Mary Russell Mitford.[49] In 1850 she published her second-hand version of the visit:

> A few years ago he was visited by a friend of mine, himself a poet of the people, who gave me a most interesting account of the then state of his intellect. His delusions were at that time very singular in their character. Whatever he read, whatever recurred to him from his former reading, or happened to be mentioned in conversation, became impressed on his mind as a thing that he had witnessed and acted in. My friend was struck with a narrative of the execution of Charles the First, recounted by Clare, as a transaction that occurred yesterday, and of which he was an eye-witness, – a narrative the most graphic and minute, with an accuracy as to costume and manners far exceeding what would probably have been at his command if sane ... Or he would relate the battle of the Nile, and the death of Lord Nelson with the same perfect keeping, especially as to seamanship, fancying himself one of the sailors who had been in the action, and dealing out nautical phrases with admirable exactness and accuracy, although it is doubtful if he ever saw the sea in his life.[50]

Mitford's version of William Howitt's July 1844 visit constructs a Clare who is out of time, and dislocated. His madness is modelled on a collapsing of fact with fiction, past with present; the sad life of the enclosed asylum in which the stories are related, contrasted with the exciting lives of the historically magnificent and unbounded. His poetic sensibility is evoked in the remnants of an ability to tell stories with an apparently insanity-proving amount of 'accuracy'. History and fantasy spill into each other, and we are to believe that Clare as a controlling subject is lost. It is instructive that Clare's stories are about glorious deaths. He plucks two male figures from distant ends of English history: meritocratic and monarchic, long distant and relatively recent – yet both figureheads, and figurations, of a nation in dire trouble. The end of these two lives were to become state-quaking moments, no matter what side of the Napoleonic or Civil wars was adopted by the teller. These popular, heroic stories of geographic extensiveness are contrasted by Mitford with observations of the teller's supposedly limited horizons. Whether Clare appreciated that his own death was likely to be less monumental than a King's or a Vice Admiral's, some twenty years before he was to die in that same asylum, is unknowable. The overall effect is pathetic: lives lost in the eye of historical storms, aped by a life lived as if plucked out of history altogether; the remembered, heroic dead, contrasted with the forgotten poet, presumed by many to be long dead, but who clings onto these tales of monumental men with an eye-witness's breathlessness. The disenfranchised, de-historicized, parochialized poet reaches desperately for security in stories of masculine power, of international consequence. The Romantic poets' concerns about fame and their longevity in the memories of future generations runs wildly, excitedly in Clare, and latches onto characters whose fame is certain to be everlasting.

Mitford asserts that Clare is the lucky beneficiary of 'the triumph of humanity and of science in the present day' that is the liberal asylum.[51] She uses Clare's example to mount an impassioned warning to peasants and their putative patrons:

> We cannot, I repeat, do too much for John Clare; he has a claim to it as a man of genius suffering under the severest visitation of Providence. But let us beware of indulging ourselves by encouraging the class of pseudo-peasant poets who spring up on every side, and are amongst the most pitiable objects in creation. One knows them by sight upon the pathway, from their appearance of vagrant misery, – an appearance arising from the sense of injustice and of oppression under which they suffer, the powerless feeling that they have claims which the whole world refuses to acknowledge, a perpetual and growing sense of injury. It is a worse insanity than John Clare's, and one for which there is no asylum. Victims to their own daydreams, are they! They have heard of Burns and of Chatterton; they have a certain knack of rhyming, although even that is by no means necessary to such a delusion; they find an audience whom their intense faith in their own

power conspires to delude; and their quiet, their content, their every prospect is ruined for ever. It is this honest and unconquerable persuasion of their own genius that makes it impossible to reason with or convince them. Their faith in their own powers – their racking sense of the injustice of all about them, makes one's heart ache. It is impossible for the sternest or the sturdiest teller of painful truths to disenchant them, and the consequence is as obvious as it is miserable ... They believe poetry to be their work, and they will do no other. Then comes utter poverty. They haunt the ale-house, they drink, they sicken, they starve. I have known many such.

Happily there is one cure, not for individual cases, but for the entire class; a slow but a sure remedy ... Education, wide and general, not mere learning to read, but making discreet and wise use of the power, and the nuisance will be abated at once and for ever. Let our peasants become as intelligent as our artisans, and we shall have no more prodigies, no more martyrs.[52]

The deluded peasant poet is doomed from the outset, and is disabled by the social and educational over-reach of his self-displacement. Aggrandized by himself and the fawning of others into a permanent state of embittered social awkwardness and inherent humiliation, the peasant poet is the product not of intermittent oases of literacy, but of a piecemeal, threadbare approach to the democracy of education. Presumably if her readers were as roundly educated as Mitford herself, they too would recognize these 'vagrant' interlopers – not just by their destitution and hunger, but also by their air of benighted grievance.

Mitford's logic takes her to a principled role for educational reform, which would have a levelling effect in raising the peasant onto a utilizable platform of pragmatic, empowering and fecund literacy and understanding, which is opposed to the barren plains of inappropriate poetic aspiration. The end result of such reform, inspired negatively by Clare's example, would be that the newly level-headed working-classes would forego poetic musings altogether.

For our conclusion, we now turn to a posthumous assessment of Clare, published in October 1864, by which time the news of Clare's actual death on 20 May had circulated nationally.[53] Clare's story is again deployed as a warning, but here is steered to say something about English society. The obituary in the Saturday supplement to the *Manchester Weekly Times* celebrates the life of a French poet called Jacques Jasmin, an Occitan or *langue d'Oc* poet who died that same month. Jasmin was Clare's junior by five years, and for the anonymous writer, of comparable social stock:

> The life of the "last of the Troubadours" certainly forms a remarkable story, and the more remarkable if we contrast it with a similar life in our own country which came to an end not many months ago, John Clare, the

peasant-poet of Northamptonshire, who died last spring, was a "troubadour" fully as inspired by the divine gift of song as Jacques Jasmin. Like the latter, too, he was born in abject poverty; and like him he sang of trees and flowers and green fields, and the simple life of labourers and peasants, the lowliest of mankind. John Clare was born in 1793, and Jacques Jasmin in 1798; and the English minstrel came out with his first volume, "Rural Life", in 1818, while his French brother followed, in 1825, with "Mi cal mouri". So for the career of both poets alike, with the additional likeness that the success and fame of both came at once upon the first publication of their works. At this point, however, the lives of the English and of the French poet begin to differ widely, ending with the one in a madhouse and an obscure grave, and the other in a public funeral and proposed marble statue. There is something singularly characteristic of the two nations in the career of these two poets. John Clare, drawn overnight from utter obscurity, by an article in the "Quarterly Review," *feted* and praised by noble lords and ladies, and made a nine days' lion in the metropolis, found himself, after his sudden access of fame, never more at home behind the plough. While, on the other hand, his proud heart revolted against living upon what seemed to him charity, and, like a true poet, hating to exhibit his poetry and himself before gaping multitudes, he at the same time found the hard labours of the field too uncongenial for his mind and his delicate physical organisation, and before long fell a victim to these antagonistic elements. But see how Jacques Jasmin, the French Clare, gets out of this fatal struggle.[54]

What follows for the 'French Clare' is a story of state honours, money, parties and gifts, the full patronage of aristocracy and royalty, and a solidly decent professional life following Jasmin's literary success as the 'coiffeur' poet (the author gets some details of Jasmin's life factually wrong;[55] Gilchrist's *Quarterly* essay on Clare appeared in May 1820;[56] while Clare's first book was in fact published in 1820). This poet-barber did well financially and lived a long, healthy life – and the 'fervour of his poetry lost nothing from his daily unromantic avocation'. In Jasmin's example – and expressly not in Clare's – the author finds that 'there is nothing to show ... that true poetry will suffer from association with any trade or handicraft'. The author makes a firm point that in contrast to other countries, England neglects its poets, and always allows them to die in penury, no matter the riches they bestow upon society through the gift of their verse (John Wilson made exactly the same point when discussing Clare's lot in 1835[57]). The author is clear that England sees and allows – indeed, *expects* – a damaging disjuncture between social position, occupation and poetic writing. The 'French Clare' illustrates that this need not be so.

Clare was always the model of the fatally doomed poor poet, a warning to any who might follow, and a nationally-defining marker of how England treats its poets, and its poor. The 'hand-producer' tradition that enabled Clare to get a foothold in the literary world could be modelled in a noble fashion in the hands of a craftsman such as Devlin, who implores us to build a community of support and sympathy for Clare. But, far more commonly, the labouring-class poet was thought to be doomed and isolated at the outset. Certainly, a sense of inevitable tragedy dominated Clare's critical reception in life, while the assumption that he would always struggle with the jarring combination of poverty and poetry – of labour and literary culture – continued to inform his literary legacy and reputation following his death.

Notes

1. 'Sketches in the Life of John Clare', *By Himself*, p. 3.
2. Ibid., pp. 2–3.
3. Roy Porter, 'Medicine', *An Oxford Companion to the Romantic Age: British Culture 1776–1832*, ed. Iain McCalman (Oxford: Oxford University Press, 1999), pp. 170–7 (p. 171).
4. *By Himself*, p. 2.
5. Ibid., pp. 60, 78.
6. Ibid., pp. 18–19.
7. Bate, pp. 252–3.
8. *By Himself*, p. 29.
9. Ibid., p. 5.
10. My transcription of the first two lines of an untitled short-form Spenserian stanza, Nor. 19, p. 6. The Oxford editors date the poem to 1845 (*Later Poems*, I, 165), which year is part of the notebook's opening inscription. The notebook also contains two doodled references to the year '49' (Nor. 19, pp. 52, 115). No other possible year dating appears. Other references – to Eliza Cook (whose poems were published in 1845 and 1848) and Dowager Queen Adelaide (who died in 1849), for example – might situate at least some of the contents towards the end of the 1840s (pp. 24, 63).
11. See Bate, p. 222.
12. See Gary Dyer, *British Satire and the Politics of Style, 1789–1832* (Cambridge: Cambridge University Press, 1997), pp. 139–42.
13. *By Himself*, p. 45.
14. For excellent considerations of death and Romanticism, see Andrew Bennett, *Romantic Poets and the Culture of Posterity* (Cambridge: Cambridge University Press, 1999), and Paul Westover, *Necromanticism: Travelling to Meet the Dead, 1750–1860* (Palgrave Macmillan: Basingstoke and New York, 2012).

15. William Wordsworth, 'Resolution and Independence', *Poems in Two Volumes*, 2 vols. (London: Longman, Hurst, Rees and Orme, 1807), 1, p. 92 (no line numbers).
16. Critics constantly complain about the neglect of Clare. For the latest contribution see John Dugdale, 'Week in Books', *Guardian*, Review section, 17 May 2014, p. 5.
17. John Taylor, 'Introduction', *Poems Descriptive of Rural Life and Scenery* (London: Taylor and Hessey, 1820), pp. 7, 9.
18. Correctives to versions of Taylor's supposed bad faith are offered by: Zachary Leader, *Revision and Romantic Authorship* (Oxford: Oxford University Press, 1996), pp. 206–61; Sales, especially pp. 66–75; Bate, especially pp. 563–75; Tim Chilcott, *A Publisher and His Circle: The Life and Work of John Taylor, Keats's Publisher* (London: Routledge and Kegan Paul, 1972), and *The Shepherd's Calendar: Manuscript and Published Version*, ed. Tim Chilcott (Manchester: Carcanet, 2006), pp. vii–xxviii.
19. See the headnote to 'The Wish', *Early Poems*, I, p. 43, and *Letters*, p. 431.
20. A brief account of this death notice is used as the springboard for a fine analysis of fame by Jason N. Goldsmith in 'The Promiscuity of Print: John Clare's "Don Juan" and the Culture of Romantic Celebrity', *Studies in English Literature, 1500–1900*, 'Nineteenth Century', 46.4 (Autumn, 2006), 803–32 (803–4).
21. *The Times*, 17 June 1840, p. 5. News of Clare's death appeared in *Morning Post*, 16 June 1840, p. 5, and 17 June 1840, p. 3; *Standard*, 16 June 1840, p. 2; *Northern Star and Leeds General Advertiser*, 20 June 1840, p. 8; *Hampshire Advertiser and Salisbury Guardian*, 20 June 1840, p. 4; London's *Examiner*, 21 June 1840, p. 398; *Belfast News-Letter*, 23 June 1840, p. 4; *Derby Mercury*, 24 June 1840, p. 1; *Trewman's Exeter Flying Post or Plymouth and Cornish Advertiser*, 25 June 1840, p. 4.
22. Allen's letter was published in *The Times*, 23 June 1840, p. 5. Corrective notes, some quoting Allen's letter at length, were published in papers like the *Leeds Mercury*, 27 June 1840, p. 7; *Hampshire Advertiser & Salisbury Guardian*, 27 June 1840, p. 4; London's *Morning Post*, 24 June 1840, p. 1; *Bradford Observer*, 25 June 1840, p. 3; *Glamorgan, Monmouth and Brecon Gazette and Merthyr Guardian*, 4 July 1840, p. 4; Edinburgh's *Caledonian Mercury*, 4 July 1840, p. 2.
23. From first admittance in 1837, Allen thought Clare was suffering from malnourishment brought on by poverty, and that hunger combined with anxiety over poverty were the root causes of his debilitation. See Pamela Faithfull, *An Evaluation of An Eccentric: Matthew Allen MD, Chemical Philosopher, Phrenologist, Pedagogue and Mad-Doctor, 1783–1845* (University of Sheffield: PhD Thesis, 2001), pp. 173–88.
24. On Allen, see Faithfull, op. cit.; Tibbles (1972), pp. 337–40; Valerie Pedlar, '"No place like home": Reconsidering Matthew Allen and his "Mild System" of Treatment', *JCSJ*, 13 (1994), 41–57; Sales, pp. 126–9; Bate, pp. 421–50.
25. *English Journal*, 1.20 (15 May 1841), 305–9 and 1.22 (29 May 1841), 340–3.

26. Cyrus Redding, 'A Word or Two with the Readers', *English Journal*, 1.1 (2 January 1841), 1–3 (1–2).
27. For an analysis of the significance of Bloomfield to Clare, see John Goodridge, *John Clare and Community* (Cambridge: Cambridge University Press, 2013), pp. 83–101, and Mina Gorji, 'Burying Bloomfield: Poetical Remains and "the Unlettered Muse"', in *Robert Bloomfield: Lyric, Class, and the Romantic Canon*, ed. Simon White, John Goodridge and Bridget Keegan (Lewisburg, PA: Bucknell University Press, 2006), pp. 232–52. For the tradition of labouring-class poetry in relation to Clare, see Bridget Keegan, *British Labouring-Class Nature Poetry, 1730–1837* (Basingstoke and New York: Palgrave Macmillan, 2008), pp. 148–71.
28. Patrick Stewart played Redding in a BBC1 programme broadcast on 8 February 1970, starring Freddie Jones as Clare. An account of Redding appears in Bate, pp. 438–41, while High Beach is central to Adam Foulds' novel *The Quickening Maze* (London: Random House, 2009).
29. The Tibbles write: 'The Appeal was commended to the public by Cyrus Redding in two articles in the English Journal … by James Devlin in the same, and by an unknown in a collection of verse entitled *Poetry*, 1841.' Tibbles (1972), p. 342. This could be *'Go to Epping!'*.
30. This is the second of two Devlin sonnets in this issue. *English Journal*, 1.23 (5 June 1841), 368.
31. The first part of Devlin's essay in the *English Journal* carries the title and authorship of 'The Trialist; or, Head-Attempts. By a Hand-Producer. A New Beginning with an Old Name', *English Journal*, 1.13 (27 March 1841), 204–5.
32. *Letters*, p. 302.
33. 'The Condition of the Poor, and their Claims', *English Journal*, 1.19 (8 May 1841), 294–6. This continues on from the 27 March essay. Devlin's brilliant work forms a consciousness-raising platform for the reception of part one of Redding's Clare coverage the following week. It was an expanded version of 'Considerations in Behalf of the Poor', *The Trialist: A Series of Attempts at Prose Composition, by One of the Operative Class* (Dover: printed for the author, 1836), pp. 97–102. This collection, on diverse matters, is interspersed with Devlin's poetry.
34. Devlin's trade-based books include *The Guide to Trade: The Shoemaker*, 2 vols. (London, 1839), *The Shoemaker, Part II* (London, 1841), *Critica Crispiana: Or, The Boots and Shoes, British and Foreign, of the Great Exhibition* (London: Houlston and Stoneman, 1852). He became increasingly reformist, as shown by the long titles of *Strangers' Homes; or, the Model lodging houses of London described and recommended, as an example of what ought to be done … for the stranger work-seeker in general; but especially as regards the humbler class of emigrants* (London: Trelawney W. Saunders, 1853) and *Contract Reform: Its Necessity Shewn in Respect to the Shoemaker, Soldier, Sailor* (London: E. Stanford, 1856).
35. E. J. Hobsbawm and Joan Wallach Scott, 'Political Shoemakers', *Past and Present*, 89 (November 1980), 86–114 (107, n. 98).

36. See David Goodway, *London Chartism: 1838–1848* (Cambridge: Cambridge University Press, 1982), pp. 159–69.
37. *The Remains of Robert Bloomfield*, 2 vols. (London: Baldwin, Cradock and Joy, 1824), I, pp. 164–6. A letter and poem of 12 June 1820 are included, addressed to Bloomfield by shoemakers Devlin and John O'Neill, and announcing their forthcoming poetry collection (untraced). Another recorded letter was sent to Lady Morgan in 1828. Morgan records an occupation-based response to Devlin's aspirations: 'What a contrast between the humble confidence that he can make good boots and shoes for gentlemen and the "fortitude from despair" with which he wrote his bad poetry! Oh! why will not every one find out his "last" and stick to it.' *Lady Morgan's Memoirs*, ed. W. H. Dixon, 2 vols., 2nd edn. (London: Wm. Allen, 1863), 2, pp. 264–5 (264).
38. A collection of poems to Clare was edited by John Lucas: *For John Clare: An Anthology of Verse* (Helpston: John Clare Society, 1997). Devlin is not included.
39. Laurence Worms, 'Wilson, Effingham (1785–1868)', *Oxford Dictionary of National Biography* (Oxford: Oxford University Press, 2004): www.oxforddnb.com.oxfordbrookes.idm.oclc.org/view/article/38136. Accessed 27 September 2014.
40. *Pierce Egan's Anecdotes of the Turf, the Chase, the Ring, and the Stage* (London: Knight and Lacey, 1827), p. 3.
41. Thomas Hood, *The Epping Hunt* (London: Charles Tilt, 1829).
42. See Bate, p. 240, and Simon Kövesi, 'John Hamilton Reynolds, John Clare and *The London Magazine*', *Wordsworth Circle*, 42.3 (Summer 2011), 226–35.
43. See Kasia Boddy, *Boxing: A Cultural History* (London: Reaktion Books, 2008), especially pp. 49–75, Tom Bates, 'John Clare and "Boximania"', *JCSJ*, 13 (1994), 5–17, and Bate, p. 438.
44. Epping Forest was revived as a boxing venue in 1816. *The Sporting Magazine* reports a succession of 'second rate' bouts in 1808 (XXXI.185, p. 265), while Egan recounts two fights near Ilford on 5 December 1816, including 'The Bow Boy' Jem Bunn who fought a sailor seconded by Randall. *Boxiana; or Sketches of Ancient and Modern Pugilism*, 5 vols. (London: Sherwood, Neely, and Jones, 1829), II, pp. 380–1 and 479. London's *Morning Chronicle* reports on these fights too: the occasion was a 'renewal of the sports in the pugilistic ring' at this location (6 December 1816, p. 3). Ilford is eight miles from High Beach.
45. Anonymous, 'Sights of Books', *Cleave's Penny Gazette of Variety and Amusement*, 26 June 1841, p. 3. The publication itself is currently lost: J. Devlin, *Go to Epping!* (London: Effingham Wilson, 1841). *Go to Epping!* is also noted as having been received by *The Spectator*, 5 June 1841, p. 547.
46. Sales is the only scholar to consider Clare in a Chartist context: the movement led to a general suspicion of working-class poetry, following Thomas Carlyle's lead especially. Sales, pp. 76–101.
47. See Tim Chilcott's *John Clare: The Living Year 1841* (Nottingham: Trent Editions, 1999).
48. *Letters*, p. 659 and n. 2.

49. See Tibbles (1972), p. 375. Both Howitts are mentioned by Devlin at the start of each part of his essay on the poor in the *English Journal* (op. cit.), while a 'country story' by Mitford is the first piece (after Redding's introduction) in the first issue, 1.1 (2 January 1841), 3–6. In the same year as his first visit to Clare, William Howitt jokingly claims that Clare was driven insane by the proliferation of police (which Howitt is against): 'it is the day of the rural police. John Clare got a glimpse of them, and it operated, as it must do on all poets—it drove him mad, and he took to an asylum'. *German Experiences: Addressed to the English; Both Stayers at Home and Goers Abroad* (London: Longman, 1844), p. 113.
50. Mary Russell Mitford, 'Readings of Poetry Old and New: Peasant Poets—John Clare', *The Ladies Companion*, V.38 (7 September 1850), 163–6 (165). This essay was included in Mitford's *Recollections of a Literary Life; Or, Books, Places, and People*, 2nd edn., 2 vols. (London: Richard Bentley, 1857), vol. 2, pp. 147–62 (first published 1852).
51. Mitford, 'Readings ... ', 165.
52. Ibid., 165–6.
53. The *Cambridge Independent* and *Northampton Mercury* are often credited as original sources for the story of Clare's death, announced in papers such as: *Birmingham Daily Post*, 30 May 1864, p. 3; *Leeds Mercury*, 30 May 1864, p. 4; London's *Daily News*, 30 May 1864, p. 5; London's *Standard*, 30 May 1864, p. 3; *Dundee Courier & Argus*, 31 May 1864, p. 3; *Sheffield & Rotherham Independent*, 31 May 1864, p. 3; *Essex Standard and General Advertiser for the Eastern Counties*, 3 June 1864, p. 4; *Hull Packet and East Riding Times*, 3 June 1864, p. 5; *Newcastle Courant*, 3 June 1864, p. 3; *Huddersfield Chronicle and West Yorkshire Advertiser*, 4 June 1864, p. 9; *London Examiner*, 4 June 1864, p. 366; *Leicester Chronicle*, 4 June 1864, p. 6; *Manchester Weekly Times: Supplement*, 11 June 1864, p. 8.
54. *Manchester Weekly Times: Supplement*, 22 October 1864, p. 339.
55. For correctives, see Samuel Smiles' biography, *Jasmin: Barber, Poet, Philanthropist* (London: John Murray, 1891).
56. *Critical Heritage*, pp. 94–100.
57. Taylor thought Wilson's (Christopher North's) 1835 *Blackwood's Edinburgh Magazine* review of *The Rural Muse* a 'very poor one' when he sent it to Clare (*Letters*, p. 628, n. 2). Wilson defended Scotland's supposed neglect of Burns by pointing to England's neglect of Bloomfield – with Clare caught unhappily in Wilson's cross-fire. 'England', Wilson writes, 'never had a Burns. We cannot know how she would have treated him – had he "walked in glory and in joy upon her mountain-sides." But we do know how she treated her Bloomfield. She let him starve' (*Critical Heritage*, p. 237).

PART III
Community

CHAPTER 8

John Clare's natural history

Robert Heyes

John Clare had a distinctive vision of the natural world and it is, at some level, impossible wholly to account for it. Some of the contributory factors can, however, be identified. One was his early training as a gardener, first in the gardens at Burghley House, then working at Newark, a centre of the horticultural trade in the early nineteenth century. The education of a gardener was thorough and far-reaching, and included botany and other branches of agricultural science. Clare's education was greatly furthered by those in his locality who shared his interests, perhaps most importantly two of the staff at nearby Milton Hall: the house steward Edmund Artis, and the head gardener Joseph Henderson. Both men were skilled all-round naturalists, although they had their particular areas of expertise. One suspects, however, that their greatest service to Clare was in showing him that study of the natural world was a legitimate area of intellectual activity, not something of which he need feel ashamed, or carry out furtively. It is never difficult, in an English village, to become labelled as 'odd', something which Clare would have wanted to avoid. As well as furthering his education, his friendships involved him in much painstaking searching of the neighbourhood for specimens. He was not a collector himself – conditions in his little cottage would hardly have permitted that – but he collected enthusiastically for various friends; fossils, archaeological specimens, plants and birds' nests and eggs were gathered, and he learned how to capture and kill butterflies and moths and pin them out on cork.

In the years between 1823 and 1825, a series of events prompted Clare to consider publishing a natural history of his own. This chapter offers a new and fuller account of this project than has been produced before, employing manuscript evidence and correspondence in order to trace Clare's overlapping, shifting plans for possible publication. Scholarly understanding of Clare's work towards a natural history has largely been based on

Margaret Grainger's *The Natural History Prose Writings of John Clare* (1983). As important and original as Grainger's book was, its editorial presentation of Clare's writings on this topic – including his so-called Natural History Letters – gives a formal gloss to his efforts that often misrepresents the context in which they were produced. A reconstruction of the circumstances under which Clare began drafting prose on natural history gives us a revealing glimpse into his struggles to move forward professionally after the initial successes of *Poems Descriptive of Rural Life and Scenery* (1820) and *The Village Minstrel* (1821). These events also suggest that, in parallel, Clare's publishers, Taylor and Hessey, were themselves wondering about how Clare might be best utilized as a marketable author with expertise on rural subjects.

Clare's ambition to produce some sort of natural history work had its beginnings in July 1823 when Taylor and Hessey sent him a copy of an anonymous work they had just published, *Flora Domestica, or the Portable Flower-Garden; with Directions for the Treatment of Plants in Pots; and Illustrations from the Works of the Poets*. James Hessey's accompanying letter, dated 14 July 1823, began:

> My dear Clare
>
> I have waited till to day that I might send you a Copy of a pretty volume just published, (on a subject that will be interesting to you) in which your Name is honourably mentioned – You must add it to your Collection for our sakes if it is not worthy a place on your Shelves for its own. You have done as much as most poets towards the investing of Flowers with Interest and Sentiment & Imagination, and our friend has endeavoured to bring into one view the pleasant labours of your poetical Brethren and to raise the flowers of the Field to a rank which they deserve to hold – Should a second edition of it ever be required many additions might be made with advantage, and I dare say you could help us to many – If you should find any little beautiful passages in the course of your poetical reading you may as well mark them for us.[1]

Clare had not been to London for a year and, because the publishers had not previously mentioned the book in their correspondence, its appearance was a surprise. It will be noted that Hessey's letter had not revealed the identity of the author, so when Clare replied, as he did immediately, on 17 July 1823, he assumed the book was the work of a man; it was in fact written by Elizabeth Kent (1790–1861), a Brighton-born writer and botanist.[2] A work combining gardening and poetry had an obvious appeal for someone like Clare, with a horticultural training and a love of verse; he expressed pride and pleasure at being mentioned by the author, and offered some reflections on the volume.

> My dear Hessey
>
> I am so pleasd with the distinction of your making a present of the "Flora Domestica" to me that I have sat down to thank you for it directly ... I am pleasd with the mention the author has made of me & not only pleasd but gratifyd & proud of it I will make a few remarks while I am hot for I shall be soon cold perhaps how pretty is the allusion to poor Keats grave I like the plan of the thing uncommonly & I think a 2nd Edit: is certain when some improvements may as certainly be made ... I will somewhere or other mark what I read of flowers.

Clare made a number of detailed comments on the contents of the book, and in a postscript added: 'I had a deal more to say but my sheet is too short – I shall read the book seriously over & give you my remarks shortly'.[3] Taylor and Hessey seized the opportunity to reprint part of this letter in the *London Magazine* for August 1823, following a lengthy extract from *Flora Domestica* which was clearly intended to advertise the work.[4] Clare repeated his sentiments in a letter to Taylor of 31 July 1823, saying he was 'uncommonly pleasd' with the book,[5] then, in the postscript to an August letter to James Hessey, he indicated that he had kept his promise: 'I have offerd some remarks about the "Flora &c" but they are for you & not the author unless any hint would furnish him with improvement if so he is welcome'.[6] These 'remarks' were published by Margaret Grainger as 'Natural History Letter I' in the *Natural History Prose of John Clare*.[7]

There is no direct evidence that, at this time, the *Flora Domestica* was leading either Clare or his publishers to consider the idea that he might construct something in a similar vein. However, when Clare visited London a year later, between 20 May and 6 August 1824, a fairly definite idea emerged in discussions with Hessey. The outlines of this initial plan can best be grasped in retrospect, through a letter from Hessey to Clare written on 2 March 1825 that accompanied a copy of Elizabeth Kent's second book, *Sylvan Sketches*. By this time, of course, Clare had been made aware of the identity of the author. Hessey wrote:

> The Volume is a new one by the author of the Book on Flowers which you liked so much and I think it is even a pleasanter book than its predecessor. The author is now at a loss for a further subject. I mentioned to her the one

> we were talking of, "The Birds", under a Promise that she should not mention it nor take advantage of it, so long as you entertain any Idea of doing it yourself. I told her that you had thought of it and that I should immediately write to you on the subject. I think she would make a very pretty volume if she knows any thing about it already. But the Poets have not been quite so familiar with the Birds as with the Trees & Flowers. Let me hear from you soon & say whether you think you have materials enough at your Command to make up such a work, or if not, whether you would like to furnish your stock of Information to the lady author. and tell me how you like her Book of Trees.[8]

It is clear, then, that Clare had discussed with Hessey some sort of project on birds, evidently a work based on the plan which Miss Kent had adopted for *Flora Domestica*, and continued in *Sylvan Sketches*: prose description interspersed with verse chosen from the works of other poets. Given Clare's later fame as a poet of birds and their nests, it may seem curious that the men were contemplating a Clare-authored work that would feature his prose alongside the poetry of others. The immediate inference to draw is that Clare evidently perceived such a work as artistically respectable,[9] even as Hessey saw it as commercially viable. After the summer 1824 visit, Hessey was determined to capture whatever momentum he and Clare had generated. Writing on 20 August 1824, a fortnight after Clare had left London, he followed up their conversation by asking:

> Have you many swallows in your part of the Country, and do they leave you early? – I should suppose a flat country like yours must be full of Insects and that the Birds which feed on them must be very numerous Flies are I believe the chief food of the Swallow the Swift the Martin &c.[10]

Clare seems to have responded promptly; his reply is lost, but writing on 7 September 1824 Hessey began:

> My dear Clare
>
> I am much pleased with your Letter, and thank you for the information you have given me about the Swallows – the observations you have made agree in the main with my favorite White of Selborne who was a very minute observer of the various branches of the Swallow Tribe. Your Devil Martin is what we called the Swift – what a beautiful provision is that which you mention & which I have not seen elsewhere noted, the tuft of feathers for the protection of the eye of this rapid bird.[11]

These were not merely pleasant exchanges regarding a shared interest, but the beginnings of a cache of material. And though it seems that Hessey was actively working to urge Clare forward with writing, there is manuscript evidence that Clare too was thinking about the project in concrete terms. In Peterborough manuscript A46 there is a brief memorandum which has not, apparently, been noticed before, probably because Clare subsequently wrote over the top of it, largely obscuring it:

		Index to the "Letters on Natural History"	
1 Letter		On Swallows Martins &c	——————————— Sent
2 D°		On the Cuckoo & nightingale	——————— Sent
3 D°		[Further on] the song of the Nightingale the pleasure of studying nature with a poetical feeling &c[12]	

The lost letter which Hessey is acknowledging is '1 Letter' in this index (not to be confused with Grainger's printed 'Natural History Letter I'). Later in his response Hessey wrote: 'I shall be very glad to hear your Accounts of the nightingale',[13] so Clare had evidently promised him such an account. Hessey repeated his request in another letter four days later, on 11 September, saying:

> I shall be very glad to see your Account of the nightingale – Some man is making a Collection of all the Poems that have been written about it, and another is puzzling himself with doubts about the nightingales singing by day, and about the expression of his Notes whether they are grave or gay – what solemn trifling![14]

Clare's response seems to have crossed in the post with Hessey's most recent letter, and must be the one listed as '2 Letter' in Clare's index; again, the letter is lost.

The item listed as '3 Letter' is clearly the one whose draft is printed as 'Natural History Letter III' by Grainger.[15] This is a reply to Hessey's letter of 11 September, and is obviously a follow-up to an earlier letter on the cuckoo and nightingale, because Clare begins by saying: 'I forgot to say in my last that the Nightingale sung as common by day as night & as often'. Later in the draft he continues his previous comments on the cuckoo: 'As to the cuckoo I can give you no further tidings that what I have given in my last'. He then goes on to talk about how he loves to 'look on nature with a poetic feeling which magnifys the pleasure'. He lists 'favourite Poems & Poets who went to nature for their images', and discusses these. Finally, in a postscript, he says:

> P.S. I can scarcly believe the account which you mention at the end of your letter respecting the mans 'puzzling himself with doubts about the Nightingales singing by day & about the expression of his notes wether they are grave or gay' – you may well exclaim 'what solemn trifling' it betrays such ignorance that I can scarcely believe it – if the man does but go into any village solitude a few miles from London next may their varied music will soon put away his doubts of its singing by day – nay he may get rid of them now by asking any country clown the question for its such a common fact that all know of it – & as to the 'expression of its notes' if he has any knowledge of nature let him ask himself wether nature is in the habit of making such happy seeming songs for sorrow as that of the Nightingales – the poets indulgd in fancys but they did not wish that those matter of fact men the Naturalists shoud take them for facts upon their credit – What absurditys for a world that is said to get wiser & wiser every day
>
> – yours &c
> J. Clare

In Clare's Index the word 'Sent' is conspicuous by its absence after '3 Letter', and it is probable that this vehement, and rather lengthy, letter remained in draft form and was never sent. Certainly, there is nothing in Hessey's correspondence which would suggest he had received it, and he usually responded to Clare's letters. It is obvious from Clare's Journal, and from Hessey's letters, that Clare was very ill for a long time in the autumn of 1824; Hessey was passing on advice from Dr Darling of Russell Square, as well as Darling's prescriptions for assorted powders, pills and blisters. Writing to Edmund Artis around this time Clare said, in a postscript: 'I will look out some MS for Mrs Artis as promisd when I get more settld in health & temper for I can do nothing now excuse a short letter'.[16] Perhaps, then, the thought of copying out a long letter for Hessey was too much, and it was never sent, in spite of the warm reception the two earlier letters had received.

But there is also the possibility that Clare's commitment to the 'Birds' plan was waning. The emphasis of Clare's project seems to have changed and broadened at this time, as indicated by his Journal entry of 11 September 1824:

> Written an Essay today 'on the sexual system of plants' & began one on 'the Fungus tribe & on Mildew Blight &c' intended for 'A Natural History of Helpstone' in a Series of Letters to Hessey who will publish it when finishd I did not think it woud cause me such trouble or I should not have began it.[17]

Despite the very definite statements here – a new title with a rather different focus, and the claim of Hessey's commitment – there is no indication that Hessey was aware of this arrangement. By 24 October 1824, little more than a month later, yet another plan was taking shape, as Clare recorded in his Journal:

> lookd into 'Maddox on the culture of flowers' & the 'Flora Domestica' which with a few improvments & additions woud be one of the most entertaining books ever written – If I live I will write one on the same plan & call it a garden of wild Flowers as it shall contain nothing else with quotations from poets & others[18]

On 25 November 1824 Clare noted in his Journal that he had received a letter from Hessey, who asked for further information about birds in Clare's locality, saying he was anxious 'to know more about the snipes and the kingfishers and the lapwings, and the wild fowl of the fens & meres'.[19] Clare recorded in his Journal, on 20 January 1825, that he had written to Hessey; this letter, once more lost, must have contained further information on local birds because when Hessey replied, on 29 January, he said: 'I have asked many persons about your black pheasant-tailed Duck but cannot meet with any one who knows what it may be'.[20] A draft of this part of Clare's letter, entitled by him 'Ducks', and mentioning 'a beautiful black bird of the duck or diver kind ... with a long pheasant like tail', is to be found in Peterborough manuscript A46.[21]

It was on 2 March 1825 that Hessey wrote the letter quoted earlier, in which he spoke of 'The Birds', and of Miss Kent's thoughts of producing a volume on the same subject. At this point Clare seems to have approached his natural history project with renewed interest and vigour. Just over a week later, on 11 March, he recorded in his Journal: 'Intend to call my Natural History of Helpstone "Biographys of Birds & Flowers" with an Appendix on Animals & Insects'.[22] This new formulation was evidently conceived as a way to combine the disparate but related topics he had been thinking about. Moreover, he seems to have realized the need for assistance if he was ever going to get anywhere, because on the same day Joseph Henderson wrote a letter that shows that the two men had had discussions about a joint project:

> With respect to the Flora of this neighbourhood I cannot satisfy myself as to any plan, except the old one of Notes on the plants mentioned in your works, a mere catalogue of the plants found in the neighbourhood might easily be made out, but that would neither meet your views nor mine. I have been thinking that if you were to take as the subject & title of a poem

> The Poets Flower Garden you would lay the best foundation for the Scheme. The woods & the fields, where Nature is Gardener, would furnish your materials & in it you might embody all the local names you are acquainted with & when we make our long talked of excursion I shall perhaps be able to help you to others, I would even go so far as to coin a few, for there are many of our most beautiful wild flowers that have no familiar English name. On these & the plants mentioned in your works generally I would write Notes, giving the Botanical name & any other remark that might be thought interesting, which with your own observations might follow on as an appendix to your works. Let me know what you think of the plan in your nixt, & when you intend to come over & se us.[23]

The plan for a collaborative venture between Clare and Henderson to produce a flora of the neighbourhood is something that is not mentioned anywhere else, either in Henderson's letters or in Clare's letters and other manuscripts, yet it was obviously something the two men had discussed in detail. When Henderson says that he has been unable to satisfy himself 'as to any plan, except the old one' he implies that this was something they had talked about over a considerable period of time. Shortly afterwards a letter, dated 22 March 1825, arrived from Elizabeth Gilchrist in London, saying: 'I am sure it will do you good to be employed with Mr Artis in a "History of your favorite Birds, & Flowers'.[24] This shows that Clare had also tried, perhaps separately from his discussions with Henderson, to enlist the help of Edmund Artis in his project. Again this is the only evidence of Clare's proposal, and no more is heard of the projected collaborations with either of his friends.

A month later, on 18 April 1825, Clare wrote in his Journal: 'Resumed my letters on Natural History in good earnest & intend to get them finished with this year if I can get out into the fields for I will insert nothing but what comes or has come under my notice'.[25] Clare's resolve was short-lived, however. Less than three weeks later, on 5 May, writing to John Taylor, he said: 'I told Hessey that I was ready to join the Young Lady in writing the History of Birds'.[26]

Much has been written about the 'Natural History Letters' over the years, a great deal of it, one suspects, by people who have never had the opportunity of looking at them and who rely on the misleading accounts of them given by Grainger and others. In her edition of *The Natural History Prose Writings of John Clare* Grainger prints fourteen of these 'letters'. The first, which I have already mentioned, is in the Berg Collection and gives Clare's publishers his first reaction to *Flora Domestica*. What Grainger describes as Letter Ia is an incomplete draft letter to Taylor and Hessey giving his second thoughts; it is to be found in Northampton manuscript 34.[27] The twelve remaining 'Natural History Letters' are part of Peterborough manuscript A49.[28]

The first thing to be said about these letters is that they are not letters at all, but draft letters. There are many such among Clare's manuscripts, some more or less complete draft letters, others drafts of a part of a letter, sometimes only a few lines; on occasion, drafts of different parts of a letter can be found in different manuscripts. Some of these draft fragments were published by Mark Storey in *The Letters of John Clare*, but by no means all of them. This is hardly surprising because it is often unclear whether a particular piece of prose is a draft of part of a letter or was written for some other purpose. The piece on 'Ducks' referred to earlier is a case in point: if we did not have Hessey's reply, mentioning the 'black pheasant-tailed Duck', we would not know that this fragment was part of a letter. The so-called 'Natural History Letters' are simply drafts, mostly partial drafts, of various length. Each is written on a bifolium and it is clear that they are mainly drafts of letters, or at least of the beginnings of letters, because they have a gap of around an inch at the top of the first page to leave room for the place, date and greeting. The exception here is what Grainger calls 'Letter XIII', which is merely a collection of notes of various lengths. The note that she refers to as a letter is not even the first item on the bifolium, merely the longest; the other notes she prints separately as Notes N to AA.[29]

Since their conservation these manuscripts have been mounted in a guard book, but originally they were sewn together with other scraps, as was Clare's practice. Grainger suggests that Clare 'stitched the leaves together to form a book before, rather than after, writing'.[30] This cannot be so, however; most of them are folded in the manner of letters of the day, and the folds are soiled, suggesting they have been carried around in someone's pocket. It would be perverse to fold, and carry around, blank sheets until they were grubby, and then open them out, stitch them together and start writing on them. In her catalogue of the Peterborough Collection Margaret Grainger describes these 'letters' as being 'addressed to his publishers, Messrs. Taylor and Hessey, at 93 Fleet Street, London'.[31] In fact, only four of the 'letters' are so addressed; it has always been assumed that the remaining letters were intended for Taylor and Hessey,[32] but consideration of their contents shows that this is very unlikely.

None of the 'Natural History Letters' in A49 begins with a greeting of any sort, and so it is impossible to know who the intended reader was.

Letter III is obviously intended for James Hessey; the postscript of this letter is a clear response to Hessey's letter of 11 September 1824, as discussed earlier. Letters II and III are the only ones which are complete drafts, signed by Clare, and addressed to Taylor and Hessey; Letters VI and VIII are also addressed to them.

When we turn to Letter X, however, Clare says, near the beginning:

> I have been seriously & busily employd this last 3 weeks hunting Pooty shells & if you are not above them I must get you to assist me in the arangment or classification of them I have been making some drawings of them for you but they are so miserable that I must send the shells with them[33]

Taylor and Hessey were men of wide interests, but conchology was not, I think, among them, and it is doubtful whether they would have felt equal to the task of arranging and classifying Clare's snail shells for him. The obvious recipient of this letter would be Joseph Henderson, a collector of shells. The letter is headed simply 'Feb^y'; it was on 11 March 1825 that Henderson told Clare: 'I am very glad to find that you have taken up the Land-Shell's in good earnest'.[34] On 7 May 1825 Clare recorded in his Journal: 'Sent some Pootys & Ferns to Henderson yesterday',[35] and on 14 May 1825 Henderson wrote thanking Clare for the shells and saying: 'I have begun to clean & arrange them & I hope to present them to you under a new face when you come over, I have found out a new habitat of them, where I expect to find a number of new varieties'.[36]

Similarly, if we look at 'Natural History Letter XI', we find, near the beginning, Clare saying: 'you asked me a long while back to procure you a Nightingales nest & eggs & I have try'd every season since to find if the birdnesting boys have ever taken one out but I have not been able to procure one'.[37] It is difficult to imagine that either James Hessey or John Taylor had a burning desire to possess a nightingale's nest; nor, had he been able to find a nest, is it easy to picture Clare parcelling it up, carrying it to Market Deeping and putting it on the London coach. However, Joseph Henderson had asked Clare to collect eggs and nests for him, and he is a much more likely recipient of the letter.

Letter IX, which is dated unambiguously 'March 25th 1825', also has features which cast doubt on Taylor or Hessey as the intended reader. At one point Clare writes: 'I think I had the good luck today to hear the bird which you spoke of last March as singing early in spring & which you so apropriatly named the mock nightingale'.[38] Hessey did not ask Clare this in person because, although Clare was in London in 1824, he did not arrive until late May; nor is such an enquiry to be found in Hessey's letters. It is, in fact, very difficult to imagine someone like Hessey, who by his own admission had little knowledge of natural history, saying anything of the sort. Later in the letter Clare writes: 'you enquired last summer wether we had any plants indegenious to our neighbourhood',[39] again a query that is not in any of Hessey's letters.

Another possible recipient of some of these draft letters is Elizabeth Kent, who Clare tried variously to ignore, assist and collaborate with over a period of about a year between early 1825 and 1826. As we have seen, the original proposal for some sort of natural history project, as discussed between Clare and Hessey in 1824, was 'The Birds'. Clare was very active in 1824 and 1825 in seeking information on birds and recording his observations, well before any collaboration with Miss Kent was mooted. On 25 May 1825 Eliza Emmerson wrote to Clare saying: 'I am happy to find you are amusing yourself with writing a history of English Birds'.[40] This was when he compiled his most extensive bird list,[41] an enormously interesting list based on the anonymously authored *Natural History of Birds*, published in two volumes at Bungay in 1815;[42] all of Clare's page references in his list are to these two volumes. Clare's own copy of this work is dated 1831, so he must have borrowed a copy.[43]

A clue to another book which he seems to have borrowed is found in his Journal entry for 5 October 1824: 'In the "Times Telescope" they rechristend me Robert Clare there went the left wing of my fame'.[44] The issue of *Time's Telescope* to which Clare is referring, with its account of 'Robert Clare', is that for 1821.[45] There is no evidence that Clare ever owned this or any other issue of *Times Telescope*; the book was probably borrowed, and the most likely reason is that it contains a long introduction on 'The Elements of British Ornithology' (pp. xi–lxxxviii), accompanied by a handsome hand-coloured frontispiece showing seven species of British birds. Another work which Clare tried, apparently unsuccessfully, to borrow at this time was Thomas Bewick's *History of British Birds*; this is clear from Henderson's letter of 11 May 1825: 'I do not know any person who has got Bewicks Birds, there is a copy of it at the Book Society's liberary at Peterboro, but it could only be obtained through a member & I beleive even they are not allowed to lend them'.[46]

Clare's collaboration with Elizabeth Kent was sporadic but energetic. The letter indicating to Hessey that he was willing to work with Miss Kent has not survived, but Hessey replied on 10 May 1825, saying: 'I told Miss Kent, the author of Flora Domestica, of your readiness to communicate any of your knowledge to her and she has in consequence availed herself of your Permission to write to you – I enclose her letter in the Parcel.'[47]

On 14 May 1825, after receiving the parcel from his publishers containing the first letter from Elizabeth Kent, Clare wrote in his Journal: 'a Note also from Miss Kent accompanied the parcel to request my assistance to give her information for her intended History of Birds but if my assistance is not worth more then 12 lines it is worth nothing & I shall not interfere'.[48] Happily Clare relented, and recorded in his Journal on 13 August 1825: 'Went to Milton wrote a Letter to Miss Kent'.[49] On 19 September 1825 she replied with a long and friendly letter from Southampton which concluded: 'P.S. I shall enquire for the letters you mention, as soon as I return to town'.[50] These were, presumably, the handful of letters which Clare had written to James Hessey about birds.

Unfortunately, due to an oversight, Elizabeth Kent did not send this letter for four months. It was finally posted, with an accompanying note, on 19 January 1826:

> My Dear Sir
>
> Upon the receipt of your last letter, I answered it, <u>as I think</u>, immediately ... Judge of my vexation in finding it among a numb[er of] letters, which had hastily been cleared out of my desk. [If] you have had leisure to think of me at all, you must think [that] I make a poor return for your kind offers of assistance. Pray accept my apology.
>
> As I did not well remember what I had said in my letter, I opened it, thinking I might wish to add something. I have only this to add, a request that you will give me any information that may have fallen in your way, with regard to the <u>situation</u> in which the different species of Wren in this country, nestle. I feel convinced that I have seen one, which I take to be the Willow-Wren, visit its nest in a hole very high in the trunk of a tree; but this is contrary to the accounts given by the naturalists. If you can enlighten me on this subject, you will oblige, My Dear Sir,
>
> Y^{rs} Truly, E Kent.[51]

What is clearly a draft of Clare's reply to this request is the note on the willow wren (denoted Note T by Grainger) in Peterborough MS A46.[52] Much of the other natural history prose in that manuscript was probably intended for Elizabeth Kent; for example, a fragment headed 'Remark on Birds of Passage' begins: 'I have often observed that many birds that are reckoned birds of passage are very bad flyers'.[53] In one of her letters to Clare she had written: 'The fact you mention, of the weak flight of birds of passage, has excited similar conjectures in the minds of many'.[54]

Clare told Taylor, in a letter written on 24 January 1826:

> I have recieved a very pleasing letter from Miss Kent & I shall answer it as quickly as possible & give her all the information about birds that I know of for I have abandoned my own intentions of writing about them myself as I think she will be able to make a much better work of them then I shoud ... I am just going to Milton for a few days were I shall write to Miss Kent[55]

It is probable that 'Natural History Letter V' is a draft used by Clare in composing his reply; this draft is dated 'Feb 7', which would be consistent with the date of the letter to Taylor, and it is almost entirely concerned with birds familiar to Clare.[56] In the draft Clare says: 'The long taild Titmouse calld with us Bumbarrel & in yorkshire pudding bags & feather pokes is an early builder of its nest'.[57] Elizabeth Kent, replying on 16 February 1826, asked: 'Is Pudding-bags a name given to the bird, or to its nest? Mrs C. Smith says she has heard the nest called Long-pokes.'[58]

This very long letter from Miss Kent is of great interest and charm.[59] Her letters show Elizabeth Kent to have been someone who had immersed herself thoroughly in the ornithological literature, but who had little first-hand knowledge of the subject; for example, she told Clare that 'I never saw the inside of but three bird's nests, in my life; and never of one in its proper situation.'[60] Clare's observations were, therefore, of great assistance to her. I would tentatively suggest that 'Natural History Letter VII' might be the partial draft of Clare's next letter to her; it is headed 'March' and internal evidence shows that it was written in 1826.[61]

Clare took his promise of help seriously, telling John Taylor on 11 April 1826: 'I have been very busy these la[st] few days in watching the habits & coming of spring birds so as to [be] able to give Miss Kent an account of such as are not very well known in books – do you publish her Vol: of Birds'.[62] Miss Kent wrote her last letter to Clare, again lengthy and detailed, in early May 1826, telling him she had finished her book, apart from the preface, but it was not too late to incorporate additional information.[63] In his reply to Clare of 20 May 1826 Taylor explained:

> I have the MS. of her Birds in hand but have not yet formed a Judgment of it, though I think from what I have seen it is as interesting as the Flora at least, & much better than the Sylvan Sketches: this last Work has not yet paid its Exp[enses] –[64]

Taylor enlarged upon this on 7 August 1826: 'Miss Kent has sent her Work, I think, to some other Publisher. I told her I would take it in the Autumn, but she wanted to sell it immediately, & I suppose has parted with it, as I have heard no more of it'.[65]

It is impossible to avoid the conclusion that Miss Kent was pushing her luck here; Taylor and Hessey, a relatively small firm of publishers for whom literature was only a sideline, had published two of her books in 1825: the second edition of *Flora Domestica*, and *Sylvan Sketches*. Expecting them to publish a third so soon afterwards was rather ambitious, particularly at a time of crisis in the publishing trade which was soon to lead to Taylor and Hessey dissolving their partnership. No more is ever heard of Miss Kent's book, which did not find a publisher 'due, Kent told the Royal Literary Fund, to the widespread collapse of London booksellers in 1826'.[66] Her manuscript, together with Clare's letters to her, and his letters to Hessey which she used, have disappeared from view.[67]

The 'Natural History Letters' are, then, no more than draft letters, for the most part partial and fragmentary draft letters, to several correspondents, among whom we can identify Taylor and Hessey certainly, and Elizabeth Kent and Joseph Henderson probably, although some of the 'letters' may, of course, have been intended for other correspondents. The only thing they have in common is that they are all about natural history topics; Clare preserved them for future use and reference by sewing them together with other rough drafts of poetry and prose. The most important thing to be said about these 'letters' is that they have no connection with 'The Natural History of Helpstone'. The two projects have traditionally been treated as identical, but the evidence shows that they were distinct, even as their imagined structures and scopes changed in Clare's mind.

A related piece of mythology is that 'The Natural History of Helpstone' foundered because of the lack of interest of Clare's publishers; there is, in fact, no evidence that they ever heard of this project. We have all of the letters which they wrote to Clare at this period, and many (perhaps most) of his letters to them, and it is never mentioned.

Another piece of lore that might usefully be challenged is that Clare was imitating Gilbert White's *The Natural History of Selborne* when he planned his 'Natural History of Helpstone'. It is doubtful whether, in 1824, Clare had read White's book; indeed, it is not certain that he had heard of it although, given that James Hessey admired the work, he had probably been shown a copy. He did not own the book until mid-March 1828, when

Hessey gave him the two-volume edition published in 1825.[68] Clare seems to have started reading it at once, since he quoted White in a letter to John Taylor written on 3 April 1828;[69] the alacrity with which he began the book suggests that it was new to him, but unfortunately he never tells us what he thought of it. White's *Selborne* was not a well-known book in the 1820s although it already had its enthusiasts, such as Hessey. It was regarded as archaic even when it was published in 1788, partly because of its epistolary style, already outmoded, but also because it was, as Stuart Piggott has written, 'a legacy of the seventeenth century approach of Aubrey or Plot'.[70] To have attempted to imitate such a book two generations later would have been to invite ridicule, and there is not a shred of evidence that Clare was doing anything of the sort. The book which provided the impetus and the inspiration for Clare's natural history prose was not *The Natural History of Selborne* but Elizabeth Kent's *Flora Domestica*.

What, then, is left of 'The Natural History of Helpstone'? As a formal collection of writings, virtually nothing, since the project existed only as a vague and constantly shifting idea in Clare's mind. That idea was an extension of 'The Birds', or, put another way, both an expansion and a contraction. It would reach beyond Clare's knowledge of his local birds to include other fauna and flora, but would limit the need for the kind of country-wide, encyclopaedic knowledge that the 'Birds' project threatened to demand. As soon as Clare actually began, however, he had had enough, as he said in his Journal after his first attempt at writing essays for 'A Natural History of Helpstone': 'I did not think it woud cause me such trouble or I shoud not have began it'.[71] While he occasionally thought of resurrecting the project in some form, as far as we can tell that was the beginning and the end of it.

If the elements of this story are sometimes confusing, this fact reflects the partial and sketchy information on which we must rely. It also, however, reflects the confusion in Clare's own mind at this time, in the affairs of his publishers, and in the book trade and the literary world generally. Clare was aware that something more was expected of him, something different; as early as December 1820 he was telling John Taylor that 'always dinging at rural things wornt do'.[72] In the early 1820s Clare was deprived of literary direction. Edward Drury, who had played such an important role in Clare's development as a poet, had left Stamford and returned to Lincoln to take a role in the family business. His other literary friend in Stamford, Octavius Gilchrist, a man with a vast knowledge of English literature and a shrewd understanding of the literary world, died in 1823. John Taylor, another source of help and direction, was increasingly preoccupied with his editorial role on the *London Magazine* after his firm took it over in 1821, and was able to devote little time to Clare; at this period almost all of the letters Clare received from his publishers were written by James Hessey. Hessey was a wholly admirable man but he lacked Taylor's capacity to inspire. Clare had many friends, both close to home and further afield, but at this period there were none able to give him the sort of guidance and advice which he needed if he was to make the most of his gifts. Clare knew that he had to develop as a writer, but was unsure which direction to pursue.

In the circumstances it is not surprising that Clare embarked on several disparate projects in the mid-1820s, particularly in prose, which ranged from the rather unlikely to the wildly improbable. His manuscripts contain many fragmentary and abandoned prose works from this period and the natural history prose writings, which overwhelmingly date from this time, are part of this succession of false starts. To summarize, Clare wrote a few (probably two or three) letters to Hessey on the subject of birds, although on the evidence of the one draft we have, and Hessey's replies, these letters did not incorporate verse as Miss Kent's work did; they were perhaps intended as raw material, to be edited later when the poetry could be added. However, Clare obviously realized that his knowledge of birds, impressive as it was, was limited to those species with which he was familiar, making it difficult for him to produce any sort of comprehensive work. As he wrote to John Taylor on 5 May 1825:

> I have such a fear of my own inability to do any thing for such a matter that I cannot enter into it with any spirit as I find that I dont know half the Swimmers & Waders that inhabit the fens & I understand that there are a many of them strangers to the Natural History bookmakers themselves that have hithertoo written about it[73]

Little wonder, then, that, when the opportunity offered, Clare was happy to throw in his lot with Elizabeth Kent and content himself with assisting her with her own book on birds.

At the time we are considering, in the mid-1820s when Clare was in his early thirties, he was an accomplished writer possessing great technical virtuosity in addition to his imaginative gifts. However, he had his limitations, and an intended prose work such as I have been discussing highlights two of these. First, whether in verse or prose, Clare frequently foundered when writing towards a preconceived plan or on a pre-selected subject. Clare wrote best when he wrote spontaneously, compelled by the spirit. But when the spirit didn't move, he was often painfully blocked.

His other problem was, more narrowly, frustration with the activity of prose composition itself. In marked contrast to his facility with verse, a facility developed over a long apprenticeship, Clare always found prose difficult, despite some notable successes with it. He had a capacious memory, and could hold even a long poem in his head; he was able to refine his verse while going about his daily business, walking the fields or digging in his garden. By the time a poem was written down the correcting had been done – it had been polished and elaborated in his mind, hence the rarity of revisions or alterations in his manuscript poetry. This method didn't work with prose, and this is perhaps the reason why we find so many fragments of prose, particularly letters, in his manuscripts: he liked to try things out on paper in a way which was rarely necessary with his poems. He would often take himself off to Milton to work on a letter or other prose work, or take his piece of paper into the fields – anywhere, in fact, where he could have peace and quiet. This is why some drafts, including most of the 'natural history letters', have been folded and look as though they have been carried around in somebody's pocket: they have been. On both counts, then, the writing of any sort of systematic prose work on natural history was always going to be difficult, and it is not surprising that, as with other prose works he started, Clare soon abandoned it.

If Clare finished no natural history prose work, however, his close studies and notes, particularly regarding bird life, produced a rich harvest in his poems. This episode brought Clare up against the limits of his knowledge, but if it showed him what he did not know he also discovered a great deal about what he *did* know, and, further, that he had a fund of knowledge about the natural world which few people could approach. This realization fed into *The Shepherd's Calendar*, on which he was working at this time, and that poem served to confirm and emphasize the fact that natural history observation, which figures little in his early work, could be a fit subject for poetry. I would not like to give the impression that Clare's poems are merely versified natural history. There is no doubt, however, that over many years he trained himself in what Constable called 'the close observation of nature'.[74] This watchfulness introduced not merely new subject matter into Clare's writing, but a new dynamic as well, which resulted in some of his most original and distinctive poetry.

Notes

I am, as always, grateful to Professor Eric Robinson for permission to quote from John Clare's unpublished writings, and to the Manuscript Department of the

British Library for allowing me to quote from the letters to John Clare. I am also most grateful to Professor Molly Mahood for reading a draft of this chapter and saving me from more than one error.

1. Eg. 2246, fols 220^{r-v}, © The British Library Board. All further references in this chapter to Egerton Manuscripts materials are © The British Library Board.
2. For accounts of Elizabeth Kent, see Ann Shteir, 'A Romantic Flora: Elizabeth Kent' in her *Cultivating Women, Cultivating Science: Flora's Daughters and Botany in England, 1760–1860* (Baltimore and London: The Johns Hopkins University Press, 1996), pp. 135–45; Molly Tatchell, 'Elizabeth Kent and *Flora Domestica*', *Keats-Shelley Memorial Bulletin*, 27 (1976), 15–18; and Daisy Hay, 'Elizabeth Kent's Collaborators', *Romanticism*, 14 (2008), 272–81. Though Elizabeth Kent is often remembered in literary histories as the sister-in-law of Leigh Hunt, Clare seems to have considered her work entirely on its own merits; there is no evidence, for example, that he viewed her books in association with the 'suburban aesthetic' sometimes associated with Hunt.
3. This unpublished letter is in the Seymour Adelman Collection, Bryn Mawr College Library, to whom I am grateful for permission to quote from it. I am also grateful to Dr Emma Trehane for finding the letter and sharing the text of it with me.
4. *LM*, 8 (August 1823), 148, reprinted in *Letters*, pp. 279–80.
5. *Letters*, p. 278.
6. Ibid., p. 281.
7. *Natural History Prose*, pp. 13–23.
8. E.g. 2246, fols 456^r–57^r.
9. Referring to the plants described in Miss Kent's first book he had said: 'the account of them is poetry' (*Letters*, p. 279).
10. E.g. 2246, fol. 370^r.
11. Ibid., fol. 377^r.
12. Pet. A46, p. R160. This fragment is difficult to decipher because of the overwriting; however, I am fairly confident in my reading apart from the two words in square brackets, which are subject to revision.
13. E.g. 2246, fol. 377^v.
14. Ibid., fol. 384^r.
15. *Natural History Prose*, pp. 36–42.
16. *Letters*, p. 306.
17. *Natural History Prose*, p. 175.
18. *Natural History Prose*, p. 195; 'Maddox on the culture of flowers' is the 1822 edition of James Maddock's *The Florist's Directory*, item 293 in the catalogue of the Northampton Collection.
19. E.g. 2246, fol. 407^v. The letter is dated and postmarked 22 November 1824.
20. Ibid., fol. 433^v.
21. *Natural History Prose*, p. 99.
22. Ibid., p. 228.
23. E.g. 2246, fols. 468^{r-v}.

24. Ibid., fol. 480^v.
25. *Natural History Prose*, p. 235.
26. *Letters*, p. 331.
27. *Natural History Prose*, pp. 24–5.
28. Throughout my discussion of these 'letters' it must be borne in mind that 'Letter IX' has disappeared and I have no information about it other than the text printed by Margaret Grainger from a transcript supplied by Professor Eric Robinson.
29. *Natural History Prose*, pp. 70–1, for 'Letter XIII', and pp. 76–80 for the remainder of the notes.
30. Ibid., p. 28.
31. Margaret Grainger, *A Descriptive Catalogue of the John Clare Collection in Peterborough Museum and Art Gallery* ([Peterborough]: [Peterborough Museum Society], 1973), p. 8.
32. For example, in *Natural History Prose*, p. 26.
33. Ibid., p. 63.
34. E.g. 2246, fol. 468^v.
35. *Natural History Prose*, p. 238.
36. E.g. 2247, fol. 25^v.
37. *Natural History Prose*, p. 67.
38. Ibid., p. 60.
39. Ibid., p. 61.
40. E.g. 2247, fol. 30^v.
41. *Natural History Prose*, pp. 123–64.
42. *The Natural History of Birds, from the Works of the Best Authors, Antient & Modern: Embellished With Numerous Plates Accurately Coloured from Nature* (Bungay: Printed and Published by Brightly & Childs. Published also by T. Kinnersly); Clare's copy is item 316 in the Northampton Collection.
43. Although Clare's bird list is undated, internal evidence shows that he must have been working on it in the Spring of 1825 (*Natural History Prose*, p. 234 n. 2(2)).
44. *Natural History Prose*, p. 187.
45. *Time's Telescope for 1821; A Complete Guide to the Almanack* (London: Sherwood, Neely and Jones, 1821); the piece on 'Robert Clare' is on pp. 195–7.
46. E.g. 2247, fol. 25^v.
47. Ibid., fol. 24^r.
48. *Natural History Prose*, p. 239. Miss Kent's letter is Eg. 2250, fol. 242^r. It is indeed 12 lines long.
49. *Natural History Prose*, p. 253.
50. E.g. 2250, fol. 245^v.
51. E.g. 2247, fol. 128^r.
52. *Natural History Prose*, p. 110.
53. Ibid., p. 108.
54. E.g. 2247, fol. 169^v.

55. *Letters*, pp. 355–6.
56. *Natural History Prose*, pp. 45–9.
57. Ibid., p. 48.
58. E.g. 2247, fol. 144^v.
59. Ibid., fols. 144^r–45^v.
60. Ibid., fol. 145^v.
61. *Natural History Prose*, pp. 51–4; for the dating of the letter see p. 54, n. 9.
62. *Letters*, p. 374.
63. E.g. 2247, fols. 169^r–70^v. The letter is undated but postmarked 4 May 1826.
64. Ibid., fol. 177^r.
65. Ibid., fol. 202^v. Margaret Grainger was wrong in saying that 'the scheme foundered for some reason not communicated to Clare' (*Natural History Prose*, p. 120).
66. Hay, 'Elizabeth Kent's Collaborators', 279.
67. Mark Storey is surely in error in suggesting that a draft fragment which he prints (*Letters*, pp. 283–4) was intended for Miss Kent. The letter was written to the author of a botanical work which had made a very favourable impression on Clare, but the picture which emerges of the book in question does not correspond with Miss Kent's *Flora Domestica*; in particular, it seems to have been an illustrated work, and Taylor and Hessey's editions of *Flora Domestica* have no illustrations. The contents of the letter also indicate a later date than the 1823 which Storey suggests. A more probable recipient would be John Claudius Loudon, to the monthly parts of whose *Encyclopaedia of Plants* Clare subscribed from 1829.
68. This is item 395 in the catalogue of the Northampton Collection. On the half-title of the first volume it is inscribed 'John Clare from his sincere friend J.A.Hessey', and on the front free endpaper is written: 'Given me March 19. 1828.'
69. *Letters*, p. 424.
70. Stuart Piggott, *Ruins in a Landscape: Essays in Antiquarianism* (Edinburgh: Edinburgh University Press, 1976), p. 121. See also P. G. M. Foster, 'Introduction' to Gilbert White, *The Natural History of Selborne: a facsimile of the 1813 edition* (London: The Ray Society, 1993), pp. viii–ix.
71. *Natural History Prose*, p. 175.
72. *Letters*, p. 114.
73. Ibid., p. 331.
74. *John Constable's Discourses*, compiled and annotated by R. B. Beckett (Ipswich: Suffolk Records Society, 1970), p. 40.

CHAPTER 9

'This is radical slang': John Clare, Admiral Lord Radstock and the Queen Caroline affair

Sam Ward

Reading through a manuscript of 'The Village Minstrel', Clare's self-appointed patron Admiral Lord Radstock paused at stanzas 107 and 108, before scrawling angrily in the margin: 'This is radical slang'.[1] Radstock's remark has emerged, for Clare scholars, as one of the defining moments of Clare's career, yet that remark has been all too often stripped of its context, its important inflections ignored or misunderstood. This chapter aims to establish clearly the contexts and meanings of Radstock's comment, some of which are directly tied to political positioning, and some of which are not (at least in the way a simple binary between Conservative and Radical would imply). In so doing, it lays the foundations for a more thorough exploration of Clare's relationships with his patrons and publishers, and opens new perspectives on Clare's experience of politics at both national and local levels.

A campaigning Christian, Radstock saw it as his moral duty to offer Clare his guidance, sending him both lengthy letters and select publications, ranging from religious tracts and sermons to works of poetry and a grammar. As a prime mover in the Society for the Suppression of Vice, Radstock was naturally keen to ensure that Clare's poetry did not offend, and he used his influence as leverage to get his way. In an account of Radstock's career published shortly after his death from apoplexy in 1825, it was noted that he was of 'an active disposition, which would not allow him to be unemployed', and so 'was constantly engaged either in patriotically contributing to the public welfare, or in benevolently promoting the welfare of his fellow-creatures'.[2] M. J. D. Roberts has calculated that the Society for the Suppression of Vice 'probably gained the most fashionable third of its early membership' through Radstock's efforts alone, and he was similarly diligent in seeking supporters for Clare.[3]

Masterminded by Radstock, a series of letters praising Clare's poetry duly appeared in the morning papers throughout the early part of 1820. Clare soon tired of this attention, complaining to Taylor about 'silly beggerly flatterys', and claiming: 'I think Ive gaind as much harm as good by it—& am nothing in debt on that quarter'.[4] Taylor also protested, writing to his brother James shortly after the publication of the third edition of *Poems Descriptive*: 'I am much annoyed by Lord R.'s puffing in the *Post* and *New Times* and am determined to put an end to it, for I cannot but think it is disgraceful to me and injurious to Clare's Fame as well as Feelings'.[5]

Puffs and reviews were one thing; calls to alter the contents of the volume quite another. For the most part Clare resisted attempts to alter his poems, yet Taylor was more pragmatic, recognizing the need to appeal to a genteel audience, as well as the detrimental effect which alienating such readers might have on sales. A letter from 'A Well-Wisher to Merit', printed in the *Morning Post* on 11 February, welcomed the prospect of a second edition of *Poems Descriptive* on the grounds that it would provide 'some substantial pecuniary relief' to Clare, but also recommended that 'some two or three poems ... be expunged, in order to make room for others of riper and purer growth'.[6] The pieces deemed 'indelicate' were quick to go. 'The Country Girl' was omitted from the second edition, while, in 'My Mary', the word 'unfit' was substituted, as Clare's Stamford friend Octavius Gilchrist put it, 'for the one which shocked the delicate sensibilities of Portland Place'.[7] By the third, published at the end of June 1820, 'My Mary' was gone altogether, as was 'Dolly's Mistake'.

While Taylor was prepared to give ground over the more bawdy material, he at first stood firm on the question of political censorship. Early in May 1820, Clare had received letters – evidently sent at Radstock's bidding – asking that he do his civic and moral duty by removing ten lines from 'Helpstone' and altering one in 'Dawnings of Genius'.[8] In the face of sustained opposition from Radstock and his allies, Clare felt trapped, and wrote Taylor a grudging request that he implement an approximation of the Radstock directive:

> Being very much botherd latley I must trouble you to leave out the 8 lines in 'helpstone' beginning 'Accursed wealth' & two under 'When ease & plenty'—& one in 'Dawnings of Genius' 'That nessesary tool' leave it out & put ***** to fill up the blank   this will let em see I do it as negligent as possible   d—n that canting way of being forcd to please I say—I cant abide it & one day or other I will show my Independance more stron[g]ly then ever   you know who's the promoter of the scheme I dare say—I have

told you to order & therefore the fault rests not with me while you are left to act as you please[9]

The sense of frustration here is palpable, yet as Alan Vardy has observed, by refusing to rewrite the lines in question, Clare continued to assert his independence while also absolving himself of the responsibility of making the proposed changes.[10] This strategy had only limited success. Shortly afterwards, Markham E. Sherwill wrote to him to advise that while he agreed 'Mr Taylor is a very sensible man, & very equal to changing the line', 'I do not think *he* ought to do it – Whatever is done must be done by y^r.self, or the poems cease to be your own'. To add insult to injury, Sherwill added: 'I wish you would endeavour to write an address to "*Gratitude*" & have it inserted in y^r. next Volume, as the first article – It w^d. please all those kind & liberal patrons you have'.[11]

If Taylor initially felt able to ignore Radstock's demands, by the autumn this was no longer possible. Writing at the end of September he gloomily informed Clare: 'Lord R. has expressed his Intention of disowning you in such strong Terms, unless the radical Lines as he called them were left out, that I conceived it would be deemed improper in me as your Friend to hold out any longer'.[12] What prompted Radstock to threaten such a drastic course of action? The answer, I would suggest, lies less with Clare's conduct than with the course of political events, the most significant of which was the so-called Queen Caroline affair.

On the accession of George IV in January 1820, the status of his estranged wife, Caroline of Brunswick, took on a new importance. Although the royal couple had formally separated back in 1797, they had never divorced, meaning Caroline's position was uncertain and, from the point of view of George and his ministers, potentially dangerous. Relations between the pair, which were already tense at best, now grew toxic when George announced his intention to remove Caroline's name from the Liturgy. This move prompted an incensed Caroline to return to England from the continent, where she had lived for the past six years, to claim her rights and privileges as queen.

'The Queen of England is at present every thing with every body', declared *The Times* on 7 June, and from then until the end of the year the affair 'dominated the national consciousness'.[13] Writing in 1823, William Hazlitt recalled that it 'was the only question I ever knew that excited a thorough popular feeling. It struck its roots into the heart of the nation, took possession of every house or cottage in the kingdom; man, woman, and child took part in it, as if it had been their own concern'.[14] As these comments indicate, Caroline's fate was widely discussed and the extent of her support was of particular concern to conservatives such as Radstock, many of whom, Thomas Laqueur notes, recognized that 'it was the power of public opinion and the entry of new groups into the political arena which constituted the real threat in the "queen's business"'.[15]

Radstock's increasing determination to purge Clare's work of anything which smacked of discontent, then, occurred against a backdrop of rapidly escalating political tension. London was the epicentre of the disturbances. The day after Caroline landed at Dover, an informant wrote to the Home Office to warn that: 'The disaffected are *all in motion* to raise the population of the Metropolis to receive her in a *triumphant* manner', adding that a number of well-known radicals were also 'endeavouring to raise a popular *commotion* on the *occasion*'.[16]

In his influential counter-revolutionary tract of 1814, *The Cottager's Friend*, Radstock had reminded the poor of their duty to 'Fear God' and 'Honour the King'.[17] 'Keep me from all self-conceit and petulance, from discontent and murmuring, and give me a meek and humble spirit', ran one of the prayers included by Radstock.[18] Vardy contends that *The Cottager's Friend* 'must be one of the most anxious documents of an anxious age', suggesting further that: 'Perhaps only in London, playing the part of the powerful rural landlord, could Radstock have produced such a pamphlet'.[19] As the Queen Caroline affair exploded into life in the summer of 1820, it must have seemed to Radstock that most of the goals he had been fighting for throughout his long career were threatened as never before. In the capital, ultra-radical ideas which had been bubbling near to the surface for a number of years burst forth to be given far wider exposure than they had ever previously received. Worse, as we shall see, such views were dispersed into the countryside, threatening the contentment and loyalty of the rustic audience addressed by him in *The Cottager's Friend*.

There is a suggestive parallel between Radstock's increasing need to exert an influence over the contents of Clare's work and the growing unrest among the labouring-classes: control of the one compensating in some measure for the failure to adequately contain the other. This is only part of the story, however, as a more detailed consideration of both the Caroline controversy and Radstock's politicized reading of Clare's poetry will make clear. At stake was the legitimacy of labouring-class discourse, an issue which was inextricably linked to ongoing debates about education, public opinion and Parliamentary reform, and which brought to the fore questions surrounding the ownership and appropriation of literary and landed property.

Anxieties about where the Queen Caroline affair might end were widely shared, and were increased by the situation on the continent, which saw popular uprisings in Spain, Portugal and Italy. 'We shall see, if we live, a Jacobin Revolution more bloody than that of France', predicted Lord Grey, the leader of the Whigs, in a letter to a friend.[20] Robert Southey, meanwhile, suggested:

> There is every probability of a more tremendous explosion than that which Lord George Gordon brought about in our childhood; and no reliance can be placed upon the soldiers. For they are not only duped by the devilish newspapers to believe that the Queen is an innocent and injured woman, but they are infected by the moral pestilence of the age, since the armies in Spain and Naples have chosen to interfere in state affairs. Before this letter can reach you the crisis will, in all likelihood, have come on. It will be a trial between the Government, supported by the civil power alone, and the mob, with the traitorous Whigs and the Press on their side,—the troops being worse than doubtful.[21]

As these examples reveal, in the period leading up to Radstock's threat to publicly disown Clare, the dangers posed by the queen's case appeared ever more serious. On 5 July the government introduced a Bill of Pains and Penalties in the House of Lords, in order to deprive Caroline of 'the title of Queen, and of all the prerogatives, rights, privileges, and exemptions appertaining to her as Queen Consort of this Realm', and to render her marriage to George IV 'wholly dissolved, annulled and made void' on the grounds of adultery.[22] The second reading of the Bill began on 17 August, at which stage, R. A. Melikan notes, 'the process assumed a judicial character'.[23] The ensuing 'trial' caught the public imagination, but the king's actions were widely condemned, especially in view of his own personal conduct.[24]

Southey's summary is particularly useful, since it brings together a number of factors which preoccupied conservative-minded contemporaries at the moment the trial began. Concerns over the loyalty of the troops became particularly acute after the mutiny of the 3rd Regiment of Guards on 15 June, especially in view of the crucial role played by armed forces in revolts on the continent.[25]

If the future looked alarming to the authorities, for radicals and others with grievances against the established order it appeared to offer real hopes of social and political change. 'The year 1820 will be a new era in history', Richard Carlile assured readers of *The Republican*: 'When there is a union between the soldier and the citizen in defence of their common right and liberties, all is sure to proceed well without bloodshed, and even without confusion'.[26] In spite of Southey's identification of Caroline's allies as 'the mob', a pejorative with specific class connotations, her cause in fact created what Rohan McWilliam calls 'communities of moral outrage'.[27] Dror Wahrman suggests that 'the most striking aspect of the Queen Caroline agitation' was its 'lack of class specificity'.[28] Public expressions of solidarity with the queen took many forms, including meetings, processions and addresses (sent to her by groups from across the country).[29] Many of the addresses were printed, together with the queen's replies – some of the most radically inflected of which were written for her by William Cobbett – and widely distributed.[30] The mixed nature of support for Caroline meant that she quickly became, in John Belchem's phrase, 'a multivocal symbol of opposition'.[31]

Having outlined the way in which widely felt anxieties about the Queen Caroline affair may have given a new urgency to Radstock's concern about '*Radical* and *ungrateful* sentiments', I want to turn to the poems themselves in order to explore what it was that made certain lines so problematic.[32] I start with 'Dawnings of Genius', since this piece has received very little attention in comparison with 'Helpstone'.[33]

In spite of its relative neglect today, 'Dawnings of Genius' was frequently singled out for praise by Clare's contemporaries, including, somewhat paradoxically perhaps, members of the Radstock circle. To a degree, this may be a consequence of Taylor's reference to it in his introduction to *Poems Descriptive*, where it is said to describe 'the condition of a man, whose education has been too contracted to utter the thoughts of which he is conscious'. 'That this would have been CLARE's fate, unless he had been taught to write', Taylor continued, 'cannot be doubted; and a perusal of his Poems will convince any one, that something of this kind he still feels, from his inability to find those words which can fully declare his meaning.'[34] As Vardy argues, many readers 'followed Taylor's lead in noting the special circumstances of the poet's life', placing enormous pressure on Clare's identification as a 'peasant poet', a class-based label which duly shifted its meaning to meet 'preconceived political and cultural assumptions and expectations'.[35] The *New Monthly Magazine* – which condemned 'Dolly's Mistake' and 'My Mary' as 'by far the worst pieces in the volume' – named 'Dawnings of Genius' as one of those 'which please us best'; while the *Gentleman's Magazine* listed it as one of the poems which 'may, for the fine tone of their sentiment, the dignity, and, withal, the warmth, tenderness, and simplicity of their style, vie with the admired productions of many, who have long ranked deservedly high in the annals of Poetic fame'.[36] Letters to the *Morning Post* from 'Q' (Sherwill) and 'Cantabrigiensis' (Chauncey Hare Townshend) also called attention to the poem, the latter describing it as 'unquestionably the most beautiful and extraordinary' in the book.[37]

Sherwill's response to 'Dawnings of Genius' is particularly interesting, since he was one of those who had acted on Radstock's behalf to recommend to Clare that a line in it be altered; indeed, 'Q's' letter – which stated that it was the 'general opinion' that there was 'great originality of idea' in the poem – was published a mere four days after he had written to Clare *in propria persona* advising him to make the change. Furthermore, both he and Mrs Emmerson praised 'Dawnings of Genius' when they wrote saying it had to be amended – the former calling it 'the best thing almost that you have written', Mrs Emmerson, 'your beautiful poem on "Genius"'.[38] Such admiration seems heartfelt, and, while it is tempting to speculate that they may not have entirely agreed with Radstock's reservations, instead I would suggest that their ambivalence is typical of a more common response to Clare's poetry, one shared by many of his earliest readers. The popularity of *Poems Descriptive* owed much to the public's hunger for a voice ostensibly unsullied by party politics, metropolitan corruption or pretensions to grandeur. However, the rapid commodification of Clare's life and work – by no means exceptional in an age which cherished literary celebrity – meant that their perceived value in the literary marketplace was very much dependent on a reader's attitude to the labouring-classes and on Clare's continued good conduct.[39] Consequently, an anxiety about where to place Clare can be detected almost everywhere in his contemporary reception.

As reported by Mrs Emmerson, Radstock attributed Clare's bitter expressions in 'Helpstone' and 'Dawnings of Genius' to his 'depressed state' at the time these pieces were written, an idea echoed by Emmerson herself, who reassured Clare that 'severe privation . . . alone induced you to exclaim against the higher classes of society'.[40] The passages were deemed 'objectionable' however, not only because they risked making Clare appear ungrateful, but because they seemed to echo the language of popular radicalism.[41] In 'Dawnings of Genius' he had described the 'rough, rude ploughman' as 'That necessary tool of wealth and pride' (line 15), but, as Sherwill cautioned: 'In your present situation, I w^d. not advise you to make what some persons might term such *an attack* on the aristocracy – It was well enough in former days, but is now illtimed'.[42]

Considering how best to accommodate the various changes insisted upon by Radstock, Taylor told Clare that he intended to cut out the couplet containing the line referring to 'wealth and pride'. It 'now reads very well', he claimed, 'in fact better than ever'. 'By this amendment', he went on, 'I avoid, what I am desirous to do, the Insertion of any Lines not absolutely yours.'[43] (Mrs Emmerson had proposed as an alternative 'With Nature! simple Nature for his guide!', a suggestion equally out of keeping with the spirit of Clare's original and with the image of wearisome toil introduced in the following line: 'While moil'd and sweating by some pasture's side'.)[44] Taylor's willingness to amend 'Dawnings of Genius' suggests that he recognized that the text was open to the kind of politicized reading which Radstock had given it. One of the recommended alterations to 'Helpstone', on the other hand, was a different matter. According to Clare, Radstock wanted the following lines omitted:

> Accursed Wealth! o'er-bounding human laws,
> Of every evil thou remain'st the cause.
> Victims of want, those wretches such as me,
> Too truly lay their wretchedness to thee:
> Thou art the bar that keeps from being fed,
> And thine our loss of labour and of bread;
> Thou art the cause that levels every tree,
> And woods bow down to clear a way for thee ...
>
> When ease and plenty, known but now to few,
> Were known to all, and labour had its due[45]

'Though I am willing to leave out the Lines beginning "Accursed wealth" which it still grieves me to do', Taylor admitted, 'I can see no Reason so imperative for complying with Lord R's further Demand that the 3rd and 4th Lines of the following Paragraph should also be omitted, viz "Where Ease and Plenty" &c for I am convinced this is at least no exaggeration'.[46]

Having drawn attention to the passages identified by Radstock as 'radical', I want to follow a little in Taylor's footsteps, and consider what made them so, and, in particular, what relationship they bore to the radical politics of the day. According to J. C. D. Clark, though 'it was established by 1802', the noun 'radical', as 'shorthand for "a proponent of radical reform"', 'seems to have gone into abeyance until after 1810, and was not common until 1819'.[47] Putting a stop to the dissemination of radical ideas was a major aim of conservatives in the period, and, since the 1790s, a series of so-called gagging acts had been introduced in an attempt to control both printed materials and public meetings. Following a resurgence of popular radicalism after the Napoleonic Wars, a fresh set of repressive measures culminating in the Six Acts of 1819 had been enacted. The dissemination of radical texts was frequently identified as dangerous, not only because it allowed subversive ideas to circulate freely, but because it made it impossible to control how such works were read and by whom. Though Radstock is highly unlikely to have suspected Clare of harbouring radical sympathies – of being 'a radical', in other words – he nevertheless clearly detected close thematic and tonal parallels between Clare's protests about inequalities in the countryside and the discourse of contemporary radicalism. As we have seen, Radstock did not altogether blame Clare for voicing complaints, but felt that these could easily be misinterpreted by readers, who might also presume that he and Clare's other post-publication patrons consented to the sentiments expressed. Jon Klancher's observations about radical discourse are useful here. This, he suggests,

> was not as much 'expressed' by a nascent working class as it formed the latter's ideological and interpretive map. Yet, like an atlas in which one map overlaps another, fitting its figural territory within another frame, the boundaries between middle-class and working-class discourses were not immobile lines but strategic shifting latitudes of force.[48]

Commenting on the effect which Radstock's cuts had on the meaning of 'Helpstone', Sarah M. Zimmerman notes that the devastation lamented by the poet in the preceding lines ('Now all is laid waste by desolation's hand,/ Whose cursed weapon levels half the land') is 'rendered more existential than political' when the agent behind it is no longer identified. 'Moreover', she insists, 'the "weapons" deplored may be found in time's arsenal, rather than among the implements of "agricultural improvement"'.[49] In this way, the poem's 'radical' components – its sharp condemnation of 'Wealth' and the disproportionate impact of enclosure on the poor – are lost. Before moving on to look at some additional reasons why Radstock's anxiety over radical elements peaked in the latter part of 1820, it is instructive to look at some material by self-confessed radicals. The two examples I've chosen touch directly on the topic of enclosure and do so in language closely resembling that used by Clare.

Just over a year before *Poems Descriptive* made its appearance, the first article in T. J. Wooler's *The Black Dwarf* for 6 January 1819 was entitled 'The Right of the Poor to the Cultivation of Waste Lands'.[50] This piece is headed by a quotation from Goldsmith's 'The Deserted Village', a key influence on 'Helpstone', which cleverly sets up the argument within:

'A time there was ere England's griefs began,/When every rood of ground maintained its man'.[51] 'Let us endeavour to obtain the soil', the article commands, 'some place whereon to stand, and to tell tyranny it is *our own*'.

> If any real wish had ever existed, to render the poor as comfortable as they ought to be, half of our miseries would have been removed ... Every thing that is done in the way of improvement, leaves them out of its operation. Look at the common enclosure acts, in which the most barefaced pillage of their rights is exhibited ... The poor may well wish to be legislators for themselves, when such legislation disgraces the statute book.[52]

In his 'deceptively titled' *Christian Policy, The Salvation of the Empire* of 1816, the veteran Spencean campaigner Thomas Evans, meanwhile, claimed that: 'Landlords ... and Landlords only, are the oppressors of the people'. 'I have lived long enough to witness the effect of enclosure after enclosure, and tax after tax', he complained, 'expelling the cottager from gleaning the open fields, from his right of the common, from his cottage, his hovel, once his own; robbing him of his little store, his pig, his fowls, his fuel; thereby reducing him to a pauper, a slave'.[53] David Worrall has recently reminded us of the 'agrarianist, redistributist, ecological sentiments' which motivated 'much of the organized radical activism which survived Spa Fields, the Pentrich Rising, Peterloo and Cato Street', and it is this strand of radicalism, taking its lead from Thomas Spence, which Radstock most likely associated with Clare's 'Radical lines'.[54] As Worrall remarks elsewhere: 'The Spencean ideology is a counter-culture firmly based upon the political and economic importance of land'.[55]

Among the written placards circulated at Spa Fields in 1816 was one 'of the most dangerous and inflammatory nature', pledging: 'no rise of bread; no Regent; no Castlereagh, off with their heads; no placemen, tythes, or enclosures; no taxes; no bishops, only useless lumber! stand true, or be slaves forever!'[56] With the onset of the Queen Caroline affair, the legislation which had been introduced in an attempt to hold back the tide of radical material momentarily failed. As early as the second week in July 1820, the Home Office was notified that men and boys had been employed

> to circulate in the Metropolis, & for 50 Miles around it, vast quantities of Bills, Placards, and Publications of a Seditious and inflamatory nature, with a view to inflame the passions of the Lower orders into acts of Violence ag[ain]st the Constituted authorities, & to interrupt the course of Justice and to stop the investigation in the House of Lords respecting the Queen.[57]

By autumn, the radicals had grown increasingly bold. On 16 October, the same informant reported that they were getting flags and standards made-up bearing 'various mottos, but particularly the following – "The Queens rights, the Peoples Liberty"'.[58] The previous month, Mr Simmons, editor of *The Boston Gazette*, had been forced to leave his home after 'there was a riot in the town ... in consequence of what appeared in the paper'.[59] Writing to Lord Sidmouth, he warned 'that a *very bad* spirit prevails in this town among the class of politicians who have Reform in their mouths but Revolution in their hearts, and who influence a large portion of the Labouring and working classes'.[60]

Direct activity by radicals, whether real or anticipated, was not the only issue of concern to conservatives worried by public interest in the Queen Caroline affair. 'The blasphemous pages of Carlisle [*sic*], whose conviction towards the close of the preceding year had given general satisfaction were confined to comparatively few readers', thundered the *Christian Observer*, 'but this contaminating topic has polluted every newspaper, and found its way to every hamlet in the kingdom'.[61] As Laqueur remarks: 'Week after week, the *Courier* or the *New Times*, staunchly reactionary though they were, carried the queen's assurances that she would "overthrow the power of faction and deliver the people from oppression"', and '[e]ven the most conservative of papers printed her claims to be what the *Loyalist* called "the French Revolutionary Leader"'.[62] Reflecting on the power of the press, the *New Times* submitted that it 'tends to give unity to public sentiment to a degree that has never existed before in any country in the world'.[63] In Laqueur's view, 'discourse about the meaning of various manifestations of support for Caroline was in fact a discourse about the power of the press and the legitimacy of a greatly expanded public opinion. The queen's cause could be, in a literal sense, popular as no previous political movement had been.'[64] Above all, it was this extraordinary diffusion of 'radical' sentiment, I would contend, that provoked Radstock to threaten to disown Clare.

A further piece of evidence which demonstrates that current events lay behind Radstock's insistence that what he regarded as politically sensitive material be omitted is provided by Taylor's reassurance that: 'When the Follies of the Day are past with all the Fears they have engendered we can restore the Poems according to the earlier Editions.'[65] Also highly significant is Radstock's choice of the phrase 'radical slang' to describe the two stanzas he objected to in 'The Village Minstrel'.

In September 1820, *The Anti-Jacobin Review* attacked the answers Caroline had publicly issued in response to the addresses she had received from her supporters. 'What motive', it asked, 'could ever induce the Queen of England to lend her name to such contemptible effusions of calumny, radical slang, self-adulation, bombast and nonsense, as are contained in these answers, we are at a loss to guess'. 'If our readers are not disgusted with what they have read', it went on, 'we will quote a few instances of the "radical slang," in which the Queen at times indulges':

> "My sympathies all harmonize with those of the *people*, we have one common interest; and that interest is *one* and *indivisible*. I should have no heart, if I did not participate in their sorrows, and condole with their *wrongs*.["]—(*Answer to Bolton*.) "The *rights of the nation* will be only a scattered wreck, and this *once free* people, like the meanest of slaves, must submit to *the lash of an insolent domination*."—(*Answer to Wakefield*.) "The improved *spirit of the age* is seen in the *intellectual advancement* through all the gradations of the social scheme."—(*Answer to Middlesex*.) "When my rights are attacked, a fatal blow is aimed at the *rights* of the people." (*Answer to Kinnoul*.)[66]

In the eyes of the *Boston Gazette* 'her Majesty's Answers promulgate Revolutionary principles ... more worthy of *King Cobbett* than Queen Caroline'! Indeed, it is quite easy to see a connection between the language used in the answers and radical discourse, for as Gareth Stedman Jones suggests: '[i]n radical discourse the dividing line between classes was not that between employer and employed, but that between the represented and the unrepresented'.[67] In a debate in the House of Commons on the restoration of the queen's name to the Liturgy, Thomas Denman, Caroline's Solicitor General, reportedly used a telling phrase when he stated that: 'If Her Majesty was included in any general prayer, it was in the prayer for all that are desolate and oppressed.'[68] 'National identity', notes Rohan McWilliam, was 'a crucial component' of the radical movement at this time 'with the queen representing the people'.[69]

Keeping these contexts in mind, it is worth looking afresh at the two 'radical' stanzas in 'The Village Minstrel':

107
There once was lanes in natures freedom dropt
There once was paths that every valley wound
Inclosure came & every path was stopt
Each tyrant fixt his sign were pads was found
To hint a trespass now who crossd the ground

> Justice is made to speak as they command
> The high road now must be each stinted bound
> —Inclosure thourt a curse upon the land
> & tastless was the wretch who thy existance pland
>
> 108
> O england boasted land of liberty
> Wi strangers still thou mayst thy title own
> But thy poor slaves the alteration see
> Wi many a loss to them the truth is known
> Like emigrating bird thy freedoms flown
> While mongrel clowns low as their rooting plough
> Disdain thy laws to put in force their own
> & every village owns its tyrants now
> & parish slaves must live as parish kings alow
>
> (lines 1084–101; *Early Poems*, II, 169)

It is noteworthy that Radstock singled out these two stanzas for criticism. The four before and two after, while also lamenting enclosure, seem not to have troubled him unduly.[70] Stephen Colclough aptly observes that the stanzas in question 'are particularly effective in indicating that the local incidents of enclosure are examples of national corruption', and as he points out, the poem succeeds 'by moving from the local to the national, enclosure is described as "a curse upon the land" suggesting both its power to alter topography and its adverse effect on the nation, and the poem goes on to argue that "every village owns its tyrants now"'.[71] Clare's decision to criticize enclosure in this fashion, his choice of language (at times reminiscent of both the queen's answers and the Spencean sentiments of Wooler and Evans), and, above all, his class identity as a peasant poet, must have greatly alarmed Radstock.

David Worrall writes that Caroline's replies reveal her awareness of the 'artisan or plebeian public sphere'.[72] Her appeal to members of the labouring-classes was singled out for criticism by the *Morning Post*, a paper with which Radstock had close connections:

> The regal pomp and dignity of the Crown of England were never so degraded, were never so debased, as by the rabble throng who have been ushered into the presence of Royalty at Brandenburgh House, and by the Radical Slang which has issued from that house in the shape of answers to addresses. It is within our own personal knowledge, that journeymen bakers, the landladies of low ale houses, and the daughters of the lowest orders, have had the honour (if such it can be called) of kissing her MAJESTY's hand.[73]

Here again, the phrase 'radical slang' is used specifically to refer to Caroline's answers, suggesting that Radstock saw clear parallels between the queen's defence of her people's liberties and the language used by Clare to protest against what he saw as the unjust and often oppressive nature of rural society. 'Slang' in this context appears to mean both 'cant, i.e., the jargon of criminals' and 'illiterate, "low" language', neither of which, from a conservative perspective, was deemed an appropriate vehicle for the expression of political ideas.[74] More than that, however, as Olivia Smith has written: 'To speak the vulgar language demonstrated that one belonged to the vulgar class; that is, that one was morally and intellectually unfit to participate in the culture.'[75]

Roger Sales has proposed that 'Radstock came to regard Clare's poetry as a vital battleground, since, if it could be shown that this particular cottager was peaceable in his station, then it could be asserted that all the others either were, or ought to be.'[76] As Colclough insightfully suggests, Clare's lines were considered radical not only because they attacked the aristocracy, 'who now made up a significant proportion of his patrons', but because they 'spoke from the perspective of the labourer, and made significant demands about his material existence'.[77] The danger was that such sentiments not only described or represented politicized spaces, they also produced them, providing the labouring-classes with a sense of agency.

As I draw to a conclusion, I am conscious that Clare's agency has barely figured in my account. My aim here, however, has been to consider some of the key issues relating to Clare *and* politics in the early 1820s and not Clare's politics as such.[78] Having said that, I think it is important to acknowledge that Clare's few surviving comments on Caroline are critical and that he regarded the whole affair with barely concealed contempt. When Caroline died in August 1821, Taylor sent him a black waistcoat to mark the occasion. Thanking him, Clare's feelings spilled out to the extent that he backtracked with an attempted excision:

> I have put on the black waiscoat you gave me for this last week & shoud have done so with the coat but it is too dandyish for this country—but it is not to mourn for the injurd quean—I hated her while living & have no inclination to regret her death—I hated her not as a woman or as a queen but as vilest hypocrite that ever existed—common sense gives me her spectacles to look upon every thing Im of no party   but I never saw such farcical humbug carried on in my life before & I never wish to see it agen for its lanched me head over ears in politics for this last twelvemonth & made me very violent when John Barleycorn inspird me—who made me side for the King & a

~~little true subject tho I was formerly as I was touchd with a stain of radicalism~~ every one has his share of humbug & I have mine.[79]

Although Clare prefigures E. P. Thompson's hasty dismissal of the Queen Caroline affair as 'humbug' in *The Making of the English Working Class*, and echoes his contemporaries by describing it with a theatrical image as a 'farce', it is the heavily deleted passage which is perhaps the most striking thing here, acknowledging as it does both the limited scope of Clare's previous loyalty to George IV ('a little true subject tho I formerly was') and an association with potentially seditious ideas ('I was touchd with a stain of radicalism').[80]

As this example plainly illustrates, political allegiances in this period were seldom as clearly defined as ideologues such as Radstock desired them to be. In December 1820, the painter Benjamin Robert Haydon recorded a meeting he had had in Kendal with 'a little Whig hater, loyal but a Queen's man—a picture of English healthy independence'. According to Haydon, this man 'loved the King, thought the Queen a whore—but he would be damned if any woman should [be] ill used, whore or no whore'.[81] Somewhat similarly, Clare's letter to Taylor indicates his independence of mind – a characteristic also apparent in his blunt refusal to do as he was told, whether that involved putting a light in his window to honour Queen Caroline or cutting lines from his poetry at the request of Radstock and his friends.[82] It further suggests that even if Clare's most anti-aristocratic seeming verse might have been viewed as contiguous with the wider radical discourse centred around Caroline, it did so because of the implicit challenge his writing posed to contemporary definitions of legitimate plebeian discourse and not because he was in any direct sense an active proponent of radical reform.

Notes

1. Nor. 3, p. 186b.
2. *The Annual Biography and Obituary for the Year 1826* (London, 1826), pp. 2–14 (p. 9).
3. M. J. D. Roberts, *Making English Morals: Voluntary Association and Moral Reform in England, 1787–1886* (Cambridge: Cambridge University Press, 2004), p. 79.
4. Clare to Taylor, 3 April 1821, *Letters*, p. 173.
5. John Taylor to James Taylor, 22 May 1820, quoted in Olive M. Taylor, 'John Taylor: Author and Publisher, 1781–1864', *London Mercury*, 12 (July 1925), 258–67 (261).

6. *Morning Post*, 11 February 1820.
7. Gilchrist to Clare, 21 March 1820, *Critical Heritage*, p. 61; Radstock lived at 10 Portland Place. *Early Poems*, I, p. 80, indicates that the word was written as 'bes—t' or 'besh–t' (as applied to a dirty baby) in manuscript, as a dash only in the first edition of *Poems Descriptive*, and as 'unfit' in the second edition.
8. As discussed below, these letters were written by Eliza Emmerson and Markham E. Sherwill.
9. Clare to Taylor, 16 May 1820, *Letters*, pp. 68–70.
10. Alan Vardy, *John Clare, Politics and Poetry* (Basingstoke: Palgrave, 2003), pp. 94–5.
11. Sherwill to Clare, 25 May 1820, Pet. F1.
12. Taylor to Clare, 27–29 September 1820, Eg. 2245, f. 225, © The British Library Board. All further references in this chapter to Egerton Manuscripts materials are © The British Library Board.
13. *The Times*, 7 June 1820. J. Ann Hone, *For the Cause of Truth: Radicalism in London 1769–1821* (Oxford: Clarendon Press, 1982), p. 307.
14. William Hazlitt, 'Common Places', *The Complete Works of William Hazlitt*, ed. P. P. Howe, 21 vols. (London: Dent, 1930–4), 20, p. 136.
15. Thomas W. Laqueur, 'The Queen Caroline Affair: Politics as Art in the Reign of George IV', *Journal of Modern History*, 54 (September 1992), 417–66 (427).
16. 'J. S.' to Sir Robert Baker, 6 June 1820, Home Office Papers, HO 40/15, f. 22. They did so 'from a *Spirit of Hostility to his Majesty*, and not from any *Loyalty or real good will* to her Majesty'.
17. Radstock is quoting here from 1 Peter 2:17 – 'Honour all men. Love the brotherhood. Fear God. Honour the King.' The contents of *The Cottager's Friend* are summarized in Vardy, pp. 88–91. Most commentators, including Vardy, have suggested that the pamphlet dates from 1816, but it had first appeared at least two years earlier.
18. Quoted in Vardy, *John Clare, Politics and Poetry*, p. 91.
19. Vardy, p. 91.
20. E. Tangye Lean, *The Napoleonists: A Study in Political Disaffection* (London: Oxford University Press, 1970), p. 118.
21. Southey to W. S. Landor, 14 August 1820, *Selections from the Letters of Robert Southey*, ed. John Wood Warter, 4 vols. (London: Longman, Brown, Green, and Longmans, 1856), 3, p. 206.
22. T. C. Hansard, *Parliamentary Debates*, n.s., vol. 2 (27 June–27 September 1820), cols. 213, 214.
23. R. A. Melikan, 'Pain and Penalties Procedure: How the House of Lords "Tried" Queen Caroline', in *Domestic and International Trials, 1700–2000*, ed. R. A. Melikan (Manchester: Manchester University Press, 2003), pp. 54–75 (p. 57).
24. For modern accounts of the trial, see E. A. Smith, *A Queen on Trial: The Affair of Queen Caroline* (Stroud: Allen Sutton, 1993) and Jane Robins, *Rebel Queen: The Trial of Caroline* (London: Simon and Schuster, 2006). A discussion of literary responses is provided by John Gardner in *Poetry and Popular*

Protest: Peterloo, Cato Street and the Queen Caroline Controversy (Basingstoke: Palgrave, 2011), pp. 157–217.
25. See Smith, *A Queen on Trial*, pp. 40–1.
26. 'The Progress of Revolution Cheering to the Lover of Liberty', *The Republican*, 4.1 (1 September 1820), 6–7 (7).
27. Rohan McWilliam, *Popular Politics in Nineteenth-Century England* (London: Routledge, 1998), p. 9.
28. Dror Wahrman, '"Middle-Class" Domesticity Goes Public: Gender, Class, and Politics from Queen Caroline to Queen Victoria', *Journal of British Studies*, 32.4 (October 1993), 396–432 (402).
29. The queen enjoyed strong support among women, on which topic see Susan Kingley Kent, *Gender and Power in Britain: 1640–1990* (London: Routledge, 1999), pp. 159–64, and Anna Clark, 'Queen Caroline and the Sexual Politics of Popular Culture in London, 1820', *Representations*, 31 (Summer, 1990), 47–68.
30. For examples of the addresses to the Queen and her replies, see Smith, *A Queen on Trial*, pp. 106–7, 112–3, 148–9, and, with a highly critical commentary, *Selections from the Queen's Answers to Various Addresses Presented to Her: Together with Her Majesty's Extraordinary Letter to the King; and an Introduction and Observations Illustrative of their Tendency* (London, 1821). On Cobbett's role, see Robins, *The Trial of Queen Caroline*, pp. 158–60, 162–4.
31. John Belchem, *Popular Radicalism in Nineteenth-Century Britain* (Basingstoke: Macmillan, 1996), p. 50.
32. Emmerson to Clare, 11 May 1820, Eg. 2245, ff. 118–20.
33. A notable exception is Johanne Clare, *John Clare and the Bounds of Circumstance* (Kingston: McGill-Queen's University Press, 1987), pp. 113–15.
34. *Poems Descriptive of Rural Life and Scenery* (London: Taylor and Hessey, 1820), pp. xiii–xiv.
35. Vardy, *John Clare, Politics and Poetry*, pp. 42, 44.
36. *New Monthly Magazine*, 13.74 (1 March 1820), 326–30 (329), rpt. *Critical Heritage*, pp. 68–73; 'Display of Native Genius. No. II', *The Gentleman's Magazine*, 91 (April 1821), 308–12 (309).
37. *Morning Post*, 15 May 1820 and 12 June 1820.
38. Sherwill to Clare, 11 May 1820, Pet. F1; Emmerson to Clare, 11 May 1820 Eg. 2245, ff. 118–20.
39. On literary celebrity, see the essays collected in *Romanticism and Celebrity Culture, 1750–1850*, ed. Tom Mole (Cambridge: Cambridge University Press, 2009).
40. Radstock to Emmerson (copy) in Emmerson to Clare, 11 May 1820; and Emmerson to Clare, 11 May 1820, Eg. 2245, ff. 118–20.
41. John Lucas suggests that several of Clare's early poems 'use exactly the language of popular radicalism that can be found in radical newspapers of the time'; 'Clare's Politics', in Haughton, pp. 148–77 (p. 155).

42. *Poems Descriptive*, p. 148; Sherwill to Clare, 11 May 1820.
43. Taylor to Clare, 27–29 September 1820, Eg. 2245, f. 225.
44. Emmerson to Clare, 24 May 1820, quoted in *Critical Heritage*, p. 62. *Poems Descriptive*, p. 148. 'Moiled' means 'hot and weary with work; tired out, exhausted', Joseph Wright, *The English Dialect Dictionary*, 6 vols. (London: Henry Frowde, 1898–1905), 4: M–Q, p. 143.
45. *Poems Descriptive*, p. 9.
46. Taylor to Clare, 27–29 September 1820, Eg. 2245, f. 225. Taylor was still unsure how to proceed in January the following year, enquiring of Clare: 'what are we to do with those 8 lines LR marked out of Helpstone?'; Taylor to Clare, 6 January 1821, quoted in *Letters*, p.135. In the fourth edition, the 'Accursed wealth' passage was finally cut, but the other lines survived.
47. J. C. D. Clark, *English Society 1660–1832: Religion, Ideology and Politics During the Ancien Régime* (Cambridge: Cambridge University Press, 2000), p. 8.
48. Jon Klancher, *The Making of English Reading Audiences, 1798–1832* (Madison, WI: Wisconsin University Press, 1987), p. 103.
49. Sarah M. Zimmerman, *Romanticism, Lyricism, and History* (Albany, NY: State University Press of New York, 1999), pp. 158–9.
50. 'The Right of the Poor to the Cultivation of Waste Lands', *The Black Dwarf*, 6 January 1819, 1–5.
51. Lines 57–8 of the poem. *The Poems of Thomas Gray, William Collins, Oliver Goldsmith*, ed. Roger Lonsdale (London: Longman, 1969), p. 678.
52. *The Black Dwarf*, 6 January 1819, 4–5.
53. Thomas Evans, *Christian Policy, the Salvation of the Empire*, 2nd edn. (London, 1820), pp. 15, 17. The description 'deceptively titled' is taken from David Worrall's '*Mab* and Mob: The Radical Press Community in Regency London', in *Romanticism, Radicalism and the Press*, ed. Stephen Behrendt (Detroit: Wayne State University Press, 1997), pp. 137–56 (p. 143).
54. David Worrall, 'Review Essay: Reassessing the "Romantic" Scene', on John Gardner, *Poetry and Popular Protest: Peterloo, Cato Street, and the Queen Caroline Controversy*, *JCSJ*, 33 (2014), 87–91 (89). Despite the leads provided by John Lucas ('Clare's Politics', p. 155) and Anne Janowitz in her *Lyric and Labour in the Romantic Tradition* (Cambridge: Cambridge University Press, 1998), a detailed comparison between Clare's work and what Worrall calls the 'radical poetic counterculture' of Spencean poets such as E. J. Blandford, Allen Davenport, and Thomas Hazard is urgently needed. P. M. S. Dawson, on the contrary, argues that: 'Of all the various strands of radicalism at the time Clare would have had least sympathy for the "physical force" Spenceans who belonged to what even the government distinguished under the term "Ultra (or Fighting) Radicals" as opposed to the constitutional radicals.' See 'Common Sense or Radicalism? Some Reflections on Clare's Politics', *Romanticism*, 2.1 (1996), 81–97 (85).
55. David Worrall, 'Agrarians against the Picturesque: Ultra-Radicalism and the Revolutionary Politics of Land', in *The Politics of the Picturesque: Literature,*

Landscape and Aesthetics Since 1770, ed. Stephen Copley and Peter Garside (Cambridge: Cambridge University Press, 1994), pp. 240–60 (p. 257).
56. *The Annual Register, or a View of the History, Politics, and Literature, for the Year 1817* (London, 1818), pp. 13–14.
57. 'J.S.' to Sir Robert Baker, 10 July 1820, Home Office Papers, HO 40/15, f. 33.
58. 'J.S.' to the Home Office, 16 October 1820, Home Office Papers, HO 40/15, f. 38.
59. Mr Simmons to Lord Sidmouth, 6 September 1820, Home Office Papers, HO 40/14, f. 254.
60. Mr Simmons to Lord Sidmouth, 7 September 1820, Home Office Papers, HO 40/14, f. 258.
61. *Christian Observer*, vol. 19 (London, 1820), p. iii.
62. Laqueur, 'The Queen Caroline Affair', 429.
63. *New Times*, 12 November 1820, quoted in Laqueur, 'The Queen Caroline Affair', 431.
64. Laqueur, 'The Queen Caroline Affair', 429.
65. Taylor to Clare, 27–29 September 1820, Eg. 2245, f. 225. As Simon Kövesi reminds us, by 1893, the very lines identified by Radstock as 'radical slang' could be used to explicitly bolster a conservative reading of Clare. See 'John Clare & ... & ... & ... Deleuze and Guattari's Rhizome', in *Ecology and the British Left: The Red and the Green*, ed. John Rignall and H. Gustav Klaus, in association with Valentine Cunningham (Farnham: Ashgate, 2012), pp. 75–88 (pp. 76, 78).
66. Review of *The Moral and Political Crisis of England: Most Respectfully Inscribed to the Higher and Middle Classes* by the Reverend Melville Horne and *A Letter from an Englishman at St. Omers to a Member of Parliament*, Anti-Jacobin Review, 268.59 (September, 1820), 66–76 (70, 72).
67. *The Boston Gazette, and Lincolnshire Advertiser*, 5 September 1820; Gareth Stedman Jones, *Languages of Class: Studies in English Working Class History 1832–1982* (Cambridge: Cambridge University Press, 1983), p. 106.
68. *The Creevey Papers: A Selection from the Correspondence and Diaries of the Late Thomas Creevey, M.P.*, ed. Herbert Maxwell, 2 vols. (London: John Murray, 1904), I, p. 304.
69. McWilliam, *Popular Politics*, p. 11.
70. In spite of two references to 'oppressions power' in stanzas 105 (line 1071) and 110 (line 1119).
71. Stephen Colclough, *Voicing Loss, Versions of Pastoral in the Poetry of John Clare, 1817–1832*, (University of Keele: PhD thesis, 1996), p. 85.
72. David Worrall, *Theatric Revolution: Drama, Censorship, and Romantic Period Subcultures 1773–1832* (Oxford: Oxford University Press, 2006), pp. 199–200.
73. *Morning Post*, 17 November 1820. On the conservative reaction to events, see Jonathan Fulcher, 'The Loyalist Response to the Queen Caroline Agitations', *Journal of British Studies*, 34.4 (October, 1995), 481–502. Brandenburgh House was the queen's residence in London during this period.
74. Definitions 3 and 5 in *Green's Dictionary of Slang*, ed. Jonathan Green, 3 vols. (London: Chambers, 2010), 3: P–Z, pp. 1012–13.

75. Olivia Smith, *The Politics of Language 1791–1819* (Oxford: Clarendon Press, 1984), p. 2.
76. Roger Sales, *English Literature in History 1780–1830: Pastoral and Politics* (London: Longman, 1983), p. 92.
77. Stephen Colclough, '"Labour and Luxury": Clare's Lost Pastoral and the Importance of Voice in the Early Poems', in *New Approaches*, pp. 77–91 (p. 87).
78. For the debate about the nature of Clare's politics, see, in particular, Lucas, 'Clare's Politics' and Dawson, 'Common Sense or Radicalism'. See also P. M. S. Dawson, 'John Clare—Radical?', *JCSJ*, 11 (1992), 17–27; Alan Vardy, 'Clare and Political Equivocation', *JCSJ*, 18 (1999), 37–48; Eric Robinson's introduction to *John Clare: A Champion for the Poor, Political Verse and Prose*, ed. P. M. S. Dawson, Eric Robinson and David Powell (Ashington and Manchester: MidNAG/Carcanet, 2000), pp. xiv–xv; and Vardy's review of the same in *JCSJ*, 20 (2001), 81–5.
79. Adapted from Clare to Taylor, 18 August 1821, *Letters*, pp. 208–9 and *Champion for the Poor*, pp. 312–13. The deleted passage, speculatively restored in *Champion for the Poor*, is not included in *Letters*.
80. E. P. Thompson, *The Making of the English Working Class* (1963; rpt. Harmondsworth: Penguin, 1980), p. 778. See also Thompson's review of Iowerth Prothero's *Artisans and Politics in Early Nineteenth-Century London: John Gast and His Times* (1978), in which he acknowledged that the affair had more importance than he had previously allowed, but still called it 'a glorious ebullition of that peculiar English genre: humbug'; 'The Very Type of the "Respectable Artisan"', *New Society* 48 (May 3, 1979), 275–7 (276). For descriptions of the affair as a farce, see Laqueur, 'The Queen Caroline Affair', 441.
81. *The Diary of Benjamin Robert Haydon*, ed. William Bissell Pope, 5 vols. (Cambridge, MA: Harvard University Press, 1960–3), 2, pp. 296–7.
82. On Clare's reluctance to illuminate his house to celebrate the abandonment of the Bill of Pains and Penalties, see Clare to Hessey, 1 December 1820, *Letters*, pp. 109–10.

CHAPTER 10

John Clare and the London Magazine

Richard Cronin

The *London Magazine* was addressed to a metropolitan readership. As he explains in his prospectus, John Scott, its first editor, chose to revive the title of a defunct magazine as a way of calling attention to a gap in the market: 'while secondary towns of the Kingdom' (the town uppermost in his mind is Edinburgh) 'give name and distinction to popular Journals, the METROPOLIS' remains '*unrepresented* in the now strenuous *competition* of Periodical Literature'.[1] Given this, it seems odd that the first issue of the magazine should feature in its opening pages Octavius Gilchrist's 'Account of John Clare, an Agricultural Labourer and Poet'.[2] Clare's obscurity – he is, as Gilchrist acknowledges, as yet 'altogether unknown to literature' – is underlined by the paper that immediately follows in which John Scott offers his tribute to the most celebrated writer of the age, the 'Author of the Scotch Novels'. Walter Scott takes second place to a provincial poet who lived 'in the neighbourhood of Stamford', the Lincolnshire market town. But Stamford, seven miles from Clare's village of Helpston, was an important provincial centre and the hub of an extensive literary network. John Scott, the *London*'s editor, had edited Drakard's *Stamford News*, a newspaper that had been launched in 1809 as a radical alternative to the long-established *Stamford Mercury*. Gilchrist had been his principal coadjutor and succeeded to the editorship of the newspaper in 1813 when Scott returned to London to edit *Drakard's Paper*, retitled in the following year as *The Champion*. Gilchrist's paper in the *London* was clearly intended to advertise Clare's first volume, *Poems, Descriptive of Rural Life and Scenery*, about to be published by the London firm of Taylor and Hessey. Taylor was an old friend of Gilchrist's and had first met Clare at Gilchrist's house in Stamford. He had already been introduced to Clare's poems by another Stamford resident, the young bookseller Edward Drury, who was Taylor's cousin. Taylor and Hessey were also intimates of John Scott. In 1817 they had published *The House of Mourning*, Scott's elegy for his dead son. After Scott's death on 27 February 1821, Taylor and Hessey bought the magazine from its founder, Robert Baldwin, and Taylor succeeded Scott as editor. These circumstances may explain the inclusion of Gilchrist's paper in the *London's* first number, but they offer no explanation of why it was that Clare went on to become so important a contributor to the magazine, by some reckonings the most prolific of all the contributors of original poetry.[3]

Roger Sales argues that the *London Magazine* made space for John Clare and Allan Cunningham, the Scottish stone mason and neighbour of Burns, in recognition of the importance of James Hogg to *Blackwood's Edinburgh Magazine*. *Blackwood's* was, after all, the magazine on which the *London* most closely modelled itself. The employment of Clare and Cunningham was a manifestation of 'the rivalry between the two journals'.[4] But this answers one question only to prompt another. Why did *Blackwood's*, a product of the most culturally sophisticated city in Britain – its principal writers, John Wilson and J. G. Lockhart, Oxford-educated Edinburgh lawyers – value so highly the contributions of the scarcely educated James Hogg? The success of the new literary magazines, the single most remarkable publishing phenomenon in the second and third decades of the nineteenth century, was gained because they catered for a new urban middle class, not often university-educated, employed most typically as clerks in trading companies, in government offices, or the offices of lawyers. The magazines supplied the new readership with the cultural baggage that it lacked.[5] When Thomas Campbell accepted Henry Colburn's generous offer to edit the *New Monthly Magazine* his own principal contribution was a series of papers of remarkable dullness on Greek poetry, but Colburn recognized their value. They reinforced the decision to appoint as editor a recognized British poet by offering a further demonstration of the magazine's cultural seriousness. The new magazines set themselves somewhat self-consciously to repair the narrowness of their readership's cultural experience – hence the inclusion of papers that surveyed the classical heritage, the older literature of Britain, and European cultural developments. The new readership was characteristically urban, and unfamiliar with the traditional culture that still survived, if precariously, in rural areas. Contributions were also needed to supply this lack. So it was that even before Wilson and Lockhart were associated with *Blackwood's*, James Hogg furnished the magazine with a series of papers under the title 'Tales and Anecdotes of the Pastoral Life', which introduced readers to 'old songs', 'strange stories of witches and apparitions' and 'anecdotes of the pastoral life'. Hogg recommended his material as 'extremely curious, and wholly unknown to the literary part of the community'.[6] As James Chandler and Kevin Gilmartin point out, 'the very act of laying claim to a rural sensibility' was itself 'a product of the metropolitan moment'.[7] John Scott already knew as much. While Hogg lives, he wrote, 'the great and final gulph of division is not yet interposed between the simplicity and elevated imagination of an innocent, religious, and patriarchal people, and the artifice and pretention of what is called refined civilization'.[8] Clare's role was to offer a similar bridge between the two cultures in Scott's own magazine. The *London*, like Leigh Hunt's *Examiner*, was a Cockney publication – Hazlitt was a leading contributor and it championed the poetry of Keats – but in Clare, Scott seems to have recognized, it had found an antidote to its own Cockneyism. Clare's poetry, as his reviewer in the *Monthly Review* put it, precisely because it was 'artless and unsophisticated', offered a salutary corrective to 'the effusions of a poet writing pastorals as he wanders through the fields to the north-east of London'.[9]

Allan Cunningham makes the point in the first of a series of papers for the *London* on 'Traditional Literature'.[10] In the provinces 'a species of rustic, or national oral literature' still survives that has been 'long since obliterated in the city'. It is, Cunningham insists, a more truly national literature than the urbane literary tradition, and a more authentic literature: 'The character of the city is not of that genuine original kind, which would incline its society to receive and retain those simple compositions that dwell in the minds and hearts of a pastoral and a rural people.'[11] The metropolitan citizen, like the typefaces in which literature was reproduced on the city's printing presses, is unindividualized, 'so smoothed down and polished, in the outward and inner man, that the original English stamp is more than half effaced'.[12] Cunningham supplied the magazine with papers designed to meet a taste that had been created principally by Walter Scott: in his collection of border ballads, *Minstrelsy of the Scottish Border*, in the poems that followed, and more recently in the Scotch novels. But, as Hazlitt noted, the taste for all things Scottish was itself a reaction against an England in which 'every foot of soil' had been 'worked up' and 'nearly every movement of the social machine' had become 'calculable'. England had once been properly represented by the strongly individual, by the idiosyncratic and the eccentric. There was 'a Parson Adams not quite a hundred years ago – a Sir Roger de Coverley rather more than a hundred', but now individuality has been erased by 'the level, the littleness, the frippery of modern civilization'.[13] It was not just character that had been lost. In a culture that was now regulated by the use of dictionaries and the operation of printers' conventions, language itself had been flattened. Cunningham offered the 'more varied and original cast'[14] of rural language as an antidote to the 'smoothed down and polished' language of the metropolis. John Taylor makes a similar point in the paper for the *London* in which he describes his visit to John Clare.[15] Taylor is at first defensive about Clare's 'provincial' language, recommending the 'philosophic mind' to 'read his thoughts, rather than catch at the manner of their utterance'.[16] But when he calls to mind those who would prefer corn to be threshed rather than thumped he registers an objection to all attempts to impose on literature a standardized diction, a policy that, as he points out, would dictate that 'Spenser and Shakespeare ought to be proscribed', since both wrote before the time at which a single group, socially and geographically defined, had succeeded in establishing its own linguistic habits as 'the true and entire "world of words" for all Englishmen'.[17] He ends by finding in Clare's diction the most decisive proof of 'the originality of his genius'. It is through his diction that Clare rescues his reader from the mass-produced language that characterized the print industry of the early nineteenth century. As Taylor puts it, Clare saves the reader from a 'cluster-language framed and cast into set forms, in the most approved models, and adapted for all occasions'.[18]

Clare's poetry, Taylor suggests, has the value that attaches to a handicraft in an age of mass production. The poetry embodies an individuality and an authenticity that have been lost in a print industry that now manufactures goods for consumption by a mass public. The paradox in making such a claim in the *London Magazine* is evident, because the new magazines were themselves amongst the most striking symptoms of the industrialization of literature of which Taylor complains, and from which Clare's poems are represented as offering relief. It is a paradox central to the literary culture of the early nineteenth century. The most striking symptom of the industrialization of print was the entirely unprecedented sale of Walter Scott's novels, the fifth of which, *Rob Roy*, might, according to Peter Garside, fairly claim to be the first example of the phenomenon that most dramatically signalled the transformation in the character of the print industry – the best seller.[19] Scott secured his phenomenal sales in part, surely, because the Scots that his best-loved characters spoke offered precisely what Taylor discovered in Clare's poems: direct access to an oral culture that was in danger of being extirpated by a literary culture issuing from the metropolitan centres of London and Edinburgh. The literary language of the metropolis was not reproduced in speech but typographically, by means of letter press. The new magazines employed writers such as James Hogg, Allan Cunningham and John Clare because they offered magazine readers, as Scott offered novel readers, the chance to rediscover an older, more authentic, and more truly national oral culture. But such promises could only be illusory. Scott's novels, for example, could not offer direct access to the oral culture of Scotland because the Scots language, as the novels reproduced it, was itself a typographical phenomenon. The novels, claims Hazlitt, 'are not so much admired in Scotland as in England':[20] they are most admired, then, by those for whom Scots is not a spoken language so much as a system of orthography. The novels, just as much as Scott's *Minstrelsy of the Scottish Border*, could preserve oral culture only by translating modes of speech into typographical conventions, which is to say that they could not preserve them at all, an uncomfortable perception not lost on James Hogg's mother, one of the principal sources for the ballads that Scott preserved in the *Minstrelsy*. Scott, she complains, had 'broken the charm' of poems that were 'made for singing and no' for reading'. Hogg adds that his mother had been proved right, 'for from that day to this, these songs, which were the amusement of every winter evening, have never been sung more'.[21]

Scott's achievement is inherently paradoxical. Hazlitt properly prefers the novels to the poems, which can claim only the status of 'a *modern-antique*': the 'smooth, glossy texture of his verse contrasts happily with the quaint, uncouth, rugged materials of which it is composed'.[22] But there is surely a very similar contrast between the 'quaint, uncouth, rugged' speech of characters such as Rob Roy and Bailie Nicol Jarvie and the elegant pages set by James Ballantyne in which that speech was encountered. I suspect that the paradox secured rather than threatened Scott's overwhelming popularity. It is certainly a paradox that writers such as Hogg and Cunningham who were building on Scott's success seem anxious to reproduce. Cunningham, for example, regrets in the first paper in his series 'Traditional Literature' that the poet has been degraded so far that he has become 'a kind of auxiliary to the city bookseller',[23] which is an odd complaint to make in a contribution to a periodical such as the *London Magazine*. In the papers themselves Cunningham offers examples of the 'rustic, or national oral literature' that he prizes, but the verse specimens are enclosed within a prose narrative of a very different character. In the second paper in the series[24] Cunningham chooses as an epigraph a vigorous 'old ballad', 'Richard Faulder of Allanbay' – 'It's sweet to go with hound and hawk, / O'er moor and mountain roamin'' – but the paper proper opens with a sentence of a polished urbanity so emphatic that it can only have been designed to point a contrast with the verse that precedes it: 'On a harvest afternoon, when the ripe grain, which clothed the western slope of the Cumberland hills, had partly submitted to the sickle, a party of reapers were seated on a small green knoll, enjoying the brief luxury of the dinner hour.' This is prose as 'smoothed down and polished, in the outward and inner man' as any of the city dwellers whose lack of 'the original English stamp' Cunningham bemoans in the paper introducing the series. It is as if he is not content to allow his old ballads to stand out by contrast with the other contributions to John Scott's metropolitan magazine – he insists on rehearsing the contrast within his own contribution. But Cunningham's magazine identity is still more ambivalent than this suggests, for Cunningham, even more emphatically than Walter Scott, is an exponent of the '*modern-antique*'. The ballads offered as specimens of 'the unwritten reliques of our poetry'[25] were written by Cunningham himself.

Cunningham's practice seemed reprehensible to serious scholars of popular literature. To William Motherwell he was one of the 'manufacturers of antique gems' who 'poison the sources of history'.[26] Cunningham had notoriously submitted some of his own compositions to R. H. Cromek, who had published them in 1810 in his *Remains of Nithsdale and Galloway Song*. But in the *London* such subterfuges were viewed more indulgently. For Thomas Hood, who joined the *London Magazine* in 1821 as 'a sort of sub-editor', Cunningham was a purveyor of 'rare old-new or new-old ballads'.[27] In John Hamilton Reynolds's squib, 'The Literary Police Office, Bow Street',[28] the charge becomes merely facetious: 'ALLAN CUNNINGHAM, a dwarf' (because Cunningham was remarkably tall) is brought up before the magistrate 'charged with a fraud upon a Mr. Cromek. Being young and little, he was handed over to the Philanthropic, as a fit place for such a heart as his'[29] (the Philanthropic Society of Mile End had been established in 1803 'for the Relief and Discharge of Persons Imprisoned for Small Debts'). When Taylor visited Clare he noted a copy of Cromek's volume on Clare's shelves, and the success of Cunningham's deception seemed to both men simply a matter for congratulation: 'he thought, as I did, that only "Auld Lang Syne" could have produced poems such as The Lord's Marie, Bonnie Lady Anne, and the Mermaid of Gallowa'. Clare, who was so great an admirer of Chatterton, could scarcely be expected to have thought otherwise.[30]

Cunningham had been born and raised in Dumfriesshire, where he had served his apprenticeship as a stonemason, but since 1810 he had worked in

London, employed by the most fashionable sculptor of the day, Francis Chantrey, as superintendent of his studio. The papers on 'Traditional Literature' are directed from 'Lammerlea, Cumberland' only by a polite fiction: in fact, Cunningham lived in Pimlico. The wide difference between the two addresses usefully offers a clue to the complexity of Cunningham's place within the literary economy of the *London Magazine*. He was a prominent member of a tight circle of London writers, and also a writer whose special function was to act as a conduit through which a popular, oral, rustic literature might enliven a magazine otherwise remarkable for the metropolitan character of its materials. Cunningham was asked, in other words, at once to take his place as one of a group of London writers, and to function as their antidote.

The defining mark of the London writers was the ease with which they were able to move between identities. Metropolitan identity was defined by its fluidity. Its most popular representative in the period was Corinthian Tom in Pierce Egan's *Life In London*, who earns his Corinthian status because he is a citizen of the whole city, equally happy 'whether he was animatedly engaged in squeezing the hand of some lovely countess of St James's, or passing an hour with a poor custard-monger in the back settlements of St Giles's'. For Tom and his country cousin Jerry all the sights of London are equally available; 'taking a turn in the evening to listen to Coleridge, Flaxman, and Soane', a visit to Newgate on the morning of an execution, a trip to the dog-pit to watch the famous monkey Jacco take on the dogs, or an evening at the Royal Academy exhibition at Somerset House, a visit to which, as Bob Logic, Tom's Oxonian friend, insists, is always 'a bob well laid out'.[31] In the course of their adventures Tom and Jerry traverse the whole of the city, and Jerry, fresh from the country, learns under Tom's tutelage to be equally at home wherever he goes. As Gregory Dart points out, the new readership that the *London Magazine* addressed, a heterogeneous group of semi-professionals, clerks, trainee lawyers, shop-keepers and craftsmen, had in common only that their place in the social hierarchy was unfixed. *Life in London* achieved its extraordinary success because it was able to 'throw itself into this experience of social indeterminacy and to turn it into a source of pleasure'.[32] Allan Cunningham's subscription from 'Lammerlea Cumberland' worked by contrast to root the series of papers in a fixed place governed by a stable social hierarchy in which identities were fully determined.

Contributions to magazines were, for the most part, anonymous. But a still more flamboyant magazine expression of the fluid identity that defined the metropolitan personality was the practice of pseudonymity. In an attack on *Blackwood's* in the *London*, John Scott suggests that it was a practice that the *Blackwood's* men borrowed from Walter Scott, who presented his own fiction under a rich variety of pseudonyms.[33] In a typically impudent gesture *Blackwood's* offered the 'names of Odoherty, Kempferhausen, Wastle, Timothy Tickler, and Lauerwinckel', pseudonyms used in the magazine often enough to have developed into house characters, as proof that its writers scorned anonymity.[34] John Scott condemns the irresponsibility that the practice encourages. It made it possible, he complains, for Wordsworth to be 'outrageously vilified, and zealously defended' in papers written 'by the same individual' (he seems mistakenly to have believed that the pieces in question were written by Lockhart rather than John Wilson). But in the very same edition of the *London* Scott had included the paper 'Christ's Hospital Five and Thirty Years Ago', in which Elia refutes the 'magnificent eulogy' of his old school that 'Mr. Lamb' had reprinted in his '"Works," published a year or two since'.[35] Pseudonymity was one of the games that the new magazines played,[36] no contributor more flamboyantly than the *London*'s T. G. Wainewright. His papers might appear under the signature of Janus Weathercock, or Egomet Bonmot, or Cornelius van Vinkbooms, and it was Wainewright, Lamb believed, who, more than any other contributor, gave the *London* its character. In 1822, he asked Hessey:

> What is gone of the Opium Eater, where is Barry Cornwall, & above all what is become of Janus Weathercock – or by his worse name of Vinksomething? – He is much wanted. He was the genius of the Lond. Mag. The rest of us are single Essayists.[37]

John Taylor secured the collegiality of the magazine by offering monthly dinners first at his premises in Fleet Street and later at Waterloo Place.[38] Clare, who attended when visiting London, remembers them fondly as presided over by John Hamilton Reynolds, 'the soul of these dinner partys'. The fellow guests included Hazlitt, 'a silent picture of severity', Charles Lamb, 'a good sort of a fellow and if he offends it is innosently done', and Henry Cary, the translator of Dante.[39] The dinners were remembered too by Thomas Hood. Hood remembers Clare sitting next to Hazlitt, distinguished from the other guests by his bright green coat: 'shining verdantly out from the grave-coloured suits of the literati, like a patch of turnips amidst stubble and fallow, behold our Jack i' the Green – John Clare' (the 'Jack i' the Green' is the figure swathed in foliage who figures in rustic Mayday celebrations). After the dinner Clare walked along the Strand arm-in-arm with Charles Lamb, while passers-by shouted after them, 'there goes Tom and Jerry' (in the Cruikshanks' illustrations to *Life in London* and in all the stage adaptations a green coat identifies Tom's country cousin, Jerry Hawthorn). Hood recalls how, on an occasion when the dinner was hosted by T. G. Wainewright, Wainewright's valet tried to exclude Clare from the gathering, taking him for an 'interloper'. The anecdote establishes Clare as at once an accepted member of the group and as an outsider. The brightness of the green coat, such a very *'countrified* suit', set against the 'editorial sables' favoured by the other guests, is, as Hood intimates, emblematic: it signals Clare's failure to blend in with his fellow contributors. The green coat makes it predictable that Hood should end his account of Clare by regretting his presence: 'Poor Clare! – It would greatly please me to hear that he was happy and well, and thriving; but the transplanting of Peasants and Farmers' Boys from the natural into an artificial soil, does not always conduce to their happiness, or health, or ultimate well doing.'[40] Hood's misgivings were widely shared. Wainewright claimed Clare's friendship in one of his Weathercock papers: 'Thy hand, friend Clare! others may speak thee fairer, but none wish thee solider welfare than Janus.' But his concern for Clare's welfare issues in a piece of advice that, even Janus admits, seems strange coming from a friend, 'visit London seldom'.[41] The same thought moved the classicist C. A. Elton to verse. In his 'Idler's Epistle to John Clare'[42] he urges the poet to quit the town: 'The paven flat of endless street / Is all unsuited to thy feet,' by which he means the feet of Clare's verse as much as the feet on which he treads the London pavements.

Elton's point is that Clare's value to the magazine depends on his maintaining his difference from the metropolitan contributors. He understands as well as Hood that Clare could only be struck by the disparity between the society that London affords him and the society available to him in Helpston. He will be left sadly 'contrasting the unlettered country company of Clod, and Hodge and Podge, with the delights of "London" society – Elia, and Barry [Cornwall, the pen-name of Bryan Waller Proctor], and Herbert [J. H. Reynolds wrote for the *London* under the pseudonym, Edward Herbert], and Mr Table Talk [Hazlitt], *cum multis aliis*'.[43] But his proper place is with Clod, Hodge and Podge. Hood's recourse to the pseudonyms so characteristic of metropolitan magazine writing is revealing. Lamb and Reynolds appear under their pseudonyms because they have assumed the unstable, shifting identity of the metropolis. The value of Clare, by contrast, depends upon his maintaining a simple, fixed identity.

The verbal figure most closely associated with metropolitan magazine identity was the pun. It is entirely appropriate that as a young man of twenty-two Thomas Hood, the most celebrated punster of the century, should have been introduced to 'Authorship in earnest' when he was appointed by Taylor and Hessey to a position at the *London*.[44] Hood took over the 'Lion's Head', the column that acknowledged unsolicited contributions, and immediately put his own stamp upon it: 'The Essay on Agricultural Distress would only increase it.'[45] The magazine dinners were also remembered for their puns. For Hood it was Lamb who was sure 'to stammer out the best pun of the evening'.[46] Clare too recalls how Lamb 'stammers at a joke or pun', but gives the palm to Reynolds, who is 'a wit and punster and very happy and entertaining in both pretentions ... there is nothing studied about them'.[47] But, as Charles Lamb explains in one of his Elia papers, punning did not simply refer to wordplay. Lamb thought of 'all non-serious subjects; or subjects serious in themselves, but treated after my fashion, non-seriously' as puns ('Distant Correspondents'[48]). The pun came to figure the principle of mobility that was so characteristic of the *London*'s writers.[49] Clare notes that one of those present at the dinners, Allan Cunningham, felt excluded from this community of punsters: 'when the companys talk is of poetry he is ready to talk 2 ways at once but when puns are up his head is down over his glass musing and silent and nothing but poetry is the game to start him into hillarity again'.[50] It is a discomfort that Wainewright believed Clare himself felt. When, in one of the *London*'s more elaborate practical jokes, the death of Elia was announced, Wainewright suggested that Clare would be relieved: never again will his 'sweetly-simple Doric phrase and accent beget the odious *pun*'. Wainewright, like Clare himself, takes punning to be inconsistent with the language of poetry, for 'love and perfect trust, no doubt, is the germ of *true* poetry'.[51]

John Scott accused *Blackwood's* of including Hogg's contributions without according him collegial status: 'in Blackwood's Magazine' Hogg 'is made to figure as an absolute Zany: he is made the Fool of the Show-cart: that is to say, he is abused, belied, disfigured – and *all under the guise of friendship and affection*'.[52] Hogg, Scott believed, was less like John Wilson and J. G. Lockhart, the other principal contributors to the magazine, than one of the magazine's characters. His proper place was not with Wilson and Lockhart but with Morgan Odoherty, Timothy Tickler, Kempferhausen and so on. It was a suspicion that was confirmed, it might be thought, in March 1823, when Hogg made his first appearance in the 'Noctes Ambrosianae', the most celebrated of all the *Blackwood's* series, supposedly offering transcripts of the regular meetings of the *Blackwood's* editorial team at Ambrose's, a tavern in Gabriel Road, Edinburgh. In March 1823, Hogg was impersonated by Lockhart, but later the column became the exclusive property of John Wilson, and Hogg, usually dubbed by Wilson the Shepherd, became his most famous character. It was a position that Hogg did not find quite comfortable. It was not simply that Hogg's identity was being appropriated by another contributor to the magazine: in becoming a character he was flattened, reduced to a type, an embodiment of rustic horse sense or of the bodily importunities that his more intellectual collocutors are apt to overlook.[53] It remains a question whether John Clare escaped a similar fate at the hands of the *London Magazine*.

The test case is the squib by John Hamilton Reynolds that appeared in the issue for February 1823, 'The Literary Police Office'.[54] The paper reports on a sitting at Bow Street of the metropolitan magistrates' court before which a wide selection of contemporary literary figures appear to answer a variety of charges. The fun is harmless enough – Wordsworth is charged with stealing a pony from Mrs Foy and a spade from Mr Wilkinson, Coleridge of spending his days asleep in Highgate. Reynolds, who published the piece under his regular pseudonym, Edward Herbert, seems most taken with the opportunities for punning that the scenario affords him: Byron is committed to Coldbath Fields 'for want of *Bayle* (which he had lent to Mr. Leigh Hunt, to assist him in his philosophical pursuits)', Southey admits 'that he lived upon the lives of others'. But the treatment of John Clare seems altogether rougher. He is accused of fathering a child upon one of the Muses, and ordered to pay maintenance of 'half-a-crown' which he is somehow to save out of his 'sixpence-a-day' even though he has 'a wife, and ten little children' to support. Clare might not have welcomed references so direct to his poverty and his domestic responsibilities, no matter how well-intentioned, but it is hard not to suspect that Reynolds is in addition hinting at some sexual misdemeanour of Clare's, well-known within his London circle, that Clare could not possibly have been happy to see rehearsed in print under so flimsy a disguise.[55] It is surely possible to argue that Clare in a piece such as this, just as much as Hogg in various of his appearances in *Blackwood's*, is 'abused, belied, disfigured – and *all under the guise of friendship and affection*'.

Responses to Reynolds's paper necessarily depend on the view taken of Clare's status within the magazine. Up to a point he was clearly accepted as an equal, included within the mobile, punning literary community of the magazine. As Hood recalls, to Lamb he was 'Clarissimus', 'Princely Clare', at his most exalted he was 'C in alt'.[56] Most of his poems in the magazine appeared anonymously, or under his own name, or his initials, J. C., but in what may have been his very last contributions he wrote, as his colleagues in the magazine so often did, under a pseudonym. He becomes Percy Green – green for his garish London coat, and to mark his role in offering readers who saw the world dulled by London smoke access through his poems to the fresh greens of the English countryside.[57] But it was two years earlier, in June 1821, that Clare made his most ingenious attempt to assimilate with the culture of the magazine. He wrote a letter to its editor, John Taylor, introducing himself as Stephen Timms, 'a countryman in a very humble way' anxious to 'rise by trying [his] tallents at poetry'. He enclosed a specimen of his work, 'Some account of my Kin, my Tallents & myself. a Poem', and promised 'halfacrown' to the editor if the poem should be printed. By masquerading as a cod version of himself, Clare claims the right to join in the self-mocking, self-referential game-playing so typical of the magazines. This, for example, is his response to those who mock his father as a 'timber merchant', by which he means, he confesses, a maker and seller of matches (George Packwood, who manufactured razor strops and paste, was celebrated for the rhymed advertisements for his products):

> is the prime strops of Packwood
> A pin the worse cause he has humbler been
> Then why – but hold – I quake at Mr B—
> Hell rap my knuckles in his magazine

It is revealing that Clare borrows the Packwood/Blackwood rhyme from a poem by Lockhart in *Blackwood's*.[58] In response Hessey reported that he and Taylor 'did not think it one of your happiest efforts – The best thing you can do is to write in your own natural Style, in which no one can excel you.' Clare's letter was not printed.[59] Instead, it was Horace Smith, the exemplary metropolitan man of letters, who took up the joke in his 'Auto-Biography of John Huggins', in which he presents 'Huggins, the Oxfordshire Toll-boy' as the worthy successor to the Bristol Milkmaid (Ann Yearsley), the Farmer's Boy (Bloomfield), the Ettrick Shepherd (Hogg), and 'Clare, the Northamptonshire peasant'. Huggins becomes a poet when he comes across 'two odd volumes of Hayley's poems, which had been given to one of [his] school-fellows by his godmother'.[60] Magazine insiders would have caught the reference to Clare's acquisition of a copy of Thomson's *Seasons*. Denied the opportunity to practice self-mockery, Clare found himself the object of the more urbane mockery of Horace Smith.

Taylor and Hessey did not want Clare to contribute playful articles of the kind contributed by the Smith brothers, Reynolds and Wainewright, but pieces written in his 'own natural style', by which they seemed to mean pieces written in the rustic dialect that was for Taylor decisive proof of the originality of Clare's genius. Except that none of the poems printed in the *London Magazine* is quite of that character. 'Childish Recollections', quoted in full by Taylor in his paper recalling his 'Visit to John Clare', is a representative *London* poem. It contains only one expression that Taylor needed to gloss, the reference to a snail shell as a 'pooty-shell'.[61] Clare omits the epigraph from Henry Mackenzie that, when the poem appeared in *The Village Minstrel*, places it within the sentimental tradition, but the tradition to which the poem belongs is clear enough without it. Clare describes a landscape of 'checquer'd fields' populated by 'shepherd boy, and neatherd'. Other passages in the poem are more distinctive, the rendering, for example, of the gurgling sounds of the running brook that Clare watches 'till bursting off it plopt / In rushing gushes of wild murmuring groans'. Several of the poems published in the *London* recall childhood experience, which is, I think, significant. Clare's childhood experience revives as it is recalled, and yet it remains an experience from which the adult observer knows himself to be excluded. As Clare puts it in 'Childish Recollections', 'Sad manhood marks me an intruder now'. Clare occupies a position in between childhood and adulthood, and just as importantly in between languages, in between the language of pastoral poetry and the language of his native Helpston. Hood was sensitive to Clare's in-betweenness: it is why Clare's green coat, 'that *very countrified* suit', seemed to him less like a peasant's costume than a species of fancy dress, the garb of 'some eccentric notable of the Corinthian order, disguised in rustic'.[62] In his 'Idler's Epistle to John Clare', Elton proves equally sensitive to the way in which the in-betweenness was registered in the diction of Clare's poems. He advises Clare to 'drive' from his head all the poets 'alive or dead', but that is because he recognizes the language in which Clare's *London Magazine* poems are written as heavily contaminated by the literary: 'Some in thy lines a Goldsmith see, / Or Dyer's tone'.[63] It is not just his residence in London but the cast of the poems that leads Elton to stigmatize him as 'Thou cockney Clare!'. It was, after all, the Cockney poets who were the exemplary in-betweeners, the poets who, as Marjorie Levinson puts it, characteristically wrote from the 'neither/nor' position, defined only by their difference from the class above them and the class below.[64]

Clare's importance to the *London* was as an antidote to the Cockneyism of much of the magazine's content, but, looked at another way, Clare might be thought of as the Cockney's mirror image. It is the point that Charles Lamb makes in his one surviving letter to Clare when he complains that Clare is too profuse in his use of slang, by which he seems to mean any language that is narrowly localized: 'There is a rustic Cockneyism as little pleasing as ours of London'.[65] Horace Smith too associated peasant poets and Cockneys. He was reminded of Huggins, he claims, when he read in the last number of the magazine 'the very affecting account of Perrinson'. Edward Perrinson, another fictitious poet, had been 'apprenticed to a grocer of Exeter' where, 'after raisin-hours, he buried himself in the classic poets' before abandoning his apprenticeship to devote himself 'to love and literature'.[66] Despite the west-country setting the parody of Keats is as evident as the parody of Clare as John Huggins. The Cockney and the peasant poet performed similar functions for the magazine. Clare's poems offered a passage out of the urban landscape in which the magazine was read to a rural England of which the magazine's readership had only a limited experience. Cockney poets offered access to high literary traditions from which readers without a university education might have felt themselves similarly excluded. So, when Reynolds introduces the magazine's readers to Warwick Castle, he approaches the aristocratic site through Keats. The Warwick Vase puts him in mind of 'Ode on a Grecian Urn', and the solemn silence of the great hall, prompts lines from *Hyperion*: 'As when, upon a tranced summer night'.[67] Cockney poets and peasant poets are close kin, both cultivating an impure language that allowed them to mediate between the magazine's readers and kinds of experience with which those readers were unfamiliar. The London street urchins who saw Clare and Lamb walking arm-in-arm and called after them 'Tom and Jerry' were more perceptive than they knew.

Hazlitt's great essay on Cockneyism, 'On Londoners and Country People', first appeared in the *New Monthly* rather than the *London*,[68] but it is crucial to my argument because the contrast that Hazlitt sets out to point between urban and rustic experience so often collapses. Even the definition of the Cockney with which Hazlitt begins – 'I mean by it a person who has never lived out of London, and who has got all his ideas from it' – contrives to transfer to Londoners the narrowness of experience more conventionally ascribed to the provincial. Hazlitt represents the Cockney as astounded by the rural: 'The country has a strange blank appearance. It is not lined with houses all the way, like London.'[69] It is an astonishment exactly mirrored in Clare's accounts of his own responses not to leaving London but to entering it: 'as we approached it the road was lind wi lamps that diminishd in the distance to stars this is London I exclaimd he laughed at my ignorance and only increasd my wonder by saying we were still several miles from it'.[70] The Cockney and the rustic Clare are alike not just in their astonishment, but in the manner in which they inspect their astonishment, taking up a position at a distance from themselves. The effect is still more pronounced in a *London* paper by the dramatist John Poole, 'A Cockney's Rural Sports':

> The country, then, is a place where, instead of thousands of houses rising about us at every turn, only one is to be seen within a considerable space; – where the sky is presented in a large, broad, boundless expanse, instead of being retailed out, as it were, in long strips of a yard and a half wide.[71]

This is a Cockney whose Cockneyism seems aberrant even to himself, and Clare can represent his own rusticity in much the same way. In the poem thanking Gilchrist for inviting him to his house, Clare represents himself as blinking, 'dazzled' by a room 'too fine for clowns to bide in', and grateful that his host should 'put clown's language on his tongue, / As suited well the Rustic's hearing'.[72] It is not just that Clare so clearly playacts his befuddlement – he assumes a posture in which he sees himself from the outside, as a clown, a rustic, as Hodge or Podge. As he travelled in Gilchrist's coach towards London for the first time, he records feeling that 'he was not the same John Clare but that some stranger soul had jumpd into [his] skin'.[73] In that feeling of separation from the self, Cockney and rustic writers merge. The Cockney and the rustic are both defined by their relationship to place, but for both placement and displacement are all but inseparable. 'A real Cockney', writes Hazlitt, is 'the most literal' of creatures and yet he also lives 'in a world of romance – a fairy-land of his own'.[74] The same thought struck John Taylor as Clare conducted him round the sites that he had commemorated in his poems, Lolham Brigs and so on: the scenes as rendered in the poems seemed, when Taylor compared them with the scenes before him, as if transformed by 'the wand of a necromancer'.[75] There is a slight but suggestive indication that Clare himself recognized his kinship with the Cockneys. When he invented a peasant poet who might act as his alter ego he named him Stephen Timms. It seems at least possible that he chose the name as a sly echo of the character in *Blackwood's* known as Tims, a 'small pale dapper young man' who makes his first appearance as an absurdly out of place guest at a Highland shooting party, where he complains that his gun has 'carried away [his] little finger' and with it 'a ring that was a real diamond'.[76] Thereafter Tims became an established *Blackwood's* character, always the archetypal Cockney, and often identified with P. G. Patmore, a frequent contributor to the *London Magazine* and John Scott's second in the duel in which he was fatally wounded.

The brief period of Clare's literary celebrity coincided almost exactly with the life of the *London Magazine*, which ran from January 1820 to June 1829. This is not, I would argue, a coincidence. Clare's fame was a product of what Gregory Dart has called the 'Cockney Moment'.[77] Like the magazine itself, Clare's success was a symptom of the rapid increase in the London population, and the development within it of a new class, aspirant and literate, but as yet unstable in its social identity. The development of that class was both cause and effect of the industrialization of literature that made the new magazines of the early nineteenth century possible. But just as urban expansion increased the value attached to the rural, the development of a print industry produced a nostalgia for an earlier time when literature was not produced by professional men of letters, a nostalgia for a literature that seemed more authentic, more English, closer to the oral literature of times gone by than literature set in smart modern type. It was a nostalgia to which the Northamptonshire peasant appealed, however factitious the appeal may have been. Clare's poems shared with the magazine that first published so many of them a mediatory function. The *London* offered its readers material that would at once entertain them and broaden their experience. Papers on London itself, papers such as Lamb's 'South-Sea House', enriched their imaginative apprehension of their own city. Papers on classical and European literature widened their cultural experience. In a paper such as 'Warwick Castle' Reynolds acted as a tourist guide to one of the great English seats but also to the version of Englishness that the building embodied. Clare's poems offered those same readers access to another version of Englishness that might otherwise have seemed to them as impenetrable as the fortified walls of the castle. Clare's poems answered to the needs of the magazine readers of the 1820s in a variety of ways, but that appeal, like the Cockney Moment itself, proved sadly short-lived.

Notes

1. *London Magazine*, 1 (January 1820), iv, henceforward *LM*.
2. *LM*, 1 (January 1820), 7–11.
3. There are already two studies of Clare's relations with the *London Magazine*, and in particular of his relations with the magazine's most celebrated

contributor: Scott McEathron, 'John Clare and Charles Lamb: Friends in the Past', *Charles Lamb Bulletin*, 95 (July 1996), 98–109, and Simon Kövesi, 'John Clare, Charles Lamb and the *London Magazine*', *Charles Lamb Bulletin*, 135 (July 2006), 82–93. I am indebted to both, but my focus is not on the role of the magazine and its contributors in Clare's literary life but on Clare's role within the literary economy of the magazine.

4. Sales, p. 34.
5. On this, see Jon P. Klancher, *The Making of English Reading Audiences, 1790–1832* (Madison, Wisconsin: Wisconsin University Press, 1987), especially pp. 47–75.
6. *Blackwood's Edinburgh Magazine*, 1 (April 1827), 25. It is entirely characteristic that Hogg's paper should be immediately followed by a paper entitled 'Remarks on Greek Tragedy'.
7. *Romantic Metropolis: The Urban Scene of British Culture, 1780–1840*, ed. James Chandler and Kevin Gilmartin (Cambridge: Cambridge University Press, 2005), p. 15.
8. *LM*, 2 (December 1820), 578.
9. *Monthly Review*, 91 (March 1820), 296.
10. *LM*, 2 (December 1820), 641–7.
11. Ibid., 641.
12. Ibid.
13. *New Monthly Magazine*, 10 (January 1824), 297–304.
14. *LM*, 2 (December 1820), 641.
15. *LM*, 4 (November 1821), 540–8.
16. Ibid., 542.
17. Ibid., 544. Taylor, as he indicated by pressing Clare to entitle his third volume *The Shepherd's Calendar*, thought Spenser an especially valuable precedent for Clare, presumably because of Spenser's self-conscious adoption in his own *Shepherd's Calendar* of rustic dialect words.
18. Ibid.
19. *The English Novel 1770–1829: A Bibliographical Survey of Prose Fiction Published in the British Isles*, ed. P. Garside, J. Raven and R. Schöweling, 2 vols. (Oxford: Oxford University Press, 2000), 2, p. 45.
20. *New Monthly Magazine*, 10 (January 1824), 300.
21. James Hogg, *Anecdotes of Scott*, ed. Jill Rubinstein (Edinburgh: Edinburgh University Press, 1999), p. 38.
22. *New Monthly Magazine*, 10 (January 1824), 299.
23. *LM*, 2 (December 1820), 642.
24. *LM*, 3 (January 1821), pp. 26–32.
25. *LM*, 2 (December 1820), 641.
26. William Motherwell, *Minstrelsy: Ancient and Modern, with an Historical Introduction and Notes* (Glasgow: John Wylie, 1827), p. v.
27. Walter Jerrold, *Thomas Hood and Charles Lamb* (London: Ernest Benn Ltd., 1930), subsequently Jerrold, pp. 99 and 116.
28. *LM*, 7 (February 1823), 157–61.

29. Ibid., 161.
30. *LM*, 4 (November 1821), 546. On Clare and Chatterton, see John Goodridge, *John Clare and Community* (Cambridge: Cambridge University Press, 2013), pp. 12–35. John Scott accepted the charge made in *Blackwood's* that 'Hogg is himself the author of some of the songs given as *Jacobite Relics*', but found that the allegation served only to prove 'the genius of the writer', *LM*, 2 (December 1820), 578. As Simon Kövesi notes, it was a ruse that Clare himself practised, successfully imposing on William Hone one of his own pastiches as an authentic poem of Andrew Marvell's. See 'John Clare, Charles Lamb, and the *London Magazine*', 91.
31. Pierce Egan, *Life in London; or, The day and night scenes of Jerry Hawthorn, esq. and his elegant friend Corinthian Tom, accompanied by Bob Logic, the Oxonian, in their rambles and sprees through the metropolis* (London: Sherwood and Jones, 1823), pp. 44, 29, 339.
32. Gregory Dart, *Metropolitan Art and Literature, 1810–1830* (Cambridge: Cambridge University Press, 2012), p. 113.
33. *LM*, 2 (November 1820), 516–7.
34. *Blackwood's Edinburgh Magazine*, 10 (August 1821), 104.
35. *LM*, 2 (November 1820), 512 and 483.
36. For a brilliant discussion of the practice, see Peter Murphy, 'Impersonation and Authorship in Romantic Britain', *English Literary History*, 59 (1992), 625–49.
37. *The Letters of Charles Lamb, to which are added those of his sister Mary Lamb*, ed. E. V. Lucas, 3 vols. (London: J. M. Dent, 1935), 2, p. 323. Wainewright had not yet been exposed as one of the century's more outrageous murderers.
38. The dinners were monthly in the years 1821–2, but became more sporadic thereafter. By 1824 they had become 'few and far between.' See Tim Chilcott, *A Publisher and His Circle: The Life and Work of John Taylor, Keats's Publisher* (London and Boston: Routledge and Kegan Paul, 1972), p. 153.
39. *John Clare's Autobiographical Writings*, ed. Eric Robinson (Oxford and New York: Oxford University Press, 1983), pp. 136–7.
40. Jerrold, pp. 112–5.
41. *LM*, 7 (January 1823), 48.
42. *LM*, 10 (August 1824), 143–5.
43. Jerrold, p. 113.
44. Walter Jerrold, *Thomas Hood: His Life and Times* (New York: Haskell House Publishers, 1968, first published 1907), p. 93.
45. *LM*, 5 (June 1822), 500.
46. Jerrold, p. 112.
47. *John Clare's Autobiographical Writings*, pp. 134–5.
48. *LM*, 5 (March 1822), 282.
49. On punning in the *London Magazine*, see Simon Kövesi, 'John Clare, Charles Lamb and the *London Magazine*', 84–5.
50. *John Clare's Autobiographical Writings*, p. 137.
51. *LM*, 7 (January 1823), 73.
52. *LM*, 2 (December 1820), 578.

53. On Hogg's emblematic status, see Ian Duncan, 'Hogg's Body', *Studies in Hogg and His World*, 9 (1998), 1–15.
54. *LM*, 7 (February 1823), 157–61.
55. For a contrasting account of the relationship between Clare and Reynolds that includes a discussion of 'The Literary Police Office', see Simon Kövesi, 'John Hamilton Reynolds, John Clare and the *London Magazine*', *Wordsworth Circle*, 42.3 (Summer, 2011), 226–35. On Clare's London adventures, see Bate, pp. 261–2.
56. Jerrold, pp. 113–14.
57. See the fine sonnet, 'Sweet brook! I've met thee many a summer's day', *LM*, 8 (July 1823), 46, and the following month 'Two Sonnets to Mary', *LM*, 8 (August 1823), 148.
58. *Blackwood's Edinburgh Magazine*, 7 (July 1820), 3.
59. For Clare's letter and Hessey's response, see *Letters*, pp. 196–8.
60. *LM*, 3 (April 1821), 375–8.
61. *LM*, 4 (November 1821), 542–3. I quote the poem in this text, in which lines are not numbered.
62. Jerrold, p. 112.
63. *LM*, 10 (August 1824), 143.
64. Marjorie Levinson, *Keats's Life of Allegory: The Origins of a Style* (Oxford: Oxford University Press, 1989), p. 5
65. *Letters of Charles Lamb*, 2, p. 328. On Lamb's one surviving letter to Clare, see Scott McEathron, 'John Clare and Charles Lamb: Friends in the Past', 102.
66. *LM*, 3 (March 1821), 322–9. Frank P. Riga and Claude A. Prance, *Index to the London Magazine* (London and New York: Garland Publishing, 1978), p. 31, suggest on internal evidence that the paper is by Reynolds. I think it more likely that it too is by Horace Smith.
67. 'Warwick Castle', *LM*, 4 (July 1821), 5–13 (7, 11).
68. *New Monthly Magazine*, 8 (January 1823), 171–9.
69. Ibid., 173.
70. *John Clare's Autobiographical Writings*, p. 141.
71. *LM*, 6 (December 1822), 498.
72. *LM*, 1 (January 1820), 7–11.
73. *John Clare's Autobiographical Writings*, p. 129.
74. *New Monthly Magazine*, 8 (January 1823), 172.
75. *LM*, 4 (November 1821), 540.
76. *Blackwood's Edinburgh Magazine*, 5 (August 1820), 605.
77. Gregory Dart, *Metropolitan Art and Literature, 1810–1840: Cockney Adventures*, pp. 1–4. I would argue that the Cockney moment was briefer than Dart supposes, beginning as the Napoleonic wars drew to a close, and ending with the 1820s.

Select bibliography

Works by John Clare

A Champion for the Poor: Political Verse and Prose, ed. P. M. S. Dawson, Eric Robinson and David Powell (Ashington and Manchester: MidNAG/Carcanet, 2000)

Cottage Tales, ed. Eric Robinson, David Powell and P. M. S. Dawson (Ashington and Manchester: MidNAG/Carcanet, 1993)

The Early Poems of John Clare 1804–1822, ed. Eric Robinson and David Powell, assoc. ed. Margaret Grainger, 2 vols. (Oxford: Clarendon Press, 1989)

"I Am": the Selected Poetry of John Clare, ed. Jonathan Bate (New York: Farrar, Straus and Giroux, 2003)

John Clare, ed. R. K. R. Thornton (London: J. M. Dent, 1997)

John Clare By Himself, ed. Eric Robinson and David Powell (Ashington and Manchester: MidNAG/Carcanet, 1996)

John Clare: Major Works, ed. Eric Robinson and David Powell with an Introduction by Tom Paulin (Oxford: Oxford World's Classics, 2004)

John Clare's Autobiographical Writings, ed. Eric Robinson (Oxford and New York: Oxford University Press, 1983)

John Clare: The Living Year 1841, ed. Tim Chilcott (Nottingham: Trent Editions, 1999)

The Journal; Essays; the Journey from Essex, ed. Anne Tibble (Ashington and Manchester: MidNAG/Carcanet, 1980)

The Later Poems of John Clare, ed. Eric Robinson and Geoffrey Summerfield (Manchester: Manchester University Press, 1964)

The Later Poems of John Clare 1837–1864, ed. Eric Robinson and David Powell, assoc. ed. Margaret Grainger, 2 vols. (Oxford: Clarendon Press, 1984)

The Letters of John Clare, ed. J. W. Tibble and Anne Tibble (London: Routledge & Kegan Paul, 1951)

The Letters of John Clare, ed. Mark Storey (Oxford: Clarendon Press, 1985)

Madrigals and Chronicles: Being Newly Found Poems Written by John Clare, ed. Edmund Blunden (London: Beaumont Press, 1924)

The Midsummer Cushion, ed. Anne Tibble and R. K. R. Thornton (Ashington and Manchester: MidNAG/Carcanet, 1979; paperback reissue 1990)

The Natural History Prose Writings of John Clare, ed. Margaret Grainger (Oxford: Clarendon Press, 1983)
Northborough Sonnets, ed. Eric Robinson, David Powell and P. M. S. Dawson (Ashington and Manchester: MidNAG/Carcanet, 1995)
Poems by John Clare, ed. Arthur Symons (London: H. Frowde, 1908)
Poems by John Clare, ed. Norman Gale (Rugby: George E. Over, 1901)
Poems, Chiefly from Manuscript, ed. Edmund Blunden and Alan Porter (London: Cobden-Sanderson, 1920)
Poems Descriptive of Rural Life and Scenery (London: Taylor and Hessey, 1820)
The Poems of John Clare, ed. J. W. Tibble (London: J. M. Dent, 1935)
Poems of John Clare's Madness, ed. Geoffrey Grigson (London: Routledge & Kegan Paul, 1949)
Poems of the Middle Period 1822–1837, ed. Eric Robinson, David Powell and P. M. S. Dawson (Oxford: Clarendon Press. Vols. I–II: 1996; vols. III–IV: 1998; vol. V: 2003).
The Prose of John Clare, ed. J. W. Tibble and Anne Tibble (London: Routledge & Kegan Paul, 1951)
The Rural Muse (London: Whittaker & Co., 1835)
The Rural Muse, ed. R. K. R. Thornton (Ashington and Manchester: MidNAG/Carcanet, 1982)
Selected Poems and Prose, ed. Eric Robinson and Geoffrey Summerfield (Oxford: Oxford University Press, 1966)
Selected Poems of John Clare, ed. Geoffrey Grigson (London: Routledge & Kegan Paul, 1950)
Selected Poems of John Clare, ed. Leonard Clark and Anne Tibble (Leeds: E. J. Arnold & Son, 1964)
The Shepherd's Calendar (London: John Taylor, 1827)
The Shepherd's Calendar, ed. Eric Robinson and Geoffrey Summerfield (Oxford: Oxford University Press, 1973)
The Shepherd's Calendar: Manuscript and Published Version, ed. Tim Chilcott (Manchester: Carcanet, 2006)
Sketches in the life of John Clare, ed. Edmund Blunden (London: Cobden-Sanderson, 1931)
The Village Minstrel and other Poems (London: Taylor and Hessey, 1821)

Select critical bibliography

Abbey, Edward, *Postcards from Ed: Dispatches and Salvos from an American Iconoclast*, ed. David Petersen (Minneapolis: Milkweed Editions, 2007)
Abram, David, *The Spell of the Sensuous: Perception and Language in a More-Than-Human World* (New York: Vintage Books, 1996)
Andrews, Malcolm, *Landscape and Western Art* (Oxford: Oxford University Press, 1999)

Ariès, Philippe, 'Introduction', in Roger Chartier (ed.), *A History of Private Life*, vol. 3: *Passions of the Renaissance*, trans. Arthur Goldhammer (Cambridge, MA: Belknap Press, 1989)
Atkinson, Juliette, *Victorian Biography Reconsidered: A Study of Nineteenth-Century 'Hidden' Lives* (Oxford: Oxford University Press, 2010)
Bachelard, Gaston, *L'air et les songes* (Paris: José Corti, 1943)
  The Poetics of Space, trans. Maria Jolas (Boston: Beacon Press, 1964)
Barasch, Mosche, *Theories of Art*, 3 vols. (London and New York: Routledge, 2000)
Barrell, John, *Poetry, Language, and Politics* (Manchester: Manchester University Press, 1988)
  The Idea of Landscape and the Sense of Place, 1730–1840: An Approach to the Poetry of John Clare (Cambridge: Cambridge University Press, 1972)
  The Spirit of Despotism: Invasions of Privacy in the 1790s (Oxford: Oxford University Press, 2006)
Bate, Jonathan, 'John Clare: Prologue to a New Life', in John Goodridge and Simon Kövesi (eds.), *John Clare: New Approaches* (Helpston, Peterborough: John Clare Society, 2000), pp. 1–16
  'New Clare Documents', *John Clare Society Journal*, 21 (2002), 5–18
  'New Light on the Life of Clare', *John Clare Society Journal*, 20 (2001), 41–54
  John Clare: A Biography (London: Picador, 2003)
  Romantic Ecology: Wordsworth and the Environmental Tradition (London and New York: Routledge, 1991)
  The Song of the Earth (London: Picador, 2000)
Bates, Tom, 'John Clare and "Boximania"', *John Clare Society Journal*, 13 (1994), 5–17
Bateson, Gregory and Mary Catherine Bateson, *Angels Fear: Towards an Epistemology of the Sacred* (New York: Macmillan, 1987)
Belchem, Jon, *Popular Radicalism in Nineteenth-Century Britain* (Basingstoke: Macmillan, 1996)
Bennett, Andrew, *Romantic Poets and the Culture of Posterity* (Cambridge: Cambridge University Press, 1999)
Birns, Nicholas, '"The riddle nature could not prove": Hidden Landscapes in Clare's poetry', in Hugh Haughton, Adam Phillips, and Geoffrey Summerfield (eds.), *John Clare in Context* (Cambridge, Cambridge University Press, 1994), pp. 189–220
Blythe, Ronald, *Talking About John Clare* (Nottingham: Trent Books, 1999)
Boddy, Kasia, *Boxing: A Cultural History* (London: Reaktion Books, 2008)
Bonehill, John and Stephen Daniels (eds.), *Paul Sandby: Picturing Britain* (London: Royal Academy, 2009)
Brown, David Blayney, 'Nationalising Norwich', in David Blayney Brown, Andrew Hemingway and Anne Lyles (eds.), *Romantic Landscape: The Norwich School of Painters* (London: Tate Gallery, 2000), pp. 24–35
Certeau, Michel de, *The Practice of Everyday Life*, trans. Steven Rendall (Berkeley: California University Press, 1984)

Select bibliography

Chambers, Douglas, '"A love for every simple weed": Clare, botany and the poetic language of lost Eden', in Hugh Haughton, Adam Phillips and Geoffrey Summerfield (eds.), *John Clare in Context* (Cambridge, Cambridge University Press, 1994), pp. 238–58

Chandler, James and Kevin Gilmartin (eds.), *Romantic Metropolis: The Urban Scene of British Culture, 1780–1840* (Cambridge: Cambridge University Press, 2005)

Chase, Malcolm, *'The People's Farm': English Radical Agrarianism, 1775–1840* (Oxford: Clarendon Press, 1988)

Cherry, J. L., *The Life and Remains of John Clare* (London: F. Warne, 1873)

Chilcott, Tim, *A Publisher and His Circle: The Life and Work of John Taylor, Keats's Publisher* (London and Boston: Routledge and Kegan Paul, 1972)

Chirico, Paul, *John Clare and the Imagination of the Reader* (Basingstoke: Palgrave Macmillan, 2007)

  'Writing Misreading: Clare and the Real World', in John Goodridge (ed.), *The Independent Spirit: John Clare and the Self-Taught Tradition* (Helpston: John Clare Society and Margaret Grainger Memorial Trust, 1994), pp. 125–38

Christensen, Jerome, *Romanticism at the End of History* (Baltimore: Johns Hopkins University Press, 2000)

Clare, Johanne, *John Clare and the Bounds of Circumstance* (Kingston: McGill-Queen's University Press, 1987)

Clark, Anna, 'Queen Caroline and the Sexual Politics of Popular Culture in London, 1820', *Representations*, 31 (Summer, 1990), 46–68

Clark, J. C. D., *English Society1660–1832: Religion, Ideology and Politics During the Ancien Régime* (Cambridge University Press, 2000)

Colclough, Stephen, '"Labour and Luxury": Clare's Lost Pastoral and the Importance of Voice in the Early Poems', in John Goodridge and Simon Kövesi (eds.), *John Clare, New Approaches* (Helpston: John Clare Society, 2000), pp. 77–91

  Voicing Loss, Versions of Pastoral in the Poetry of John Clare, 1817–1832 (University of Keele: PhD thesis, 1996)

Collis, Stephen, *The Commons* (Vancouver: Talonbooks, 2008)

Constable, John, *John Constable's Discourses*, ed. R. B. Beckett (Ipswich: Suffolk Records Society, 1970)

Corbin, Alain, *Village Bells: Sound and Meaning in the Nineteenth-Century French Countryside* (New York: Columbia University Press, 1998)

Cronin, Richard, 'In Place and Out of Place: Clare in the *Midsummer Cushion*', in John Goodridge and Simon Kövesi (eds.), *John Clare: New Approaches* (Helpston: John Clare Society, 2000), pp. 133–48.

Crossan, Greg, 'Clare's Debt to the Poets in his Library', *John Clare Society Journal*, 10 (1991) 27–41

  'Thirty Years of the *John Clare Society Journal*: A Retrospective Survey', *John Clare Society Journal*, 31 (2012), 5–22

Dart, Gregory, *Metropolitan Art and Literature, 1810–1830* (Cambridge: Cambridge University Press, 2012)

Dawson, P. M. S., 'Common Sense or Radicalism? Some Reflections on Clare's Politics', *Romanticism* 2.1 (1996), 81–97
'John Clare—Radical?', *John Clare Society Journal*, 11 (1992), 17–27
DeWint, Harriet, *A Short Memoir of the Life of Peter DeWint and William Hilton RA*, in John Lord (ed.), *Peter DeWint 1784–1849: 'For the Common Observer of Life and Nature'* (Aldershot: Lund Humphries, 2007), pp. 78–89
Duncan, Ian, 'Hogg's Body', *Studies in Hogg and His World*, 9 (1998), 1–15
Dunn, David, 'Nature, Sound Art, and the Sacred', in David Rothenberg and Marta Ulvaeus (eds.), *The Book of Music and Nature* (Middletown, CT: Wesleyan University Press, 2001), pp. 95–107
Dyer, Gary, *British Satire and The Politics of Style, 1789–1832* (Cambridge: Cambridge University Press, 1997)
Esmail, Jennifer, *Reading Victorian Deafness: Signs and Sounds in Victorian Literature and Culture* (Athens: Ohio University Press, 2013)
Espinasse, Francis, *Literary Recollections and Sketches* (London: Hodder and Stoughton, 1893)
Faithfull, Pamela *An Evaluation of An Eccentric: Matthew Allen MD, Chemical Philosopher, Phrenologist, Pedagogue and Mad-Doctor, 1783–1845* (University of Sheffield: PhD Thesis, 2001)
Faye, Emmanuel, *The Introduction of Nazism into Philosophy in Light of the Unpublished Seminars of 1933–1935*, trans. Michael B. Smith (New Haven: Yale University Press, 2009)
Fischer, Ernst, *Von der Notwendigheit der Kunst*, trans. Anna Bostock (London: Penguin Books, 1963)
Foltz, Bruce V., 'Heidegger, Ethics and Animals', *Between the Species*, 9.2 (Spring 1993), 84–9
Foster, P. G. M., 'Introduction', in Gilbert White (ed.), *The Natural History of Selborne: A Facsimile of the 1813 Edition* (London: The Ray Society, 1993), pp. viii–ix
Fromm, Harold, 'Ecocriticism at Twenty-Five', *Hudson Review*, 66.1 (2013), 196–208
The Nature of Being Human: From Environmentalism and Consciousness (Baltimore: Johns Hopkins University Press, 2009)
Fulcher, Jonathan, 'The Loyalist Response to the Queen Caroline Agitations', *Journal of British Studies*, 34.2 (1995), 481–502
Fulford, Tim, 'Cowper, Wordsworth, Clare: The Politics of Trees', *John Clare Society Journal*, 14 (1995), 47–59
'Personating Poets on the Page: John Clare in his Asylum Notebooks', *John Clare Society Journal*, 32 (2013), 26–48
Gage, John, *Colour and Culture* (London: Thames and Hudson, 1993)
Colour in Art (London: Thames and Hudson, 2006)
Gardner, John, *Poetry and Popular Protest: Peterloo, Cato Street and Queen Caroline Controversy* (Basingstoke: Palgrave, 2011)
Garside, P., J. Raven and R. Schöweling (eds.), *The English Novel 1770–1829: A Bibliographical Survey of Prose Fiction Published in the British Isles*, 2 vols. (Oxford: Oxford University Press, 2000)

Goethe, Johann Wolfgang von, *Theory of Colours* (1810), trans. Charles Lock Eastlake (London, 1840)

Goldsmith, Jason N., 'The Promiscuity of Print: John Clare's "Don Juan" and the Culture of Romantic Celebrity', *Studies in English Literature 1500–1900*, 46 (2006), 803–32

Goodridge, John (ed.), *The Independent Spirit: John Clare and the Self-Taught Tradition* (Helpston: John Clare Society and Margaret Grainger Memorial Trust, 1994)

John Clare and Community (Cambridge: Cambridge University Press, 2013)

'"Three Cheers for Mute Ingloriousness!": Gray's *Elegy* in the Poetry of John Clare', *Critical Survey*, 11.3 (1999), 11–20

and Simon Kövesi (eds.), *John Clare: New Approaches* (Helpston: John Clare Society, 2000)

and Kelsey Thornton, 'John Clare the Trespasser', in Hugh Haughton, Adam Phillips and Geoffrey Summerfield (eds.), *John Clare in Context* (Cambridge, Cambridge University Press, 1994), pp. 87–129

Goodway, David, *London Chartism: 1838–1848* (Cambridge: Cambridge University Press, 1982)

Gorji, Mina, 'Burying Bloomfield: Poetical Remains and "the Unlettered Muse"', in Simon White, John Goodridge and Bridget Keegan (eds.), *Robert Bloomfield: Lyric, Class, and the Romantic Canon* (Lewisburg, PA: Bucknell University Press, 2006), pp. 232–52

John Clare and the Place of Poetry (Liverpool: Liverpool University Press, 2008)

Grainger, Margaret, *A Descriptive Catalogue of the John Clare Collection in Peterborough Museum and Art Gallery* ([Peterborough]: [Peterborough Museum Society], 1973)

Haraway, Donna, *Simians, Cyborgs and Women: The Reinvention of Nature* (New York and Abingdon: Routledge, 1991)

The Companion Species Manifesto: Dogs, People, and Significant Otherness (Chicago: Prickly Paradigm Press)

When Species Meet (Minneapolis: University of Minnesota Press, 2008)

Haughton, Hugh, 'Progress and Rhyme', in Hugh Haughton, Adam Phillips and Geoffrey Summerfield (eds.), *John Clare in Context* (Cambridge, Cambridge University Press, 1994), pp. 51–86

and Adam Phillips, 'Introduction: Relocating John Clare', in Hugh Haughton, Adam Phillips and Geoffrey Summerfield (eds.), *John Clare in Context* (Cambridge, Cambridge University Press, 1994), pp. 1–27

and Adam Phillips and Geoffrey Summerfield (eds.), *John Clare in Context*, (Cambridge: Cambridge University Press, 1994)

Hay, Daisy, 'Elizabeth Kent's Collaborators', *Romanticism*, 14 (2008), 272–81

Heidegger, Martin, '... Poetically Man Dwells...', in *Poetry, Language, Thought*, trans. Albert Hofstadter (London: HarperPerennial, 1971)

Introduction to Philosophy: Thinking and Poetizing, trans. Phillip Jacques Braunstein (Bloomington and Indianapolis: Indiana University Press, 2011)

'Letter on "Humanism"', trans. Frank A. Capuzzi, *Pathmarks* (Cambridge: Cambridge University Press, 1998), pp. 239–76
Logic: The Question of Truth, trans. Thomas Sheehan (Bloomington and Indianapolis: Indiana University Press, 2010)
Schwarzen Hefte, in Gesamtausgabe, IV: Abteilung: Hinweise und Aufzeichnungen, Band 94: Überlegungen II–VI, Schwarze Hefte 1931–1938, ed. Peter Trawny (Frankfurt am Main: Vittorio Klostermann, 2014)
'The Age of the World Picture', in trans. William Lovitt, *The Question Concerning Technology and Other Essays* (New York: Harper Row, 1977), 115–54
Hobsbawm, E. J. and Joan Wallach Scott, 'Political Shoemakers', *Past and Present*, 89 (November 1980), 86–114
Hone, J. Ann, *For the Cause of Truth: Radicalism in London 1769–1821* (Oxford: Clarendon Press, 1982)
Houghton-Walker, Sarah, *John Clare's Religion* (Farnham: Ashgate, 2009)
Hulme, T. E., 'Romanticism and Classicism', in Patrick McGuinness (ed.), *T. E. Hulme: Selected Writings* (London: Routledge, 2008), 68–83
Janowitz, Anne, *Lyric and Labour in the Romantic Tradition* (Cambridge: Cambridge University Press, 1998)
Jasper, David, *The Sacred Desert: Religion, Literature, Art, and Culture* (Oxford: Blackwell, 2007)
Jerrold, Walter, *Thomas Hood and Charles Lamb* (London: Ernest Benn, 1930)
Thomas Hood: His Life and Times (New York: Haskell House Publishers, 1968; first published 1907)
Jones, Gareth Stedman, *Languages of Class: Studies in English Working Class History 1832–1982* (Cambridge: Cambridge University Press, 1983)
Jordan, Michael, *The Beauty of Trees* (London: Quercus, 2012)
Jordan, Sarah, *The Anxieties of Idleness* (Lewisburg: Bucknell University Press, 2003)
Kaplan, Fred, *Thomas Carlyle: A Biography* (Ithaca: Cornell University Press, 1983)
Keegan, Bridget, *British Labouring-Class Nature Poetry, 1730–1837* (Basingstoke and New York: Palgrave Macmillan, 2008)
'Broadsides, Ballads and Books: The Landscape of Cultural Literacy in *The Village Minstrel*', *John Clare Society Journal*, 15 (1996), 11–19
Kent, Susan Kingley, *Gender and Power in Britain: 1640–1990* (London: Routledge, 1999)
King, James, *William Cowper* (Durham, NC: Duke University Press, 1986)
Klancher, Jon P., *The Making of English Reading Audiences, 1798–1832* (Madison, WI: Wisconsin University Press, 1987)
Kövesi, Simon, 'Beyond the Language Wars: Towards a Green Edition of John Clare', *John Clare Society Journal*, 26 (2007), 61–75
'"Her Curious House Is Hidden": Secrecy and Femininity in John Clare's Nest Poems,' *John Clare Society Journal*, 18 (1999), 51–63
'John Clare, Charles Lamb and the *London Magazine*: "Sylvanus et Urban"', *Charles Lamb Bulletin*, 135 (July 2006), 82–93

'John Clare's "I" and "eye": Egotism and Ecologism', in Amanda Gilroy (ed.), *Green and Pleasant Land: English Culture and the Romantic Countryside* (Leuven and Paris: Peeters, 2004), pp. 73–88

'John Hamilton Reynolds, John Clare and the *London Magazine*', *Wordsworth Circle*, 42.3 (Summer, 2011), 226–35

Lamb, Trevor and Janine Bourriau, *Colour: Art and Science* (Cambridge: Cambridge University Press, 1995)

Laquer, Thomas W., 'The Queen Caroline Affair: Politics as Art in the Reign of George IV', *Journal of Modern History*, 54 (September 1992), 417–66

Leader, Zachary, *Revision and Romantic Authorship* (Oxford: Oxford University Press, 1996)

Lean, E. Tangye, *The Napoleonists: A Study in Political Disaffection* (London: Oxford University Press, 1970)

Leopold, Aldo, *A Sand County Almanac and Sketches Here and There* (New York: Oxford University Press, 1949)

Levinson, Marjorie, *Keats's Life of Allegory: The Origins of a Style* (Oxford: Oxford University Press, 1989)

Lucas, John, 'Clare's Politics', in Hugh Haughton, Adam Phillips and Geoffrey Summerfield (eds.), *John Clare in Context* (Cambridge, Cambridge University Press, 1994), pp. 148–77

(ed.), *For John Clare: An Anthology of Verse* (Helpston: John Clare Society, 1997)

John Clare (Plymouth: Northcote House, 1994)

MacWilliam, Shirley, 'The Sound of Bells and Bellies: Acoustic Authority and Sound Effects', *Circa*, 85 (1998), 22–7

Martin, Frederick, *The Life of John Clare* (London and Cambridge: Macmillan, 1865), 2nd edn., ed. Eric Robinson and Geoffrey Summerfield (New York: Barnes and Noble, 1964)

McCalman, Iain, *Radical Underworld: Prophets, Revolutionaries and Pornographers in London, 1795–1840* (Oxford: Clarendon Press, 1993)

McEathron, Scott, 'John Clare and Charles Lamb: Friends in the Past', *Charles Lamb Bulletin*, 95 (July 1996), 98–109

'John Clare, William Hilton, and the National Portrait Gallery', *John Clare Society Journal*, 32 (2013), 5–25

McKusick, James C., 'Beyond the Visionary Company: John Clare's Resistance to Romanticism', in Hugh Haughton, Adam Phillips and Geoffrey Summerfield (eds.), *John Clare in Context* (Cambridge, Cambridge University Press, 1994), pp. 221–37

Green Writing: Romanticism and Ecology (New York: St. Martin's Press. 2000)

McWilliam, Rohan, *Popular Politics in Nineteenth-Century England* (London: Routledge, 1998)

Melikan, R. A., 'Pain and Penalties Procedure: How the House of Lords "Tried" Queen Caroline', in R. A. Melikan (ed.), *Domestic and International Trials, 1700–2000* (Manchester: Manchester University Press, 2003), pp. 54–75

Mishan, E. J., *The Costs of Economic Growth* (London: Staples Press, 1967)

Mole, Tom, (ed.), *Romanticism and Celebrity Culture, 1750–1850* (Cambridge: Cambridge University Press, 2009)
Morton, Timothy, *Ecology without Nature: Rethinking Environmental Aesthetics* (Cambridge: Harvard University Press, 2007)
  The Ecological Thought (Cambridge: Harvard University Press, 2010)
Murphy, Peter, 'Impersonation and Authorship in Romantic Britain', *English Literary History*, 59 (1992), 625–49
Payne, Roger, 'Humpbacks: Their Mysterious Songs', *National Geographic*, 155 (January 1979), p. 24
Pearce, Lynn Banfield, 'John Clare and Peter DeWint', *John Clare Society Journal*, 3 (1984), 40–9
Pedlar, Valerie, '"No place like home": Reconsidering Matthew Allen and his "Mild System" of Treatment', *John Clare Society Journal*, 13 (1994), 41–57
Phillips, Adam, 'The Exposure of John Clare', in Hugh Haughton, Adam Phillips and Geoffrey Summerfield (eds.), *John Clare in Context* (Cambridge, Cambridge University Press, 1994), pp. 178–88
Piggott, Stuart, *Ruins in a Landscape: Essays in Antiquarianism* (Edinburgh: Edinburgh University Press, 1976)
Porter, Roy, 'Medicine', in Iain McCalman (ed.), *An Oxford Companion to the Romantic Age: British Culture 1776–1832* (Oxford: Oxford University Press, 1999), pp. 170–7
Powell, David, *Catalogue of the John Clare Collection in the Northampton Public Library* (Northampton: Northampton Public Library Collection, 1964)
Purcell, Rosamund, Linnea Hall and René Corado, *Egg and Nest* (Boston MA.: Harvard University Press, 2008)
Reynolds, Joshua, *Discourses on Art*, ed. R. Wark, 2nd edn. (New Haven and London: Yale University Press, 1997)
Richards, Thomas, *The Imperial Archive: Knowledge and the Fantasy of Empire* (London: Verso, 1993)
Riga, Frank P., and Claude A. Prance, *Index to the London Magazine* (London and New York: Garland Publishing, 1978)
Robbins, Jane, *Rebel Queen: The Trial of Caroline* (London: Simon and Schuster, 2006)
Roberts, M. J. D., *Making English Morals: Voluntary Association and Moral Reform in England, 1787–1886* (Cambridge: Cambridge University Press, 2004)
Roe, Nicholas, *John Keats and the Culture of Dissent* (Oxford: Oxford University Press, 1994)
Sales, Roger, *English Literature in History 1780–1830: Pastoral and Politics* (London: Longman, 1983)
  John Clare: A Literary Life (Basingstoke: Palgrave, 2002)
Schafer, R. Murray, *The Soundscape: Our Sonic Environment and the Tuning of the World* (Rochester: Destiny Books, 1977)
Seeney, Michael, *A Six Foot Three Nightingale: Norman Gale, 1862–1942: A Biographical Essay and Check-List*, Occasional Series 7 (Oxford: Eighteen Nineties Society, 1998)

Sha, Richard, *The Verbal and the Visual Sketch in British Romanticism* (Philadelphia: University of Pennsylvania Press, 1998)
Shteir, Ann, *Cultivating Women, Cultivating Science: Flora's Daughters and Botany in England, 1760–1860* (Baltimore and London: John Hopkins University Press, 1996)
Simpson, David, 'Is the Academy Ready for John Clare?', *John Clare Society Journal*, 18 (1999), 70–8
Smith, David N., *Sounding / Silence* (New York: Fordham University Press, 2013)
Smith, E. A., *A Queen on Trial: The Affair of Queen Caroline* (Stroud: Allen Sutton, 1994)
Smith, Olivia, *The Politics of Language 1791–1819* (Oxford: Clarendon Press, 1984)
Sölle, Dorothee, *Beyond Mere Obedience: Reflections on a Christian Ethic for the Future* (Minneapolis: Augsburg, 1970)
Spacks, Patricia Meyer, *Privacy: Concealing the Eighteenth-Century Self* (Chicago: University of Chicago Press, 2003)
Steeple, John, 'About Bells', *The Aldine*, 9.4 (1878), 140–1
Steinberg, S. H., 'Statesman's Year-Book: Martin to Epstein', *Journal of Library History*, 1.3 (1966), 153–66
Stevenson, Struan, *So Much Wind* (Edinburgh: Birlinn, 2013)
Storey, Mark (ed.), *Clare: The Critical Heritage* (London: Routledge & Kegan Paul, 1973)
  The Poetry of John Clare (New York: St Martin's, 1974)
Tatchell, Molly, 'Elizabeth Kent and Flora Domestica', *Keats-Shelley Memorial Bulletin*, 27 (1976), 15–18
Taylor, Olive M., 'John Taylor: Author and Publisher, 1781–1864 II', *London Mercury*, 12 (July 1925), 258–67
Thompson, E. P., *The Making of the English Working Class* (1963; reprinted Harmondsworth: Penguin, 1980)
Thornton, R. K. R., 'The Raw and the Cooked', *John Clare Society Journal*, 24 (2005), 78–86
  'What John Clare Do We Read?', *PN Review*, 31.4 (March–April, 2005), 54–6
Tibble, J. W. and Anne Tibble, *John Clare: A Life* (London: Cobden-Sanderson, 1932; revised edn., London: Michael Joseph, 1972)
  John Clare: His Life and Poetry (London: Heinemann, 1956)
Vardy, Alan, 'Clare and Political Equivocation', *John Clare Society Journal*, 18 (1999), 37–48
  John Clare, Politics and Poetry (Basingstoke: Palgrave Macmillan, 2003)
Wahrman, Dror, '"Middle-Class" Domesticity Goes Public: Gender, Class, and Politics from Queen Caroline to Queen Victoria', *Journal of British Studies*, 32.4 (October 1993), 396–432
Walters, H. B., *Church Bells of England* (London: Oxford University Press, 1912)
Wang, Orrin N. C., 'Introduction: Romanticism and Conspiracy', *Romantic Circles Praxis Series* (August 1997), www.rc.umd.edu/praxis/conspiracy/wang/owint2.html

Ward, Sam, '"To List the Song & Not to Start the Thrush": John Clare's Acoustic Ecologies', *John Clare Society Journal*, 29 (2010), 15–32

Weiger, Sarah, '"Shadows of Taste": John Clare's Tasteful Natural History', *John Clare Society Journal*, 27 (2008), 59–71

Westphal, Joseph, *Colour: Some Philosophical Problems from Wittgenstein* (Oxford: Blackwell, 1987)

White, Lynn, 'The Historical Roots of Our Ecological Crisis', *Science*, 155.3767 (10 March, 1967), 1203–7

Wittgenstein, Ludwig, *Remarks on Colour*, ed. G. E. M. Anscombe, trans. Linda McAlister and Magarete Schättle (Oxford: Blackwell, 1978)

Worrall, David, 'Agrarians against the Picturesque: Ultra-Radicalism and the Revolutionary Politics of Land', in Stephen Copley and Peter Garside (eds.), *The Politics of the Picturesque: Literature, Landscape and Aesthetics Since 1770* (Cambridge: Cambridge University Press, 1994), pp. 240–60

'*Mab* and Mob: The Radical Press Community in Regency London', in Stephen Behrendt (ed.), *Romanticism, Radicalism and the Press* (Detroit: Wayne State University Press, 1997), pp. 137–56

'Review Essay: Reassessing the "Romantic" Scene', *John Clare Society Journal*, 33 (2014), 87–91

Theatric Revolution: Drama, Censorship, and Romantic Period Subcultures 1773–1832 (Oxford: Oxford University Press, 2006)

Zimmerman, Sarah M., *Romanticism, Lyricism, and History* (Albany: State University of New York Press, 1999)

Index

Abbey, Edward, 88–9
Abram, David, 103–4
Allen, Matthew, 2, 10n6, 60, 153–4, 163n23
Anti-Jacobin Review, 200
Ariès, Phillippe, 73n5, 74n9
Artis, Edmund, 75–6n49, 169, 174, 176
Athenaeum, 138, 139
Atkinson, Juliette, 119, 142n8
Auden, W. H., 80

Bachelard, Gaston, 86, 105
Baldwin, Robert, 210
balladry, 143n49, 211, 213–14
Barrell, John, 40, 57, 61, 62, 75n39
Bate, Jonathan, 7, 8, 13n30, 60, 105, 119, 141n3, 147
Beattie, James, 38, 39, 43
Belchem, John, 194
Bewick, Thomas, 179
Bible, 41, 53, 88, 89, 108–9, 110, 112
  'Ecclesiastes', 89
  'Psalms', 53
Biographical Magazine, 138
Birns, Nicholas, 7, 69, 105
Black Dwarf, 197
Blackwood's Edinburgh Magazine, 166n57, 210, 216, 218–20, 223–4, 226n30
Blake, William, 53, 103
Bloomfield, Robert, 1, 4, 154, 155, 156, 220
Blunden, Edmund, 5–6
Boston Gazette, 199, 200
Boswell, James, 10n4
Boyce, see Boyse, Samuel
Boyse, Samuel, 155
Brighton Magazine, 138
Buddhism, 102–3
Bunyan, John, 53
Buonaparte, Napoleon, 83
Burghley House, 169
Burke, Edmund, 51
Burns, Robert, 4, 143n49, 149, 155, 159, 166n57, 210

Burton, Robert, 45
Byron, George Gordon, 39, 54, 156, 158, 219
  'Stanzas for Music', 54

Cambridge Independent, 166n53
Campbell, Thomas, 210
Carcanet, 8
Carlile, Richard, 193
Carlyle, Thomas, 119, 120, 122–5, 138, 139, 140, 165n46
Caroline of Brunswick, *see* Queen Caroline
Cary, H. F., 55n16, 216
Castlereagh, Lord (Robert Stewart), 198
Catholicism, 117n63
Cato Street Conspiracy, 64, 198
Certeau, Michel de, 63, 71
Champion, 209
Chandler, James, 211
Chantrey, Francis, 215
Chartism, 156, 158, 165n46
Chatterton, Thomas, 121, 125, 149, 155, 159, 214
Cherry, J. L., 5
Chilcott, Tim, 8, 105
Chirico, Paul, 42
Christensen, Jerome, 75n40
Christian Observer, 199
Christianity, 99, 101, 102–3, 108–11, 189
Clare, Johanne, 63, 205n33
Clare, John
  and alcohol, 87, 119, 148
  and charity, 61, 111, 130, 161
  and enclosure, 6, 23, 53, 57, 69, 79–96 *passim*, 107, 127, 197–8, 200, 201
  and punctuation, 6, 18, 21, 42
  and radicalism, 7, 58, 62, 156, 189–208 *passim*, 205n41, 206n54, 207n65
  and religion, 97–117 *passim*
  as biographical subject, 1–2, 5–6, 7, 43–4, 118–145 *passim*, 154
  bird poems, 31–6, 57–76 *passim*, 75n35, 105–6
  editions, 5–6, 7, 8–9, 11n9, 190, 199

239

death, 118, 119, 147, 148–9, 158, 160, 166n53
death, erroneous reports of, 153
institutionalization and mental health, 2–3, 44, 46, 52, 53, 60, 87–8, 134, 140, 153, 158–9, 166n49
malnourishment and weakness, 2–3, 146–7, 153
patronage, 1–2, 9, 189–91, 197, 202
poetry
  'August', 25–7
  'Birds in Alarm', 34
  'Birds Nests', 58–9, 73
  'Childish Recollections', 221
  'The Chiming Bells', 108, 110
  'The Country Girl', 190
  'Dawnings of Genius', 190, 194–6
  'Dolly's Mistake', 190, 194
  'The Eternity of Nature', 32
  'Evening Bells', 107–8
  'The Fallen Elm', 51
  'The Fern Owls Nest', 34
  'First Love', 147
  'The Flitting', 19, 48–9, 105
  'Gipsy Camp', 46–7, 56n19
  'The Gypsies Evening Blaze', 19
  'Hedge Sparrow', 31–3
  'Helpstone', 62, 88, 190, 194, 195–7, 206n46
  'Infants are but cradles for the grave', 148
  'Invite to Eternity', 151
  'The Lament of Swordy Well', 89–90
  'The Land Rail', 33, 34
  'Lines on Cowper', 44
  'Lines Written While Viewing Some Remains of an Human Body in Lolham Lane', 147
  'The Mores', 23, 81–2, 85–6, 92
  'My Mary', 190, 194, 204n7
  'The Nightingales Nest', 33–4, 57, 65, 66–9
  'The Nuthatch', 34
  'The Parish', 110
  'The Partridges Nest', 34
  'The Pettichaps Nest', 33, 57, 59, 69, 70–1
  'Pleasant Places', 21–2
  Poems Descriptive of Rural Life and Scenery, 6–7, 58, 59, 60, 150, 170, 190, 194, 195, 197, 209
  'Prayer in the Desert', 111
  'O could I be as I have been', 53
  'Old Poesy', 19
  'One monday morning sour & loath', 152
  'Out of Door Pleasures', 19, 20, 21
  'The Reed Bird', 34
  'Remembrances', 82–3, 111
  'The Request', 110
  'The Robins Nest', 33, 105
  'The Rooks Nest', 34
  The Rural Muse, 63, 153
  'Sabbath Bells', 107–8
  'Sand Martin', 66, 106, 75n43
  'Shadows of Taste', 23–4, 110–11
  The Shepherd's Calendar, 8, 20, 25–7, 127–8, 153, 185, 225n17
  'The Sky Lark', 63
  'Snow Storm', 41–2
  'Soldiers Grave', 151
  'Song Last Day', 151
  'Sonnet' ('The silver mist more lowly swims'), 20
  'Spring', 19, 24
  'Stanzas' ('There is a land of endless joy'), 111
  'The wind blows happily on everything', 18–19
  'The Thrushes Nest', 32, 106
  'This leaning tree with ivy overhung', 110
  'To Dewint', 24–5
  'To John Clare', 59, 73
  'To the Snipe', 52–3, 65–6, 69, 75n43, 105
  'The Tramp' ('He eats a moments stoppage to his song), 91–2
  'The Village Minstrel', 189, 199, 200–1
  The Village Minstrel, 4, 62, 170, 221
  'The Winters Come', 44–5
  'The Wish', 151–2, 154
  'The Wood Larks Nest', 58
  'The Wry Necks Nest', 33, 35
  'The Yellow Hammers Nest', 32, 57, 59, 69, 70, 71
  'The Yellow Wagtails Nest', 33, 57, 59, 69, 70, 71–2
poverty, 146–66 *passim*
prose
  'Autobiographical Fragments', 108–9
  'Autobiography', 52
  'Autumn', 112–13
  Bird List, 33, 75n37, 179, 187n43
  'Essay on Landscape', 22, 30–1
  'Essay on Political Religion', 113
  Natural History Letters, 17, 35, 169–88 *passim*
  'Natural History of Helpstone', 174–83
  'A Remarkable Dream', 113
  'Sketches in the Life of John Clare', 20, 146–8
reception and reputation, 1, 3–7, 149–60
use of colour, 17–37 *passim*
Clare, John Parker, 141n3
Clare, Patty, 60
Clark, Leonard, 6
Cleave's Penny Gazette, 156
Cobbett, William, 194

Index

Cockneyism and Cockney School of Poetry, 156, 221–4, 227n77
Colburn, Henry, 210
Colclough, Stephen, 201, 202
Cole, Thomas, 82
Coleridge, Samuel Taylor, 22, 215
Collier, Mary, 3
Collins, William, 40
Collis, Stephen, 97, 98, 109, 114n7
Conder, Josiah, 23
Constable, John, 29, 30, 185
Conway, Moncure Daniel, 139–40
Cotman, John Sell, 29
Courier, 199
Cowper, William, 38–56 *passim*
   'The Poplar-Field', 38, 48, 49
   The Task, 44, 45, 62–3
   'Yardley Oak', 50–1
Craik, George, 137, 144n59
Crimean War, 121, 131–4
Cromek, R. H., 214
Cromwell, Oliver, 44
Cronin, Richard, 45
Crowson, Daniel, 106–7
Cruikshank, George, 156, 217
Cumberland, 214–15
Cunningham, Allan, 128, 155, 210–16, 218
Cunningham, John, 43

Dante, 45, 55n16, 216
Dart, Gregory, 215, 224, 227n77
Dawkins, Richard, 100
Dawson, Paul, 6, 75n37, 206n54
Defoe, Daniel, 53
Delacroix, Eugène, 28, 36
Denman, Thomas, 200
Dennett, Daniel, 100
Dermody, Thomas, 155
Devlin, James Dacres, 154–8, 162, 164n29, 164n33, 164n34, 165n37
DeWint, Peter, 22–7, 30, 31, 34–5
   'August', 25–7
   'The Staith, Lincoln', 30
Dickens, Charles, 1–4, 10n3
Disraeli, Benjamin, 121, 144n66
Drury, Edward, 183, 209
Duck, Stephen, 3
Dunn, David, 97
Dyer, John, 43, 221

Edinburgh, 209, 210, 212, 219
Egan, Pierce, 156, 165n44, 215
Elton, C. A., 217, 221

'Idler's Epistle to John Clare', 217, 221
Emerson, Ralph Waldo, 124, 139
Emmerson, Eliza Louisa, 2, 61, 62, 67, 179, 195, 196
   'On Reading The Nightingale's Nest by John Clare', 67
Encyclopaedia of Plants, 188n67
English Journal, 56n19, 154–6
Epping Forest, 46, 154, 156–8, 165n44
   and boxing, 156, 165n44
Evans, Thomas, 198, 201

Faithfull, Pamela, 10n6, 163n23
Ferguson, William, 4
Fischer, Ernst, 86–7, 89–90
Flaxman, John, 28, 215
Forster, John, 1, 3, 10n8
Foulds, Adam, 164n28
French Revolution, 59, 61, 64, 193, 199
Fromm, Harold, 100
Frost, Robert, 72
Froude, James Anthony, 140
Fulford, Tim, 47, 51, 52, 62

Gage, John, 28, 29
Gainsborough, Thomas, 29
Gale, Norman, 5, 11n17
Garside, Peter, 212
Gentleman's Magazine, 194–5
George IV, 191, 193, 198, 203
Gifford, William, 130
Gilchrist, Elizabeth, 176
Gilchrist, Octavius, 119, 129–31, 161, 183, 190, 209–10, 223
Gilmartin, Kevin, 211
Girtin, Thomas, 29
Glover, Jean, 4
Goethe, Johann Wolfgang von, 28, 126
Goldsmith, Jason, 59, 60, 66
Goldsmith, Oliver, 38, 43, 53, 197–8, 221
   'The Deserted Village', 53, 197–8
Goodridge, John, 12n26, 43, 51, 55n3, 55n10, 58
Gorji, Mina, 53, 75n43
Grainger, Margaret, 6, 8, 63, 170–1, 173, 176–7, 180, 187n28, 188n65
Gray, Thomas, 40–1, 43, 150
Grey, Charles, (Earl Grey), 193
Grigson, Geoffrey, 6
Grinnell, Paul, 84

Habermas, Jürgen, 58
Haley, William, 10n4
Hambler, Clive, 84–5
Haraway, Donna, 99, 100, 106

Haughton, Hugh, 3, 36n2, 63, 67, 68, 72
Haydon, Benjamin Robert, 203
Hazlitt, William, 191, 211, 213, 216, 217, 222–3
　'On Londoners and Country People', 222–3
Heidegger, Martin, 99, 100, 102, 103–5, 111, 114n12, 116n43
Helpston (village), 61, 75–6n49, 106, 127, 134, 146, 174–5, 182, 209, 217, 221
Helpstone, *see* Helpston (village)
Henderson, Joseph, 75–6n49, 169, 175–6, 178–9, 182
Hessey, James, 62, 170–80, 182–4, 209, 216, 218, 220, 221
High Beach (asylum), 153, 154, 158, 164n28, 165n44
Hobsbawm, Eric, 156
Hogg, James, 4, 210–1, 213, 218–19, 220, 226n30
Homer, 46
Hood, Edwin Paxton, 5
Hood, Thomas, 156, 214, 216–18, 220, 221
Houghton-Walker, Sarah, 109
Howitt, William and Mary, 158, 166n49
Hughes, Frieda, 85
Hulme, T. E., 104, 115n37
Hunt, Leigh, 186n2, 211, 219

Ingres, Jean-Auguste-Dominique, 28

Jasmin, Jacques, 160–1
Johnson, Samuel, 2, 10n4, 45
Jones, Freddie, 164n28
Joyce, Mary, 133, 158

Kaplan, Fred, 124
Keats, John, 1, 171, 211, 222
　'To Autumn', 64
Keegan, Bridget, 39, 65
Kent, Elizabeth, 170–2, 175–6, 179–84, 186n2, 188n67
Kövesi, Simon, 67, 105, 207n65, 226n30, 227n55

Lamb, Charles, 216–18, 220, 222, 224, 224–5n3
　'Distant Correspondents', 218
　'South-Sea House', 224
landscape aesthetics, 18, 22–5, 27–31
landscape painters and painting, 17, 22, 25, 27–31, 34–5, 37n18
Laqueur, Thomas, 192, 199
Leopold, Aldo, 90
Levinson, Marjorie, 221
Lincolnshire, 25, 209
Lockhart, J. G., 210, 216, 218–19, 220
London, 17, 44, 118, 120, 121, 127, 129, 130, 132, 134, 139, 148, 156, 170–2, 174, 176–9, 182, 192, 198, 209, 211–24
London Magazine, 9, 129, 156, 171, 184, 209–27 *passim*

Lord, John, 30–1
Loudon, John Claudius, 188n67
Loyalist, 199
Lucas, John, 10n3, 165n38, 205n41, 206n54

Mackay, Charles, 4–5, 11n10
Macmillan, Alexander, 120, 122, 124–7, 135–9, 144n66
Manchester Weekly Times, 160
Martin, Frederick, 1, 2, 5, 118–45 *passim*
　nationality, 118, 120, 141–2n8
　Alec Drummond, 121, 122, 131–35
　Life of John Clare, 118, 122, 124–31, 138
　Statesman's Year-Book, 118, 120–1, 124–6, 135–9
Marx, Karl, 81–2, 92, 93
McKusick, James, 40
McVay, Scott, 100
McWilliam, Rohan, 194, 200
Melikan, R. A., 193
Michelangelo, 28, 29
Mid-Northumberland Arts Group (MidNAG), 8
Miller, Hugh, 4
Milton (village), 180, 181, 185
Milton Hall, 75–6n49, 169
Milton, John, 39, 45
　Paradise Lost, 46
Mishan, E. J., 79–80, 91
Mitford, Mary Russell, 158–60, 166n49
Mole, Tom, 58, 59–60
Monbiot, George, 87
Monet, Claude, 29
Monthly Review, 211
Morgan, Lady (Sydney Owenson), 165n37
Morland, George, 23
Morning Post, 153, 190, 195, 201
Morton, Timothy, 98–9, 101–4, 106
Motherwell, William, 214

Nesbitt, Dr P. R., 9–10
New Monthly Magazine, 194, 210, 222
New Times, 199
Newark (village), 169
Newton, Isaac, 28
Northampton Mercury, 166n53
Northborough 34, 52, 61, 65

Packwood, George, 220
Palgrave, Francis, 38
Patmore, P. G., 224
Payne, Roger, 100
Peterborough, 83–4, 128, 177
Peterborough Today, 83–4
Peterloo Massacre, 62, 64, 198
Petrarch, 132
Phillips, Adam, 3, 69

Index

the picturesque, 22, 31, 152
Pomfret, John, 43
Poole, John, 223
   'A Cockney's Rural Sports', 223
Porter, Alan, 3, 5, 10–11n8
Porter, Roy, 146
Powell, David, 6, 75n35, 75n37
Pre-Raphaelites, 29
Price, Uvedale, 22
Proudhon, Pierre-Joseph, 5, 93

Quarterly Review, 130, 161
Queen Caroline, 191–4, 198–203

Radstock, Admiral Lord John, 62, 74n26, 129, 189–208 *passim*
   'The Cottager's Friend', 192
Ramsay, Allan, 4
Randall, Jack, 156, 158, 165n44
Redding, Cyrus, 56n19, 154, 164n28
Reform and Reform Movement, 57, 62, 156, 164n34, 192, 196, 199, 203
Regency era, 156, 198, 206n53, 212
Republican, 193
Reynolds, John Hamilton, 214, 216–22, 224, 227n66
   'The Literary Police Office', 214, 219
   'Warwick Castle', 222, 224
Reynolds, Joshua, 28–9
Richards, Thomas, 121
Richardson, Alan, 10n4
Riley, Bridget, 28
Roberts, M. J. D., 189
Robinson, Eric, 6, 75n35, 75n37, 118–19, 142n8, 185, 187n28
Roe, Nicholas, 64
Romanticism, 2, 6–7, 39, 54, 64, 82, 91, 98, 101, 103, 104, 106–7, 149, 159, 212
Royal Academy, 24, 28, 30, 215
Royal Literary Fund, 1, 182
Rubens, Peter Paul, 28, 29
Runge, Philipp Otto, 28

Sales, Roger, 5, 165n46, 202, 210
Sandby, Paul, 29
Schafer, R. Murray, 108
Scotland and Scots identity, 4, 29, 84, 95n9, 95n10, 132, 134, 143–4n49, 166n57, 209, 210, 211–13
Scott, Joan Wallach, 156
Scott, John, 209–11, 212, 214, 216, 218, 224
   House of Mourning, 209
Scott, Walter, 130, 143n49, 209, 211, 212–14, 216, 218
Scott-Keltie, John, 139

Seeney, Michael, 11n17
Shakespeare, William, 212
Sherwill, Markham, 191, 195
Sidmouth, Viscount (Henry Addington), 199
Simpson, David, 6–7
Six Acts, 62, 197
Smiles, Samuel, 5, 166n54
Smith, Horace, 220–1, 222, 227n66
Smith, Olivia, 202
Smith, William Henry, 144n66
Soane, John, 215
Society for Suppression of Vice, 189
Society of Painters in Water-Colours, 29–30
Southey, Robert, 193, 194, 219
Spa Fields, 198
Spacks, Patricia Meyer, 58
Spanish Ornithological Society, 84
Spectator, 5, 131, 133, 145
Spence, Thomas, 198
Spencean poets, 206n54
Spenser, Edmund, 212, 225n17
Spenserian verse, 39, 162n10
Stamford (village), 129, 130, 147, 183, 190, 209
Stamford Mercury, 209
Stamford News, 209
Stedman Jones, Gareth, 200
Steinberg, Sigfrid Henry, 126, 127, 138, 141–2n8
Stephen, Sir James, 140
Stevenson, Struan, 95n9
Stewart, Patrick, 164n28
Storey, Mark, 8, 177, 188n67
Summerfield, Geoffrey, 6, 118–19, 141–2n8
the supernatural, 97, 98, 146, 210
Switzerland, 79–80
Symons, Arthur, 5, 11n17

Tannahill, Robert, 4, 155
Taylor, John, 40, 42, 60, 61, 62, 119, 127–9, 148, 150, 156, 163n18, 166n57, 170, 171, 176–8, 181–2, 183–4, 190–1, 194, 196, 199, 202, 203, 206n46, 209–10, 212, 214, 216, 218, 220, 221, 223
Tennyson, Alfred, 1, 38, 132
Thompson, E. P., 203, 208n80
Thomson, James, 38, 39, 40–3, 52, 54, 220
   'Winter', 41
Thornton, Kelsey, 6, 8
Tibble, Anne and J. W., 6, 119, 154
Times, 2, 153, 191
Titian, 27, 28
Townshend, Chauncey Hare, 195
Trades Union Movement, 5
Turner, J. M. W., 29

Ufford (village), 107

Vardy, Alan, 46, 191, 192, 194
Varley, Cornelius and John, 29
Victorian culture, 1–2, 4–6, 7, 118, 119, 120, 121, 125, 158–161
Victorian era, 206–7

Wahrman, Dror, 194
Wainewright, Thomas Griffiths, 216–8, 221, 226n37
Wang, Orrin, 64
Wesley, John, 109
Westminster Review, 131
Whitaker, Joseph, 124

White, Gilbert, 172, 182–3
White, Lynn, 101, 102
Wilson, Effingham, 156
Wilson, John (a.k.a. Christopher North), 161, 166n57, 210, 216, 218–9
Winckelmann, Johann Joachim, 28
Wooler, T. J., 197, 201
Wordsworth, William, 1, 5, 21, 39, 40, 52, 149–50, 155–6, 216, 219
Worrall, David, 198, 201, 206n54

Yearsley, Ann, 220

Zimmerman, Sarah, 197

Lightning Source UK Ltd.
Milton Keynes UK
UKHW02f2346200518
322891UK00019B/269/P